an {unSTOPPABLE} force

daring to become the church <u>GOD</u> had in mind

By Erwin Raphael McManus

Group

Loveland, Colorado

D E D I C A T I O N

To my wife, Kim; my son, Aaron; my daughter, Mariah; my daughter in the Lord, Pati; and her husband, Steve.

To my brother, Alex; his wife, Adriana; and their children, Michael, Erica, and Lucas.

To Mosaic.

It is the journey together we share and cherish.

It is the adventure we have found in his calling.

Sojourners each of us upon this divine landscape.

Explorers of dangerous mysteries.

AN UNSTOPPABLE FORCE: DARING TO BECOME THE CHURCH GOD HAD IN MIND
Copyright © 2001 Erwin Raphael McManus

Visit our Web site: **www.grouppublishing.com**

Visit Mosaic's Web site: **www.mosaic.com**

CREDITS
Creative Development Editor: Paul Woods
Chief Creative Officer: Joani Schultz
Copy Editor: Lyndsay E. Bierce
Contributing Editor: Colin Johnson
Research Director: Jennifer Cho
Stenographer: Holly Rapp
Study Question Contributors: Dave Auda, Eric Bryant, Gerardo Marti, Janice Sakuma
Book Designer: Jean Bruns
Art Coordinator: Colin Johnson
Computer Graphic Artist: Joyce Douglas

All original artwork was created by Mosaic artists.
    Contributing Artists: Joy Cha, José Fernandez, Masako Inoue, Stephen Lo, Ronald Lopez, Anthony Oronoz, Kevin Osgood, Melvin Rivera, Carlos F. Salaff

Cover Designer: Jeff A. Storm
Cover Illustrator: Carlos F. Salaff
Production Managers: DeAnne Lear, Peggy Naylor

Unless otherwise noted, Scripture taken from the HOLY BIBLE, NEW INTERNATIONAL VERSION®. Copyright © 1973, 1978, 1984 by International Bible Society. Used by permission of Zondervan Publishing House. All rights reserved.

Library of Congress Cataloging-in-Publication Data

ISBN 0-7644-2306-1

10 9 8 7 6 5 4 3 2 1   10 09 08 07 06 05 04 03 02 01

Printed in the United States of America.

CONTENTS

ACKNOWLEDGMENTS

My failures are my gift to others. My successes are the gift of others to me. Even my failures find sweet memories through the gift of friendship and community. I would like to thank a few of the many people who have shared the journey with me, both in times of failure and pain and in times of success and joy.

No one fits this description more than my partner in life, Kim. Together, we have found the oneness that Christ's love alone makes possible. I would also like to express my gratitude for my son and daughter, Aaron and Mariah, who have supported me in this effort and both encouraged me and put up with the new baby in our family, known as "the book." Your lives inspire me to live with vision and courage.

King David had his inner circle, known as "The Three," that fought at his side, and beyond them his thirty mighty men. I have known such individuals. I would like to express my deepest gratitude to the elders and their wives, who have stood at my side through even the most dangerous and difficult of journeys: Robert and Norma Martinez, Greg and Debbie SooHoo, Enrique and Felipa Vazquez, Rick and Susan Yamamoto, and Paul and Cyndi Richardson. You have my profound respect, admiration, and love.

While I carry the title of Lead Pastor, the reality is that I serve with an extraordinary leadership team. They not only give me the context from which I stand, but their friendship adds immeasurable joy to my life. To all who serve and have served with me on the staff of Mosaic, please know how grateful I am for your contribution. A special word of thanks to Janice and Steve Sakuma, Dave and Tami Auda, Gerardo and Laura Marti, David and Carrie Arcos, Eric and Debbie Bryant, Joel and Susan Catalan, Alex and Adriana McManus, Joyce Chao, Norm and Carolyn Sillman, Jaime and Belinda Puente, Robbie and Missy Sortino, and Shelly Martin—who while making a huge contribution to this chaos-generating team also brought strength and calm. All of you left your footprints on the path. Thanks for bringing your machete to clear a way in the jungle.

For years I have felt a responsibility to put on paper the stuff in my heart and head. With each effort I became more convinced that it was stuck permanently inside me. Then God sent a series of miracles. Their names were Cindy Nakamura, Jennifer Cho, Shiho Inoue Johnson, her husband Colin Johnson, and Holly Rapp. Without Colin and Holly there would not be a book. I am indebted to all of you. Thanks for believing I had something important to say.

I could have never imagined writing this book with only words. The language of Mosaic involves images, movements, sounds, and experience. At the epicenter of this creative community are those for whom art is their first language. I want to thank Melvin Rivera, José Fernandez, Anthony Oronoz, Ronald Lopez, Stephen Lo,

Kevin Osgood, Joy Cha, Masako Inoue, and Carlos Salaff for the art gallery that exists within these pages. Your contribution brings inspiration that results in worship. May your work rekindle the spirit of creativity in all of us.

Mosaic was once The Church on Brady. I followed a pastor who poured his life into his congregation. It was his combination of intellect and passion that compelled me to come with my family to this community of faith. I want to express my appreciation for the twenty-five years of ministry Tom Wolf and his wife, Linda, gave to God's people here in east L.A., and to their partner in ministry, Carol Davis.

So many incredible people have richly blessed me throughout my spiritual journey. They fill the pages of this book. I would like to take this opportunity to acknowledge a few of the people who God has used at critical intersections in my life. Thank you, Karric and Barbara Price, Gene Kelsey, Gary Goodin, Bob Weatherly, Jose Moseley, Delores Kube, David and Sue Cobb, Roy Fish, Jerry and Fern Sutton, Greg Bourgond, and Jim Henry. I would also like to thank Inez Armstrong, who always seemed to know when to send that word of encouragement that kept me moving forward. And thank you all from Life Community who came to L.A. with Kim and me to change the world. The heart of this book is your story. You know who you are, and our lives are forever interwoven.

And to the person most responsible for teaching me to love risk and change, to embrace the entrepreneurial spirit, and to live the life of an explorer, I want to thank Alby Kiphuth for your gift to me. You are one unique person, Mom! I love you.

I would also like to thank the people at Group Publishing. The way you have treated me, it would be easy to forget that I am not royalty. Thank you, Thom and Joani, for giving me this opportunity to get these thoughts out to those who are facing the same challenges as we are at Mosaic. Thank you, Paul Allen, for being a friend to us here in L.A. and being our cheerleader. I would like to give my deepest expressions of gratitude to Paul Woods, who not only became my editor, but also my Barnabas and friend. To work with people you enjoy is a gift from God.

Finally, I would like to express my dismay at the goodness of God toward me and confess that I have received far beyond his reasonable generosity. Thank you, Lord Jesus, that you are willing to pour living water into such broken vessels. I pray that you are pleased with the content of this work.

And to those of you who now choose to journey with me through the pages to come, let us remove all excess baggage, for the road ahead requires that we be fleet of foot.

Advancing the Invisible Kingdom,
Erwin Raphael McManus

F O R E W O R D

{ *by Rick Warren* }

This inspiring book is written by a survivor. Eight years ago, my friend Erwin McManus was called to pastor a church with a great history in urban Los Angeles. The Church on Brady was known for its creative pastor, its diversity, and its heart for missions. Most church consultants would have recommended that Erwin not accept the leadership of the church for three reasons. First, he would be following a great senior pastor who served for twenty-five years and created a unique culture. Second, the church had been at a plateau for fifteen years and in decline for a few years. Third, the congregation was landlocked on three-fourths of an acre on a one-block street. Conventional wisdom would say, "You'd be a fool to try to change a church with so much history. You'll be martyred." Transitioning this church for a different twenty-first–century ministry would be difficult and painful. But Erwin stepped out in faith and accepted the challenge. Now he has led the church through a process of transition and renewal that is amazing, even changing the name of the church to Mosaic (which, by the way, I think is one of the coolest names for any church). He has not only survived the transition, but he has grown and thrived. That is rare.

To get the most out of this book, pay close attention to the metaphors and stories. If you want to lead people, regardless of whether they are modern or postmodern, boomers, gen-Xers, or millennials, you must learn their metaphors, use the right metaphors, and change the metaphors when necessary. If you change the metaphors, you can change the world! Jesus did. That's what being a "cultural architect" or spiritual leader is all about.

This book models what a postmodern, purpose-driven church can look like. Every church is called to fulfill five eternal purposes that Jesus gave in the Great Commandment and the Great Commission. These purposes never change. But the styles and methods we use to fulfill these purposes MUST change with every new generation and target. And how you say it makes a difference. Mosaic uses five elemental metaphors to represent the five New Testament purposes: Evangelism as "Wind," Fellowship as "Water," Service as "Wood," Worship as "Fire," and Discipleship as "Earth." These images are poetic, deeply profound, and perfectly match the church's target of reaching artists, cultural creatives, and those attracted by aesthetics and images in the Los Angeles basin.

For twenty-five years I've taught pastors that "the church is a Body, not a business. It is an organism, not an organization! It is a family to be loved, not a machine to be engineered, and not a company to be managed." Pastoring is an art. It has nothing to do with being a CEO. It's all about servanthood and authenticity and taking risks in faith. In this book you find story after story that illustrates these timeless truths.

I love Erwin's self-deprecating humor. It's an endearing trait that I've found in all pastors who are greatly used by God. Too many Christian leaders take themselves way too seriously and don't take God seriously enough. Humor and humility come from the same root word.

Most of all, I love this book because Erwin loves the church. I've read too many self-serving critics of the church who attack straw men, use their books to vent unresolved personal anger issues, and never really give any useful insights for helping churches change and be healthier. Erwin, like a true leader, wastes no time criticizing or attacking others. Instead he dreams and focuses on what the church can be. This book is not the theories of an academic, a pollster, or a pundit. It's written by a real pastor who serves in the real trenches of local church ministry, day in and day out. He understands what ministry is really like.

So read it and learn. Read it with an open mind. The moment you think you've got the ministry all figured out, you're finished—in ministry and life. Growing churches require growing leaders. This book will help you along the way.

Rick Warren
Lead Pastor, Saddleback Church
Author, *The Purpose-Driven Church*

FOREWORD

{ *by Brad Smith* }

Ve all have mornings when it's hard to wake up. Perhaps it's forty minutes of guilt-ridden dozing, hitting the snooze alarm every eight minutes. Perhaps it's sitting in a trance, watching the long line of slow-moving taillights on the freeway ahead. But then there is the feeling that hits after the second cup of coffee or after an hour of morning exercise. Same day, different awareness. We feel alive, active, and fully awake. We realize how much we would have missed otherwise.

An Unstoppable Force is an abrupt opening of the window shade, revealing that we've all been hitting the snooze button for decades. On the other side of this book is a different faith, a new awareness, a new excitement, and a new burden that the need is even greater than we realized before. In talking with hundreds of church leaders each year, I've seen two movements of God that seem to cross all boundaries of denominations, geography, and church styles. *An Unstoppable Force* certainly hits the bull's-eye on both.

First, we see church leaders progressing beyond the church growth movement of the 1980s, which opened up a new awareness of the culture around us. They're also moving beyond the church health movement of the 1990s, which created a new emphasis on intentional discipleship. What church leaders are increasingly talking about is church dispersion. We've worked so hard to get people inside the church and on a path to maturity; how do we now move them back outside of the church to serve in the marketplace, the community, and the world? Church growth and church health really don't make sense without church dispersion; yet that may prove to be the most difficult task yet. We like comfort. We like safety. It is a daunting task to change church from a place that serves consumers to a place that creates servants. *An Unstoppable Force* tackles this challenge head-on.

Second, the role of church leaders is changing. In the last two decades, pastors have been told that they must be good preachers...Er, actually, we meant teachers...Uhh, more accurately, leaders...Well, what we really mean is visionary CEO types...Wait, that's not it...We really meant system builders and equippers. Now we see that church leaders must be spiritual directors: builders of the culture and creators of the soul of the church. *An Unstoppable Force* provides great wisdom on building the internal culture, or ethos, of a church without succumbing to a faddish role. And it also provides a demonstration of how that happens. This is a book of timeless wisdom, explained in a present perspective that seeps authenticity and reality.

Erwin McManus is unusually qualified to write this book. I first knew him as we pastored churches about a mile apart in the shadow of downtown Dallas. For years he has been a trusted friend and mentor in new ways of understanding God, the church, and spiritual maturity. He is now the pastor of a vibrant church community that is on an authentic journey to wholeness in the heart of Los Angeles. Mosaic is certainly a unique church. It is multicultural, multiethnic, multi-locational, and in a rocket ride of transition. It is a rare work of God to see so many principles that other churches merely talk about come to reality in one community. It is evident that Erwin holds this jewel lightly: It is not a product of five transferable steps; no one person created it; and while Erwin is a great leader, he knows he is not what maintains it or keeps it on track.

An Unstoppable Force is not about easy steps, but it is a journal of what God is doing in an amazing congregation, explained in ways that can be applied—but not mimicked—in the churches of those who read this book. This book is probably best read with a leadership team. It fosters challenging dialogue. It does not attempt to mechanize something that can only be achieved organically and spiritually.

At Leadership Network, we spend our days looking for innovative, God-empowered churches. Mosaic is a pioneer among pioneers. We have sent many church leaders to Mosaic to see the future firsthand. This book is cheaper than a plane ticket and perhaps good incentive to go anyway after reading it. Better yet, it convicts me, and hopefully you as well, that we have been pursuing a slumber-filled Christianity. The light of God on my comfortable Christian life might tempt me to squint and to snuggle deeper into the warm bedcovers of complacent Christianity. I am thankful that Erwin has opened the window shade so wide that God can use this book to jolt me to a new awareness of God's intention and God's purpose for me and his church.

Brad Smith
President, Leadership Network

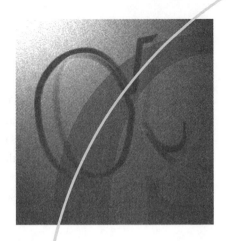

The vast ocean of the unknown
can only be navigated
through the compass of an ancient text.

The maps that will guide you
reflect a noble past

ANCIENT
TEXT
willing to decode the present context.

The journey you have embarked upon
searches not for the world you've known
but for the mysteries of the future textures.

PRESENT
CONTEXT

FUTURE
TEXTURES

ORIGINS
FINDS THE
FUTURE
IN THE BEGINNING.

A movement begins.
> Defying tradition.
> Strangely sacred yet sacrilegious.
> Without title or privilege.
> Revolutionary.
> Out of obscurity into history.

A movement begins.
> Against all odds.
> Uniting reverence with relevance.
> Unstoppable.
> Questioning everything
> and answering only to God.

ORIGINS FINDS THE FUTURE IN THE BEGINNING.

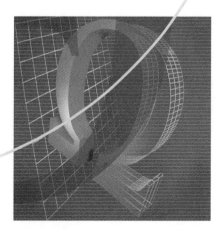

To explore
we must first excavate.

To discover
we must first recover.

To reframe
we must first reflect.

To imagine
we must first examine.

To move forward
we must first step back.

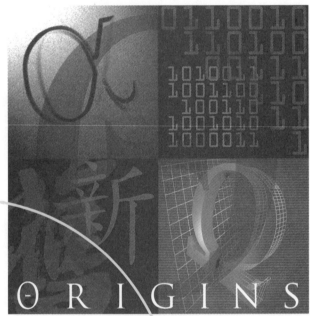

ORIGINS
FINDS
THE FUTURE
IN THE
BEGINNING.

ΘRIGINS

In 1926, Fritz Lang made a film that was more profound than it was popular. In this stark black and white silent film, he painted a picture of man's future in relationship to technology. The film is called *Metropolis*. It's a warning that man's dependence on technology may one day make him technology's slave. Lang was an early prophet against our eager surrender to the modern world. His prophecies were fulfilled as people exchanged communities for efficiency and found themselves to be nothing more than machines. The image is of an efficient yet sterile society which lacks any emotion, compassion, or love.

Recently, new warnings have arisen through images such as *The Matrix*, in which machines lead us to an unconscious state of illusion and we relinquish our reality for a perception of comfort and entertainment. Another such image is that of *Star Trek's* Borg, a callous integration of human and machine in which the value of the individual and the preservation of human uniqueness are lost to communal conformity.

It's not that the product of technology is unappealing. We work faster and better. Unimaginable conveniences become commonplace expectations. From cell phones to DSL, we have the world at our fingertips. In some ways, technology organizes the mess in our lives, yet it offers us convenience so quickly that sometimes we forget to stop and ask the question, "Is organization the best thing for everyone in every situation?"

THE PERFECT CUSTOMER

We have embraced the conveniences of the assembly line, the efficient, and the standardized and have grown in disdain for the chaotic, the unpredictable, and the disorganized. We've been all too willing to give up having it our own way just to get it faster, quicker, and easier. And so the planet is marked by golden arches, symbols of our willingness to relinquish uniqueness and line up for more of the same.

It's not that we don't like diversity, options, and choices because we clearly do. We want our color options, size options, and style options. We just want them in a way that brings us greater convenience and doesn't complicate our lives. We want everything tailored to our specific tastes, while at the same time, we want it available without any effort on our part.

COMMITTED TO AN INSTITUTION

The contemporary church has chosen the same course. We have chosen standardization over uniqueness. We have chosen predictability over surprise. And without realizing it, to our own regret, we have chosen comfort and convenience over servanthood and sacrifice. But in the end, what we have chosen is organization over life, and this, perhaps, is the fundamental dilemma we face— that at best the church is seen as a healthy organization.

The church is seen as the religious equivalent of IBM or Microsoft. If the church is not running well, then the solutions clearly lie in the best business practices available. The pastor becomes the CEO, and the success of the church is in its ability to move from a mom and pop business to a conglomerate. And *Robert's Rules of Order* becomes the guiding text rather than the pattern of the apostolic church.

The problem is that we treat the church as an organization instead of an organism. Even an elementary reading of the New Testament would make it clear that the church is the body of Christ. The church in her essence is a living system. Whenever we see the church through the template of an organization, we begin creating an institution. When we relate to the church as an organism, we begin to awaken an apostolic ethos, which unleashes the movement of God. The power and life of God's Spirit working in his people result in nothing less than cultural transformation.

BECOMING A SPIRITUAL ENVIRONMENTALIST

In this book we'll use several different metaphors to describe pastoral leadership, the first of which is the pastor as a spiritual environmentalist. He has the unique task of leading the people of God to become who they really are. For a species to survive and propagate in a given ecosystem, at least five basic characteristics need to be present. One, a balanced ecosystem; two, environmental adaptation; three, spontaneous reproduction; four, the nurturing instinct; and five, life-cycle harmony. These same principles apply to the birth, growth, and multiplication of churches throughout the world. The spiritual environmentalist centers the church around these five arenas.

A BALANCED ECOSYSTEM

When God creates, he creates with relational integrity. Everything is connected and fits together. This is true not only in the physical realm, but even more so in the spiritual. The Bible tells us that when man sinned, all creation groaned.

Those who study science have told us that a butterfly fluttering its wings in South America could, in some sense, be the primary cause of an avalanche in Antarctica. This level of complexity strikes us as new and innovative, and yet the Scriptures have advocated this kind of interconnection for thousands of years. The idea that the sin of one man and one woman could send a disruption throughout the entire cosmos is an extraordinary description of the organic connection between all of nature.

The pulling of one piece of fruit from the tree of the knowledge of good and evil was the primary influence of famines that spread across deserts, tsunamis that swallow up villages, earthquakes that shake the earth, and the unpredictable force and violence of nature. According to Scripture, everything is connected, and every action has at least some effect on the whole.

In the same way the church is a part of the whole; she is both influenced by the world around her and called to influence the world in which she exists. Too often the church does not realize that she is a part of a greater societal and spiritual ecosystem and that her role is to be the very fiber that produces health within that ecological system. This is why a balanced ecosystem is of primary importance in the Genesis design. And just as it is critical for all living beings to live within a balanced ecosystem, the church can only thrive in the context of healthy relationships.

We are accustomed to speaking of the great commission, but it is the commandment that Jesus calls "great." The commission erupts out of the great commandment: "Love the Lord your God with all your heart and with all your soul and with all your mind." The second is this: "Love your neighbor as yourself." There is no commandment greater than these. The gospel flows best through the establishing of significant relationships that are authentic and healthy. When relationships become stagnant and the community of Christ closes itself to the outside world, the result is an institution rather than a movement.

In a balanced ecosystem, the church has a proper relationship to God, and its people have a proper relationship to one another and to an unbelieving world. The measure of our spiritual health must be examined against our stewardship in relationship to a world that's lost and broken. Jesus viewed a person's

15

claim to love God and a person's actions toward the outsider as inseparable.

Through a gracious invitation by Willow Creek, we brought over thirty of our leaders to experience the Willow Creek conference in Barrington, Illinois. We were struck by many things during our time there. As wonderful as everything was, what amazed me most of all was that ordinary, everyday Christians were inviting their friends and bringing them to experience the Gospel. It's pretty simple, but seeker services don't work if there are no seekers in the service.

I was struck with the same reminder at Saddleback in Lake Forest, California. Here's a community of faith that keeps getting people up to the plate. The Saddleback community of faith is organically connected to the community of Lake Forest and beyond. The life of the church is inseparable from the life of the world around them. There is a balanced ecosystem with God and with one another and with their world.

ENVIRONMENTAL ADAPTATION

The second environment deals with an external factor, and that factor is change. Every living system that is fruitful and multiplies is required to adapt to the environment in which it has been placed. Species that thrive are species that adapt. Species that do not adapt to change do not survive because change is an ever-present reality. This is the difference between macroevolution and microevolution. This is not describing the change of one species into another species, for God clearly created each species according to its own kind, but it is the improvement of a species within its own kind.

We don't have to go any further than human beings to see the unique capacity for adaptation and change. Imagine the Olympians of the 1890s attempting to compete with gold medalists of the 1990s. Even the great heroes of the past, such as Jesse Owens, would fail to qualify to compete against the world-class athletes of today. In basketball we've seen six-foot-six-inch centers give way to six-foot-six-inch guards. We see fourteen-year-olds winning Olympic golds in gymnastics, performing feats considered impossible only twenty years ago. We've watched football players get bigger and faster. In the one area that we would seem to have the least control—our physical development—we've watched extraordinary advances take place.

What is often described as improvement is really nothing more than adaptation—either change or die. The same is true for the local church. If we accept the premise that the church is an organism, then we know that the church has the capacity for environmental adaptation. A part of the design of the church is to be able to make positive change while keeping her essence at the core.

Over the past forty years, the communities around many churches have changed dramatically, yet the church has stayed the same. Somewhere in the community's transformation, the church disconnected. And since the transition began incrementally, the local congregation was either unaware or unconcerned. The church must acclimate to a changing world, or she will destine herself to irrelevance or even extinction.

What this means for the pastor as spiritual environmentalist is that he must understand the changing environment in which his church has been called to serve. One of those dramatic changes in our environment is the shift from words to images. To do church in a way that is entirely text-driven is the kiss of death. People simply do not read; they observe. We have a culture raised on watching. Beyond the emergence of a post-literate society, we have a culture raised on entertainment.

We need to adapt to capturing images that communicate truth and to move from static to dynamic communication systems. Our culture is not only multisensory; it is multilayered. We receive information not only through all of our senses, but also through multiple senses at one time. That's why for us worship many times encompasses not only the teaching of the word and worship through song, but also the use of sculpture, painting, dance, aromas, and film.

Whether a church decides to relocate to an environment in which it can thrive or to readapt to the environment that is emerging around them, change is still inevitable. It must not be seen as a necessary evil but a God-given tool. For the first-century church, difficult and challenging environments caused her to thrive. The first-century church erupted out of a context of persecution. The church is designed to thrive on the edge of change and in the center of history. The church was designed to thrive in our radically changing environments.

SPONTANEOUS REPRODUCTION

Every living creature was created with the capacity to create life. Even the plants bear seeds. A non-reproducing species would itself live only one generation, but a species that reproduces—barring natural catastrophe—will live as long as time exists. Species do not have to be taught to reproduce. It is inherent in their nature. In much of the church, however, this characteristic seems to be missing. The church must be released to do that which comes naturally.

Years ago my wife, Kim, took me to her home in the mountains of North Carolina. She grew up on a farm with her foster parents, Theodore and Ruth Davis. Theodore was walking me around the farm, and he introduced me to a mule. He went on to explain that a mule was a combination of horse and donkey. This seemed a little weird to me, so I asked him why they didn't just use a horse or a donkey. He explained that while horses are very bright in comparison to donkeys, they're not as strong. And donkeys, while they're very strong, are not bright enough to do the work necessary. When you combine the two, you get the perfect combination for the task required. But he went on to explain to me that, while mules are good for work, they cannot reproduce.

Mules are best known for being stubborn and sterile. In some ways they illustrate all too well what happens when man begins to play God. All too often we have to acknowledge such a description in our manmade churches. Churches that are born by God have the capacity for spontaneous reproduction that is a result of an internal force that drives a species. When the church is a vibrant organism, life is reproduced over and over again. Vibrant Christians reproduce new believers, vibrant small groups reproduce new communities of faith, and vibrant churches become the catalysts for an apostolic movement.

THE NURTURING INSTINCT

Just as the instinct to nurture is characteristic of all creatures, it is so in the living church. She must care for her young and be sensitive to what is necessary for their spiritual survival. The apostolic church has a natural instinct for appropriate and healthy nurture.

Insufficient nurture can be seen when new converts too easily and too often fall away, and excessive nurture can be seen when those that we consider mature Christians have yet to embrace the mission of Christ in a personal way. The first one creates too big of a back door and the second one creates a logjam at the front door. An apostolic environment nurtures the full and dynamic expression of faith, love, and hope.

LIFE-CYCLE HARMONY

The final dynamic in God's design is life-cycle harmony. This is simply the realization and embracing of one's own birth, life, and death. It can be sobering to realize that a major portion of our lives is given to preparing the next generation for life. Each generation is connected to the generation before it and the generation that follows. In the prime of our lives we begin the process of replacing ourselves.

When a healthy relationship exists within the life cycle, a selflessness of giving oneself away is created. The more one focuses on one's own living, the less one is concerned about giving life to others. The only way church buildings stay filled through generations is if the church lives and dies and is born again over and over. Soon we realize that the church is not the same church it was twenty years ago or even four years ago. To make the kind of impact in human history that God desires, we must find our fulfillment and the rightness of this life cycle.

In the end, it is not so much about prolonging or perpetuating our own life as about giving new life to others.

Nature's most inspiring example is the salmon working its way upstream for the sole purpose of spawning a new generation, even at the cost of her own life. Whether an instinct tells a salmon that it's time to die or that it's time to give birth even at the cost of death, I am uncertain. But what I know is that even nature declares that life and death are inseparable.

It is no different for the church. Jesus reminds us that unless a seed first dies, it cannot produce life. He tells us that unless we lose our own lives, we will never live. It should be of no surprise to us that when the church awakens an apostolic ethos, she will be committed to giving herself away that others may live.

One of the most difficult things in the world for a doctor must be to tell someone that he or she is dying. Sometimes treatment is given to alleviate some of the suffering by dealing only with the symptoms. We tend to do that in the church as well. The truth is, if churches wait too long to die to themselves, then they ensure that they will die by themselves.

A church near the beaches of Santa Monica gathers each week with the ten remaining members whose average age is at best in its seventies. They cannot decide what to do. They are paralyzed by the fear of death and the lack of life. Around the country, churches that were once over a thousand in attendance have literally ceased to exist. The life cycle is a curious thing: No matter how you approach it, you die. If you die to yourself early and cel-ebrate the giving of life, you find celebration and joy, even in death. Our future is not to be found in our preservation but in our investment.

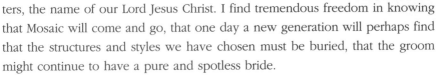

I don't think it's incidental that the church is a "she" and not a "he." The church is the bride of Christ, and Jesus is the groom. The bride gives up her name when she marries the groom. The names of our churches—our identities as unique local churches—must be absorbed by the only name that mat-ters, the name of our Lord Jesus Christ. I find tremendous freedom in knowing that Mosaic will come and go, that one day a new generation will perhaps find that the structures and styles we have chosen must be buried, that the groom might continue to have a pure and spotless bride.

We need to live our lives with the faithfulness we would have if we knew Jesus were coming back today, but with the wisdom that he may not return for another thousand years or more. We need to swim upstream, whether it's because we have an instinct that our lives are coming to an end or because somehow we know it's our duty to get to the place where we give new life at whatever cost. The church must always strive to be giving birth to the future. When awakened, an apostolic ethos has no fear of death but finds its life in dying to itself and living for Christ.

In our quest to engage the future, we must go back to the beginning. Our destiny is found in our origins. For the church to escape the paralysis of institutionalization, she must find her identity in her essence as a spiritual organism. This is both the starting point and the finish line. The pastor is perhaps, first and foremost, a spiritual environmentalist who awakens the primal essence of the church.

SPONTANEOUS LIVING

Roland Allen, in *The Spontaneous Expansion of the Church*, observed that the churches in China seemed to flourish whenever the missionaries were forced to leave. He concluded that the church of Jesus Christ has within her the capacity for spontaneous expansion, and that is what happens naturally when the church is healthy and vibrant. Within every local church, an apostolic ethos is waiting to emerge. It lies dormant within every genuine community of faith, though perhaps latent and asleep. It is my hope and prayer that through reading these pages, you will be inspired to awaken an apostolic ethos.

❝The best way to predict the future is to create it.❞ —PETER DRUCKER

FUEL FOR THOUGHT

1. Are our relationships right and pleasing to God?
2. What steps toward reconciliation can we take to restore broken relationships?
3. What changes are critical for us to make in order to thrive in our mission field?

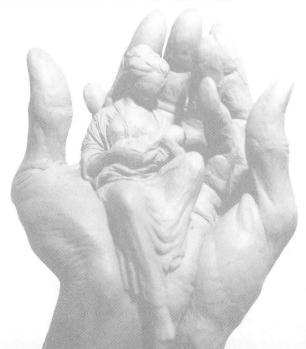

"Now there is in Jerusalem near the Sheep Gate a pool...Here a great number of disabled people used to lie—the blind, the lame, the paralyzed. One who was there had been an invalid for thirty-eight years. When Jesus saw him lying there and learned that he had been in this condition for a long time, he asked him, 'Do you want to get well?'

" 'Sir,' the invalid replied, 'I have no one to help me into the pool when the water is stirred. While I am trying to get in, someone else goes down ahead of me.'

"Then Jesus said to him, 'Get up! Pick up your mat and walk.' At once the man was cured; he picked up his mat and walked" (John 5:2-9).

Even when we are paralyzed, Jesus asks, "Do you want to get well?" In our frustration we might explain how we have longed for healing and health but have been incapable of obtaining it. We might express our pain that no one cared enough to help us get what we needed. Yet two things become clear: What we have been trying to access for our cure may not be what we really need, and Jesus won't fix what we want to keep broken. Paralysis in our churches has resulted in atrophy. We have too often been looking in all the wrong places for our healing and restoration. It's Jesus who gets us up on our feet and commands us to walk. But first we have to answer his question.

0 Atrophy

"Then the church throughout Judea, Galilee and Samaria enjoyed a time of peace. It was strengthened; and encouraged by the Holy Spirit, it grew in numbers, living in the fear of the Lord.

"As Peter traveled about the country, he went to visit the saints in Lydda. There he found a man named Aeneas, a paralytic who had been bedridden for eight years. 'Aeneas,' Peter said to him, 'Jesus Christ heals you. Get up and take care of your mat.' Immediately Aeneas got up. All those who lived in Lydda and Sharon saw him and turned to the Lord" (Acts 9:31-35).

ZERO
MOVEMENT

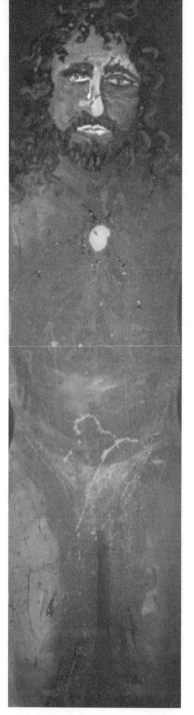

CHAPTER NONE

ATROPHY

Atrophy (n) 1. a wasting away of the body or of an organ or part, as from defective nutrition or nerve damage; 2. degeneration or decline as from disuse; 3. a decrease in size, a wasting away, deterioration, or diminution; to waste away, wither, or deteriorate.

NO SURVIVORS

About ten of us were sitting in a small duplex in south Dallas, looking toward the future possibilities for impacting our community with the gospel. The other nine were still uncertain of my qualifications; I was the new guy on the block. For decades these faithful few had given their lives to serve their impoverished neighborhood. Because they faced some of the highest crime and murder rates in the country, their task was made all the more difficult.

This was my first official pastorate, and at fifty dollars a week, I was certainly overpaid. As I overviewed all our assumed-to-be-minimal assets, I suddenly discovered that we had over $20,000 in the bank! Not bad for a handful of people ministering to a community that was predominantly on welfare. I soon learned that this money was the gift of generous believers who supported our work. When I insisted that we use the funds to reach the city rather than to maintain a financial net for the church, one of the two other men in the meeting frantically declared, "But we must survive!"

I will never forget the look on their faces when I promised that I would either lead us to impact the city or—in the effort—close our doors. I was a very young believer at the time and only in my twenties, but I was sure that there was no promise in the Bible that insured survival. Once survival has become our supreme goal, we have lost our way.

The New Testament word for "witness" is the same as for "martyr." We have come to know martyrs as those who have died for the faith. They didn't survive, but they died facing the right direction. Around the world, Christian families, tribes, and communities have been persecuted and brutally killed for their faith. They didn't survive. Yet they left a witness. The purpose of the church cannot be to survive or even to thrive but to serve. And sometimes servants die in the serving.

> **The purpose of the church cannot be to survive or even to thrive but to serve. And sometimes servants die in the serving.**

It is not difficult to understand why a church would want to disconnect from the world around it. Just watching the five o'clock news can make a person want to give up. If our perception is that people don't care anyway, if our conclusion is that no one is really open to the truth, and since there's overwhelming evidence that the hearts of individuals and the heart of society seems to have hardened beyond repair, it is no wonder that churches have become spiritual bomb shelters. Yet the church is not called to survive history but to serve humanity. As with each individual, there is a difference between living and existing for the church.

The life of the church is the heart of God. The heart of God is to serve a broken world. When Jesus wrapped a towel around his waist, he reminded us that only he could wash away our sin. The church cannot live when the heart of God is not beating within her. God's heartbeat is to seek and save that which is lost. The church exists to serve as the body of Christ, and it is through this commitment to serve that we are forced to engage our culture.

The serving that we are called to requires direct contact. You cannot wash the feet of a dirty world if you refuse to touch it. There is a sense of mystery to this, but it is in serving that the church finds her strength. When she ceases to serve the world around her, she begins to atrophy. In pathology, atrophy is the wasting or decreasing in size of any part of a body. When the church refuses to serve the world, she begins to waste away. She finds herself deteriorating, withering, and losing her strength. Like a muscle that has been locked away in a cast, the church shows the signs of atrophy that become evident when the cast is removed. It is difficult to ignore the reality that the church has lost significant muscle tissue. All around us, we find evidence that the church of Jesus Christ in our contemporary society is not what she once was.

RUNNING ON EMPTY

If only we could summarize the problem of the American church by simply saying that most churches are not growing. But it's worse than that. Even to say that churches are declining and closing their doors is not to speak of the real tragedy. This may seem strange, but the real tragedy is not that churches are dying but that churches have lost their reason to live! Dying is a natural and noble part of life. All too often we take the promise that the gates of hell will not prevail against the church as a guarantee that no local church will ever close its doors. How could we ever gather this from the one who told us that, unless a seed dies first, it cannot bear fruit? Before we can even begin to explore how the church can really live, we must first be willing to die. We must be willing to die to our conveniences, our traditions, and our preferences—everything that places us above others.

> We are in grave danger when we have the most people and the most money in our history.

About ten years ago, I read a report stating that nearly five hundred churches in Texas closed their doors in a period of one year. The report attributed these closings to a lack of finances and loss of people. It seemed strange to me that a church's final stages would inevitably be defined by this cause. In fact, the very opposite is true. The life cycle of a church is just like a bell curve. Decline begins right after the highest point. In a church's peak moment, she has the most people and the most money. I know it sounds counterintuitive, but churches begin to decline when things are going well. We are in grave danger when we have the most people and the most money in our history. Success often blinds us to the real forces of atrophy. The risk and innovation that brought us success are often abandoned to preserve success. Many times we lose our momentum because we are afraid to lose the success we've achieved, and before we know it, we discover that we are running on empty.

PREPARING FOR THE PAST

It may seem inconceivable, but not long ago the job of church growth consultant did not exist. In fact, church growth seminars and dying churches were virtually unheard of. Although most churches were essentially in plateau, there was a sense of the church as a place of permanence and stability. You just hung your sign outside, and the appropriate parishioners found their way there. The primary role of the pastor was caretaker/teacher, and many times even the role of evangelist was left to someone who came from out of town.

One could almost predict that the development of the Master of Divinity degree would serve as the religious equivalent to the M.B.A. Seminaries began to produce what local churches perceived they needed: godly men who had a professional understanding of theology, pastoral care, and management. Pastors were valued for their ability to bring and keep order rather than for their ability to bring and lead change. The reality was that pastors were being equipped to preserve the past rather than to create the future. We became known for being traditional rather than transformational. The ritual replaced the radical. The pastor/teacher replaced the apostle/evangelist.

The Church soon lost her momentum and had less and less to manage. Seminaries were producing pastors who were ready for their pulpits but not for the challenge. Pastors found themselves experts in Biblical exegesis, but novices in cultural exegesis. The rapid shifts in society only added to their dilemma. We knew something was wrong, but we couldn't quite place it. America was turning from a Christian-friendly nation to, at best, Christian-indifferent. The playing field was definitely changing, and we were unprepared for the new rules.

I have a friend named Frank who I literally met on the road to seminary. I needed a ride from Orlando to the Dallas-Fort Worth Metroplex, and he happened to be going to seminary at the same time. We jumped into his car, enthusiastic about our upcoming experience in seminary. We were going to prepare to reach the world for Christ.

I'll never forget the day Frank told me about sitting in a course on religious education and administration. He could hardly describe the feeling he had when he realized that, not only did he have the exact same professor that his father had an entire generation earlier, but he

> We've spent millions of dollars preserving our music and hymnals rather than creating worship that expresses the culture in which we live.

was also working through the exact same material and was being taught the exact same philosophy of ministry and organizational systems. It was as if the world had not changed in thirty years.

We in the church seemed to be unaware that the world of Frank, Sr. was not the same as the world of Frank, Jr. This is the "frank" reality. If this were the exception, it would perhaps be unfair to isolate this educational anomaly. But the truth is, this is more the rule. We've spent millions of dollars preserving our music and hymnals rather than creating worship that expresses the culture in which we live. And while we find it difficult enough to change in areas related to style, sound, and structure, in more substantive areas of change we lack even the wisdom to change. Not only is the world around us changing, but so is the church within us.

I live in Los Angeles, and I pastor a Southern Baptist church. If you check your map, Los Angeles is still on the West Coast. It seems that California Southern Baptists are perpetually faced with the issue of cultural identification.

Overwhelmingly, Southern Baptist churches in California started as satellite churches for transplanted Southerners. It is a new thing to find a Southern Baptist church in California that is actually full of people from outside of the Bible Belt, but it is happening. It is happening not only in California but all over the world. And it should seem strange to us that there are Southern Baptists in China and Southern Baptists in Africa and Southern Baptists in India and Southern Baptists in Latin America, because the truth of the matter is that none of those people are Southern. Yes, they are Baptists in doctrinal conviction, but the cultural designation demands an identification that is inconsistent with reality.

Although we refuse to change our name, Southern Baptists have become International Baptists. And if we were to factor in the diminishing value of denominational identification, it would be more accurate to say that Southern Baptists have gone from International Baptists to Global Christians.

Though the world and the church are changing, the decision-makers in the church have often been unprepared to face the new realities. A few decades ago, the church began to realize that our home turf had become a mission field, and very few were called to missions. As pastors became desperate, the church growth forum erupted onto the scene. In a sense, the birthplace of the church growth movement was the barren womb of the modern church. The solutions to the modern church problem were developed with our modern tools. Church growth became a science, where it had once been an art form. And it didn't take the church where it needed to go.

Rather than organizing people to accomplish a corporate purpose, the apostolic church painted divine portraits on the canvas of the human spirit. We need to look back to that Church of our origins—and to unleash the true essence of Christianity. A leader for the future church must move from corporate executive to spiritual artisan.

THE GREAT DIVIDE

Living within a Christian context, it becomes easy to divide according to theological distinctions. The difference between a Baptist and a Methodist actually used to matter to people. In many ways we seem to have had too much time on our hands. Just look at how many kinds of Baptists there are—Southern, Northern, Conservative, American, Swedish, Cooperative, Free-Will, and Seventh Day, just to name a few. While we were dividing among ourselves, we missed the growing divide that really mattered. We were losing the battle for the lives of people who were without Christ.

66We must transform the fragments into a mosaic.99

From within this context, the contemporary parachurch movement has emerged. When we are truly "on mission," nuances become secondary to the primary

mission of the church. The parachurch created a missiological rather than a theological environment. If you believed that the Bible held the solutions for man's problems, knew that Jesus was the only hope for a lost and broken world, and were willing to do something about it, then you qualified to be on the team.

In many ways the emergence of the parachurch reflects the paralysis within the local church. When we stopped calling youth to the mission of Christ, Youth With A Mission emerged. When we ignored the opportunity to reach university students, Campus Crusade emerged. When we settled for church attendance and neglected discipleship, Navigators emerged. When we hesitated to call men to the role of spiritual leadership, Promise Keepers emerged. Yet while the parachurch was rallying and mobilizing men and women whose hearts were longing to serve Christ, it was at the same time accelerating the spiritual anemia and decline of the local church. The church became a fortress from the world rather than the hope of the world. This disconnection from our present context exemplifies the need for holistic ministry. Seekers are looking for spiritual integration. This means that we must provide community with cause and meaning with healing. Having one without the other only leaves us fragmented. We must transform the fragments into a mosaic.

THE GREAT AWAKENING

Some claim that it was on June 17, 1963, that the end began. That was the day prayer was removed from public schools. Christians argued about this date as if everything was fine on Tuesday and then fell apart on Wednesday. I am certainly not saying that this was not a sad day for followers of Christ; but this assessment is not only naïve, it is indicative of our disconnection to the real crisis. The crisis did not begin when prayer was removed from public schools but when we stopped praying. This event was not the starting place of our cultural decline but the result of years of the church's diminishing influence on society.

Many people have described this as a cultural war, and our view often seems rooted in a perspective that it is a battle of the churched against the unchurched. Whether it is in the arena of political perspectives or government policy, we tend to speak about the shift from a Christian worldview as if it were instigated and implemented by those who were outside of the church's reach.

Our language communicates a deep cultural chasm that assumes tremendous distance between the conflicting parties. But if we look more closely at what is really happening, we will be even more disturbed. Very little distance remains between those who we feel affirm Christian values and those who seem committed to the elimination of those values from the American conscience. If anything, we have had an over-churched leadership base in the last thirty years. Jimmy Carter's campaign swept with surprising success behind the theme of being "born again." Ronald Reagan is often seen as the contemporary Gideon for the Christian Right. The Bushes are Methodist, and both Bill Clinton and Al Gore are Southern Baptist. In fact, President George W. Bush openly professes his conversion to Jesus Christ. The individuals who have held the highest position in our nation's government are extraordinarily rooted in an evangelical history. If we find any of them lacking in what we consider to be a Christian value system, it is not because they were unchurched, but it could perhaps even be said that it is because they were churched. I feel confident that a closer examination would prove this to be true throughout our society.

From athlete to actor, musician to politician, both those who advocate the heart of God and those who seem to war against him have many times been the product of the Western church. The problem has not been that these individuals of significant influence were outside of the sphere of the church's influence, but that, in fact, they sat in the center of the church and remained unchanged at the core.

America's best atheists are children of the church. It is rare to find a person

> **America's best atheists are children of the church.**

who is a passionate enemy of the church who has never had contact with her. The diminishing influence of the American church on American society is not simply because fewer people are going to church, but fewer people are going to church because of the diminishing influence of Christ on the church itself.

The church, at best, fell asleep. It might be fair to say that we lost the power to transform culture. We accommodated to a culture that was, for us, user-friendly. We equated being a good citizen with being a good Christian. We lived without persecution and soon found ourselves without conviction. We didn't lose America; we gave her away! In our panic and powerlessness, we turned to political means to seek to regain what we once had through spiritual awakening. Yet as a moral majority we could not accomplish what God could through Gideon's few.

The world around us was clearly shifting. What we couldn't figure out was why it seemed so disconnected from the influence of the Christian faith. Christianity had become a world religion. It carried all the trappings that came with that distinction. What appeared to be America's giant was in reality more like Dorothy's Oz. If Christianity was king in this land, then the emperor had no clothes! The church was no longer the shaper of modern culture, but, in fact, modern culture had become the shaper of the church. This should be our great awakening. The world changed, and we didn't. The world changed for the worse because we didn't change at all. The world changed for the better, and we missed the change. The world waits for the church to once again become God's agent of change.

THE SECULAR NATION

Do you remember all the voices warning us that America was becoming a secular nation? Do you remember believing it? We were convinced that the great enemy of our time was Secular Humanism. Too many of us still believe this. While our nation systematically eliminates overt Christian influences from the public arena, America's new grass-roots religion is not atheism but pantheism. Even with the public schools advocating evolution and removing creation science, belief in God is nearly at 100 percent. Even with the bombardment of modernity's materialism, rationalism, existentialism, and empiricism, our society continues its spiritual quest. America is an extraordinarily spiritual society.

Today we are not moving towards a godless land but to a land with many gods. We are more mystical than ever. We are more open than ever. We are more searching than ever. We are more inquisitive than ever. The reality is that America is not becoming a secular nation but more spiritual than it has been in perhaps one hundred years. From Deepak Chopra to Oprah Winfrey, we live in the era of the techno-spiritual guru. From New Age literature to pop psychology, our bookstores are full of spirit-based self-help books. The Psychic Network is as readily available as TBN. God talk is everywhere. From *Touched by an Angel* to *The X-Files*, from *The Matrix* to *Magnolia*, the quest for the spiritual permeates our contemporary visual literature. The biting truth is that this country is not rejecting spirituality but Christianity.

> **Is it possible that it wasn't the nation that was becoming dangerously secular but the church?**

The indictment that we must receive is that the Christian faith as we express it is no longer seen as a viable spiritual option. Masses gave the church a try and left wanting. We accuse them of not being willing to surrender to God; they accuse us of not knowing him. People are rejecting Christ *because* of the church! Once we were called Christians by an unbelieving world, and now we call ourselves Christians and the world calls us hypocrites. Is it possible that it wasn't the nation that was becoming dangerously secular but the church? We were neither relevant nor transcendent. We have become, in the worst of ways, religious. We are the founders of the secular nation.

THE BIBLE COMMUNITY FELLOWSHIP CHURCH

"We're looking for a church that meets our needs." It seems like I've heard this one a thousand times. The phenomenon of church shoppers has profoundly shaped the contemporary church. The entire conversation is not about relevance but convenience. The focus is not in serving the world; the church itself became the focal point. Our motto degenerated from "We are the church, here to serve a lost and broken world" to "What does the church have to offer me?" This move has made the pastor the only minister, while making the members the only recipients of ministry. What is lost in this process is an army of healers touching the planet.

In many ways the emergence of the suburbs and the realities of "white flight" paved the way for the community church. After World War II, we experienced growing prosperity and peace. The suburbs were born out of the post-war 1950s. They served as our shelter from the problems in the world. We lived in this intersection between rural values and urban conveniences. Over the next twenty years, the suburbs also became the urban refuge. While our cities experienced urban decay and our society began to destabilize, we were able to hide outside the center.

> **The cultural environment became comfortable, and the gospel shifted from a church "on mission" to a church that supported missions.**

These massive and sprawling planned communities were created wherever baby boomers wanted to colonize. Understandably, these communities could be characterized by a few emerging and identifiable patterns: homogenous, educated, and white-collar. These suburbs birthed the community church, which is—in itself—a good thing. Starting churches everywhere they are needed is always important. Yet at the same time, we can attribute much of our present dilemma to the role that the community church has played. The portrayal of the church as a fortress became a prevailing value. The church became a refuge from the world rather than a force in the world. Predictability and stability became dominant themes. The cultural environment became comfortable, and the gospel shifted from a church "on mission" to a church that supported missions.

Another aspect of our culture that emerged from this era was the concept of customer service. We both expect and demand to be treated as consumers. "If you want my patronage, you had better cater to my needs." This type of ideology became a reality for the church. In both traditional and contemporary churches, the member became the customer to whom the product was tailored.

He walked confidently up to me on a Sunday morning. It was clear that he knew his way around a church. He kind of stood out since he was wearing a suit and tie. Our cultural apparel is much more casual than that. He introduced himself and explained that he had been attending for a little over a month. He informed me that the teaching met his standards, that the music was acceptable, and that he was pleased with what he found in the children's and youth ministries. He went on

to explain that he was married and had several children. When I asked him where they were, he explained that they were not yet allowed to attend. He wanted to check us out for several weeks before he brought his family. He wanted to make sure the products and services were in line with what he felt his family needed. This wasn't about theology; this was all about customer service.

On another day Alex, one of our pastors, was engaged in an intense conversation with one of our more gifted artists. He was a longtime attendee who did not want to be a member. Like many from a church background, he had a tendency to see the church through a critical filter and proceeded to express his criticisms. Alex stopped him to establish a frame for the rest of the conversation. "Remember, this isn't about you."

Unfortunately, for too many people, when the conversation is no longer about them, there's not much left to be said. We've been taught that we are the center of the universe, and we evaluate everything on its ability to meet our needs. Some of the best communicators of the Scriptures who I know have had people leave their churches for the express reason that they're not being fed. I know that we are the sheep of God, and sheep require the Shepherd to feed them, but there must come a time when we become shepherds who feed others.

> **Are we too much about us getting fed and too little about us exercising our faith?**

Is it really all about us being fed? I think it might be important to remember that over 60 percent of Americans are overweight or even obese. Is it possible that this is also true in the arena of personal spirituality? Are we too much about us getting fed and too little about us exercising our faith?

Too many of our statements about the crisis in the American church center on the superficial arena of style and neglect to go to the core issue of self. At the core of so much of the resistance the church is experiencing is the preservation of selfishness and self-centeredness. It is one thing to have a preference; it is another to demand that one's preferences be honored above the needs of those without Christ.

For some churches, maintaining a standard of hymns and pews has been more important than the changing world around them. Now we have to live with the reality that, all too many times, we kept our traditions and lost our children. For others, the real issue became the tension between relevance and revolution. We became the masters of programming and, strangely enough, knowledgeable of the Bible. The focus deteriorated to formatting around the desires of Christians. In the process, we lost our immediacy and responsiveness to obeying God's call to reach the nations. While we have seen a few wonderful examples of congregations that never lost their apostolic calling, the formerly revolutionary church soon became the community church. The community church must now once again become the revolutionary church. What seems radical must become normal.

SAFE THEOLOGY

Out of the community church context has come an unending parade of pop and bumper sticker theologies—the kinds that give us comfort for all the wrong reasons. One of these in particular has both misguided the church and diluted the calling on every believer who is shaped by it. You've heard it said that the safest place to be is in the center of God's will. I am sure this promise was well intended, but it is neither true nor innocuous. When we believe that God's purpose, intention, or promise is that we will be safe from harm, we are utterly disconnected from the movement and power of God.

> **If those who prepare for leadership are looking for the safe place, who will lead the church into the dangerous places?**

I remember sitting in the home of a pastor and his wife just after they had finished seminary. They were tremendously gifted and had chosen to serve in a small community of a few thousand residents. We began to talk about their future, and I suggested they move to a major metropolitan center, such as Los Angeles. I was stunned not so much by their response, but by the rationale behind it. With great passion, they told me that God would never expect them to do that. God would never subject their children to the danger and corruption of the city. I remember leaving that night, wondering what was happening to the church. If those who prepare for leadership are looking for the safe place, who will lead the church into the dangerous places?

Somehow we have missed the reality of the biblical experience. From Abraham to Paul, those who followed God were subjected to great dangers. Paul describes his journey with Jesus as anything but safe.

In 2 Corinthians 11:23-28, Paul writes, "Are they servants of Christ? (I am out of my mind to talk like this.) I am more. I have worked much harder, been in prison more frequently, been flogged more severely, and been exposed to death again and again. Five times I received from the Jews the forty lashes minus one. Three times I was beaten with rods, once I was stoned, three times I was shipwrecked, I spent a night and a day in the open sea, I have been constantly on the move. I have been in danger from rivers, in danger from bandits, in danger from my own countrymen, in danger from Gentiles; in danger in the city, in danger in the country, in danger at sea; and in danger from false brothers. I have labored and toiled and have often gone without sleep; I have known hunger and thirst and have often gone without food; I have been cold and naked. Besides everything else, I face daily the pressure of my concern for all the churches."

The truth of the matter is that the center of God's will is not a safe place but the most dangerous place in the world! God fears nothing and no one! God moves with intentionality and power. To live outside of God's will puts us in danger; to live in his will makes us dangerous.

On my first Friday night in south Dallas, I felt overwhelmed by the intensity of the neighborhood. I was trying to find the duplex where a handful of believers were meeting that night. After realizing that I was lost, I suddenly became aware of how hard my heart was pounding. I was gripped in sheer fear. I stopped my car in the middle of Grand Avenue and cried out to the Lord to give me courage. I waited for one of the many verses that I had memorized to enter my head: "Greater is He that is in me than he that is in the world," "I can do all things through Christ who strengthens me," "Fear not for I am with you, says the Lord," "Be strong and of good courage." But none of these verses came to mind. Instead, the Spirit of God sent crashing into my mind a verse that I had never put to memory: "To live is Christ and to die is gain." This was not the word of encouragement I was looking for from the Lord. Yet it rang in my head over and over again as I sat there in my car. It was clear. Following Jesus is a dan-

> **"Only dead men can follow the God of the Cross."**

gerous undertaking. He was willing to die on our behalf. The Father was not only willing to let himself die, but he commanded it. The only way that I could truly follow God was to die to myself and to live for him. Only dead men can follow the God of the Cross.

How could we ever think the Christian faith would be safe when its central metaphor is an instrument of death? It is not a coincidence that baptism is a water grave depicting death and resurrection. It is no less significant that the ongoing ordinance of the Lord's Supper is a reminder of sacrifice. How did we ever develop a safe theology from such a dangerous faith?

We love to focus on those who were thrown to the lions and lived, thrust into the fire and not burned; people "who through faith conquered kingdoms, administered justice, and gained what was promised; who shut the mouths of lions, quenched the fury of the flames, and escaped the edge of the sword; whose weakness was turned to strength; and who became powerful in battle and routed foreign armies. Women received back their dead, raised to life again" (Hebrews 11:33-35a). But the Scriptures are clear that safety is not the promise of faith. The writer of Hebrews also says that "others were tortured and refused to be released, so that they might gain a better resurrection. Some faced jeers and flogging, while still others were chained and put in prison. They were stoned; they were sawed in two; they were put to death by the sword. They went about in sheepskins and goatskins, destitute, persecuted and mistreated—the world was not worthy of them. They wandered in deserts and mountains, and in caves and holes in the ground. These were all commended for their faith, yet none of them received what had been promised" (Hebrews 11:35b-39).

THE PERFECT STORM

I hope, by this time, you have noticed that I have attempted to assess some of the fundamental causes for the decline of the church. Have you also noticed that none of them deal with the outside environment? So much has been written on the changing canvas of society. Certainly, generational and cultural shifts are significant and need to be addressed.

> **The church must raise her sails and move with the Spirit if we are not to be left behind.**

Yet it is my conviction that these are not the essential reasons for the loss of momentum and the atrophy of the church. These rapid and dramatic changes have made for rough sailing these last fifty years, but they are not sinking the boat. There is no perfect storm out there that can sink the church of Jesus Christ. No matter how much or how rapidly culture changes, the church is designed to prevail. Yet, with each culture shift, it is painfully obvious that the church has become an institution rather than a movement.

The distinction lies in the fact that institutions preserve culture, while movements create culture. Many times those who attempt to preserve a dissipating culture will also join it in its ignoble demise. Everything about your culture may be born and rooted in the work of the Holy Spirit. But the Spirit of God moves like the wind, leaving a still silence where he once blew and beckoning us to where he now stirs. The church must raise her sails and move with the Spirit if we are not to be left behind. It is not enough to simply hang on; we must boldly move forward.

In the end, the crisis is always spiritual. Admittedly, radical changes outside the church demand an even more radical sacrifice from within the church. We understand this when we consider the realities of life for believers in persecuted countries. We champion their sacrifice and willingness to stand for Christ, even at the cost of their own lives. Yet we consider laying aside our traditions and cultural preferences as an unreasonable expectation. From my own experiences, I know that the only storm that can sink a church is the one that rages from within.

Just like urban legends, there are church legends: stories of churches splitting over the color of carpet; pastors being fired for baptizing a person of color; emergency business meetings being called, gathering inactive members for the purpose of firing a too-active pastor. I know of a church that fired its pastor after the church grew over a thousand in its first year. I also know of a dying congregation that sold its church to a community center so that the new church that had rented its property and had grown to four hundred in just a couple of years could never take over the property. Why? Because the new church didn't fit the old congregation's theological constructs.

Like urban legends, the church legends that haunt our recent history reveal more about us than we perhaps care to know. In the end, atrophy is never simply about style; it is always about the substance of servanthood. It is about a people who are willing to submit to the Lordship of Christ, no matter what the personal implications.

I had my reservations, but not long ago I accepted the role of working as a church interventionist. I had held conversations with the lay leadership before the present pastor came, so there was a level of trust between us. A small coalition surrounded the finance chairman in a mean-spirited movement to fire their pastor the week of Christmas. It was the same time of the year that a pastoral firing was initiated the year before.

They called the association to establish this intervention team, and the opposing leadership agreed that, whatever the association's recommendation was, they would adhere to it. After a thorough investigation of the charges against the pastor and the actual circumstance that led to this crisis, the intervention team overwhelmingly supported the pastor and, in the process, reprimanded those involved in the opposing action.

> **You can change the name, but if you don't change the heart, the atrophy will kill you in the end.**

Immediately after the judgment of the intervention team was announced at the business meeting, the same coalition proceeded to call a meeting to continue the process of firing the pastor. I will never forget sitting in the office, talking to the chairman of finance, walking through the Scriptures with him, and asking him if he understood that what he was doing was against the teachings of Jesus. He calmly said, "Yes." Wondering if I had somehow confused him or made myself unclear, I again referred to the Scriptures and asked him if he understood what Jesus was saying and that he was consciously disobeying the teachings of Christ. And he again said he understood that he was disobeying Christ—and was going to proceed.

With the pastor sitting to my right and the senior deacon sitting by him in support of his leadership, I was struck with the reality that here was the source of a perfect storm. When those who hold positions of leadership in the church of Jesus Christ stand opposed to the very heart of God and refuse to submit their lives to his Word, it is the death of the life of that church. As an outside intervention team, we could only watch as a room full of people who had no spiritual vitality, but still held membership in the church, voted the pastor out. They soon reversed every initiative that he had launched with the purpose of impacting their community. With the movement now stopped, the institution was secure.

The irony in all of this is that the church had changed its name to New

Hope. You can change the name, but if you don't change the heart, the atrophy will kill you in the end. All the changes in the world, minus the heart of God, equal zero movement.

> ❝We often look so long and so regretfully upon the closed door, that we do not see the ones which open for us.❞ —ALEXANDER GRAHAM BELL

FUEL FOR THOUGHT

1. Is the unstated goal of our congregation to survive?
2. How oriented is our church toward servanthood?
3. How well does our approach toward worship and evangelism reflect the needs and culture of our unchurched community?
4. What storms within threaten to sink our church?
5. How could we mobilize our church to serve a broken world?
6. In 2 Corinthians 11:23-28 Paul describes how he faced many fears in his mission. What fears do you face in your own?
7. What do we need in order to die to live for others?
8. How can we catalyze the shift from getting fed to exercising faith?

"But Jesus immediately said to them: 'Take courage! It is I. Don't be afraid.'

" 'Lord, if it's you,' Peter replied, 'tell me to come to you on the water.'

" 'Come,' he said.

"Then Peter got down out of the boat, walked on the water and came toward Jesus. But when he saw the wind, he was afraid and, beginning to sink, cried out, 'Lord, save me!'

"Immediately Jesus reached out his hand and caught him" (Matthew 14:27-31a).

HE TELLS YOU TO TAKE COURAGE. YOU ARE INSPIRED AND OVER-whelmed to go where no one has gone before. You enter an experience only possible when you are moving towards Jesus. Then it happens. You see the invisible. Peter walked on water, and that's strange enough. But then he saw the wind! Not the waves. Not the effects of the wind. He saw the wind! And then he was afraid. To follow Jesus is to engage the invisible. To lead the church is to advance the invisible kingdom. And so much becomes visible. You begin to see the gates of hell. You begin to see the powers and principalities. You begin to see the field, white to harvest. You begin to see the wind that rages against any who dare to follow Christ. Who will not shrink back? Who will become an unstoppable force? Only those who see the invisible!

"By faith Moses, when he had grown up, refused to be known as the son of Pharaoh's daughter. He chose to be mistreated along with the people of God rather than to enjoy the pleasures of sin for a short time. He regarded disgrace for the sake of Christ as of greater value than the treasures of Egypt, because he was looking ahead to his reward. By faith he left Egypt, not fearing the king's anger; he persevered because he saw him who is invisible" (Hebrews 11:24-27).

FIRST MOVEMENT

C H A P T E R   O N E

FRICTION TRACTION

I engage in a peculiar habit whenever I have the opportunity to travel: making my way to the center of the city and walking the streets. I never really feel that I understand a nation or a people until I've had a chance to visit their city. It's not enough to drive a rental car through it or to see it from overhead from an airplane window. You have to walk the streets. You have to feel the environment in which the people live, hear their voices, and have the strange and unusual sounds of their language seep through your ears into your mind.

I love to walk down lesser-traveled streets where, oftentimes, there are small markets and open-air restaurants. The smells that fill those streets bring you closer to the soul of the city. Sometimes you're captured by aromas that instantly cause you to salivate. Like the siren, the city pulls you in to eat foods that you could not possibly identify, with the hope that the taste you experience will somehow match the aroma that pulled you in. Other times your nostrils are filled with the stench of decay and desperation. Some cities overwhelm you with a smell that travels long distances, beyond their busiest roads. The weather and the experiences, whether fragrant or foul, are important to understanding and experiencing the essence of a city.

Bangkok is one of these cities that I've explored over the years. I must admit that, from my first experience, it was not my favorite. While the street markets are intriguing to experience, not to mention great places to pick up bargains, they are surrounded with some of the darkest realities of urban life. From every direction, you are reminded that Bangkok is one of the epicenters of child prostitution and a global exporter of AIDS and various other STDs. At the same time, by walking down virtually any street in the city, the careful observer will find countless numbers of "spirit houses"—miniature houses which grace the lawns of most residences and decorate the most ornate buildings. These structures serve as spiritual hotels for evil spirits as a way to keep these spirits at bay.

> **"The city temple reminds us that Bangkok is essentially a spiritual city with an impoverished soul."**

At the heart of the city there is the Wat Phra Kaeo Temple—the city's spirit house. The city temple reminds us that Bangkok is essentially a spiritual city with an impoverished soul. From the elderly that I would watch pleading with the spirits for help to the dark brown colors of the rivers that flow through the city, Bangkok's need is inescapable.

I should have known from the start that, as much as I intended to never return to Bangkok (a city whose name, like Los Angeles, also means "City of Angels"), I would one day have an inseparable relationship with the soul of the city.

A MIRACLE IN BANGKOK

It happened last March. We had just finished a week of ministry in Kanchanaburi. Forty-two of us had gone together to serve over five hundred believers who, once a year, came together for refreshment and retooling. This was our day off. We were back in Bangkok.

With mixed feelings, I reluctantly joined the group that was going to the night market to pick up last-minute gifts for our families and friends back home. Like a mother with too many children at the mall, I was trying to watch everyone in our group. I had warned them of the traffic. It was intense and extremely dangerous, and I instructed everyone to stay together and look out for one another. Like a bad script, my warnings seemed to foreshadow the very experience that I was going to have.

I had taken my children, Aaron and Mariah, on this trip. I felt that this experience would expand both their vision and burden for a world without Christ. Aaron had crossed the street with the first twenty or thirty people. I turned around to instruct the other group to begin to cross, but as the light turned red, eight-year-old Mariah darted across the street before I could stop her. I could almost feel the weight of the car as it hit her head-on. Just a few feet away, I watched helplessly as her body bent around the hood of the car before it was thrown like a rag doll onto the streets of Bangkok.

It was nothing less than a surreal moment. Hundreds of sparrows were flying overhead. I could only describe them as manic. They seemed to be out of their minds, flying in a frenzied manner and making a noise that begged for release from a torment that we could not understand. I later came to know that it was the practice of the city to capture these sparrows, place them into wooden cages, and take them to places of worship for the purpose of having people impute their sins upon them in hopes of finding forgiveness and mercy. I know this may sound crazy, but I can only say that everyone who was with me would agree that somehow those birds seemed to express a connection, if not a transference, to demonic oppression. Under the ominous cloud of the birds, on the busiest street, at the heavily populated intersection, and amidst the multitude of cars, my little girl lay crumpled on the hard concrete.

I rushed over to her and bent down to pick her up, but before I could do so, she stood on her own. Not a bone was broken. As I held her in my arms, the police arrived and insisted that we rush Mariah to the hospital. The driver of the car implored us to come with him for medical care as a large crowd gathered around us. Somehow all I could say was, "Mariah is a follower of Jesus Christ. God has protected her. She's fine." Rather than uttering the words, I felt more as if I was hearing them. It was as if someone else was saying them, and I was simply observing.

I was told later of a peculiar phenomenon that people observed that day. At the moment that our group of fifty or more surrounded my little girl and began to pray, all the sparrows overhead stopped flapping their wings. They stopped their insane ranting. For a moment there seemed to be peace in the soul of Bangkok.

My little girl is my miracle from Bangkok—proof that God has a significant purpose for her life. It's taken some time for her to regain the courage to cross the street. You can imagine the memories that her eight-year-old mind has had to deal with.

> It's not that we haven't tried. It's that when we ran across the street, we got hurt—hit head-on and banged up pretty bad.

AFRAID TO CROSS THE STREET

The first time she stood at the edge of a sidewalk, she was paralyzed. At first I would have to carry her across. Soon it would only require that I hold her hand. And now, once again, I face the parental challenge of keeping her from crossing the street on her own.

Why is this experience so important to our present conversation? Because the church is afraid to cross the street. It's not that we haven't tried. It's that when we ran across the street, we got hurt—hit head-on and banged up pretty bad. And because we are the church, and we have a resilience that even we cannot understand, we somehow got up and walked away from the accident. Somehow our bruises healed, and we live to try again—except we are too afraid.

The church stands at the edge of the sidewalk, paralyzed, afraid to cross. Sometimes the memories are overwhelming. Sometimes we need someone to carry us, and other times just to hold our hand. But this chapter is about coming to where, even if we've tried to cross the street and failed to make it across, even if we've experienced the pain of getting hit head on, we can regain the courage to get to the other side. What's across the street from your church? Could it be that God has called you to step out of your safety and cross over and engage this world?

Mariah joins the family tradition of colliding with cars. For me, like Mariah, it seemed to come out of nowhere. It would be so much easier to avoid the oncoming collision if our peripheral vision was better or if we had at least somehow just seen it coming.

When I talk to pastors and church leaders, I rarely find people who do not have it in their hearts to touch the world with the love of Christ. Often the exact opposite is true. Many are followers of Jesus Christ who are deeply burdened with the human condition. They care deeply about what God cares about; they understand that Jesus came to seek and save that which is lost; they know their churches should relevantly and powerfully impact the world around them; but they just can't seem to get across the street. Unseen obstacles keep knocking them down. It's hard to gain momentum when, every time you pick up speed, you crash into something. It's bad enough to get hit by a speeding car because you were running somewhere and didn't see it. My experience was different.

RUNNING SCARED

My first car crash was quite the opposite. When I was about twelve years old, my brother and I had seen a horror film at the house across the street, and then we had to go home in the dark. I was so scared of getting caught by the same creatures that I had just watched for two hours that I ran with the speed of fright. All I could think about was reaching the safety of my house.

I know it seems strange, but I never saw it. I ran straight into my parents' station wagon that was parked in front of our yard. I don't mean I clipped it, touched it, or brushed it. I mean I ran smack head-on into a stationary vehicle.

This is probably more descriptive of our present condition than being hit by moving cars. We're running scared, and because we are, we're hitting the cultural obstacles rather than overcoming them. In Deuteronomy 2, there's a peculiar story of God shaping his people and transforming them from slaves to conquerors. It is one thing to be set free; it is another thing to become free.

The Lord says to Moses and his people, "Set out now and cross the Arnon Gorge. See, I have given into your hand Sihon the Amorite, king of Heshbon, and his country. Begin to take possession of it and engage him in battle. This very day I will begin to put the terror and fear of you on all the nations under heaven. They will hear reports of you and will tremble and be in anguish because of you" (Deuteronomy 2:24-25).

This was Israel's defining moment. This was the battle in which God was going to establish them as his people. Through this victory, God was going to place the fear of God in all the nations who worshipped false gods. His instructions were absolutely clear, "Go pick a fight, engage them in battle, and today I will give you victory."

Surprisingly enough, the very next verse tells us that Moses sent messengers to Sihon, King of Heshbon, with this message: "Let us pass through your country. We will stay on the main road; we will not turn aside to the right or to the left. Sell us food to eat and water to drink for their price in silver. Only let us pass through on foot…until we cross the Jordan into the land the Lord our God is giving us" (Deuteronomy 2:26-29).

If you read these two passages separately, you could hardly place them at the same event. Israel's response to God's command that they engage and conquer was to offer a compromise of peace. They simply couldn't or wouldn't believe that God would keep his word. While God was committed to establishing them as a people of his presence and power, they were more than willing to settle for much less than that. All they wanted was to survive.

Shortly after this the text says, "But Sihon king of Heshbon refused to let us pass through. For the Lord your God had made his spirit stubborn and his heart obstinate in order to give him into your hands, as he has now done" (Deuteronomy 2:30). And then it says, "The Lord said to me, 'See, I have begun to deliver Sihon and his country over to you. Now begin to conquer and possess his land'" (Deuteronomy 2:31).

> **Often it is God who forces circumstances upon us in which it becomes necessary for us to rely on God's goodness.**

This passage teaches us a very peculiar thing about God. His approach toward us is often to invite us to believe in him and move in his power. God's first choice is to search for a heart that is wholly his and then strongly support it. But many times that is not the condition of our hearts. Often it is God who forces circumstances upon us in which it becomes necessary for us to rely on God's goodness.

Since Israel did not have a heart to trust God, God hardened the heart of

Sihon—made his spirit stubborn and provoked him to go to war against Israel. God did all of this so that Israel would begin to conquer and possess the land. In short, what God did was bless Israel by forcing them to engage in a battle that they were afraid to fight. As a result of this, Israel not only experienced victory in that one particular battle but discovered that there was no city too strong for them and that the Lord delivered them all.

AS THE WORLD TURNS

In the same way, the church is God's agent for redeeming the earth to himself. We are called to engage in the battle for which Jesus Christ died. Matthew tells us that the kingdom of God is forcefully advancing, and forceful men take hold of it. Jesus reminds us that the church will crash against the very gates of hell. Paul describes us through the imagery of soldiers of light, dispelling the kingdom of darkness.

For two thousand years the church has been called by God to encounter culture through his transforming power. I am convinced that many of the global trends that have brought fear and concern to the contemporary church are the very act of God, in a sense, hardening the heart of Sihon king of Heshbon. He will force us to engage the battles at hand. He will do whatever is necessary to reorganize this planet until we have nowhere to run and nowhere to hide.

For two thousand years Jesus has commanded us to go and make disciples of all nations. We have, at best, given this command nominal adherence. It seems now that God has brought us to a place in history where he is bringing the nations to us. And while we may perceive that the challenge is intensifying, it is perhaps within this very context that the church will discover most powerfully what it means to go, conquer, and possess the land.

> **The culture from which the church has been dominantly informed and formed has positioned the church to be either antagonistic or ineffective in the emerging global scenario.**

Several global movements are, in many ways, presenting countermovements to the contemporary church. These movements have had both sweeping and dramatic impacts on the culture in which we serve. The culture from which the church has been dominantly informed and formed has positioned the church to be either antagonistic or ineffective in the emerging global scenario.

While there are many current books that describe the significant part of the phenomenon known as postmodernism, I would like to approach some of these issues from the perspective of globalization. For if postmodernism is the best description of what's happening on the Western scene, globalization is the panoramic view of this historic shift.

We're going to look at a few of these globalization issues from the perspective that the very movements that create friction for the contemporary church are the same ones from which we can generate traction. Friction is what hinders us, slows us down. But traction is what helps us get going and enables us to launch a movement!

RADICAL MIGRATION: A MOVING STORY

The first significant global shift is the emergence of radical migration. Sometimes we forget that, in the past, the world has essentially been stationary. It was extraordinary for a person to ever leave home, meet foreign peoples, and settle elsewhere. Jesus never traveled more than thirty miles from his hometown during his adult life.

While visiting Pennsylvania I learned a new phrase which I had never heard before. People kept talking about being "married to the land." While visiting the university town of Penn State, I was working from the assumption that most of the community moved there to receive their education only to move somewhere else. However, many times when I asked people where they planned to live long term, they would look surprised and say, "Well, I'm married to the land," which meant that they were never going to move. It wasn't an option. It wasn't anything they would ever consider. They had deep roots and probably considered anyone who wasn't married to the land to be nothing more than an educated transient.

This was the real world of the past—the world from which the American church was formed. Even though we are a nation launched by pilgrims and pioneers—where the American spirit is unmistakably marked by adventure—the American people, in the end, did settle. The churches were a part of the land—hallmarks of stability and continuity. All over America, next to churches lie cemeteries that have no more than a half dozen last names on all the tombstones. They were family churches. If you had lived in their community for twenty years but you were not born there, you were still an outsider.

MEET YOUR NEW NEIGHBOR

Nothing is inherently wrong with this description, except in the context of radical migration. When churches have been informed by continuity, and then suddenly there's sociological discontinuity, responses may range from racism to irrelevance. At no time in history has human movement in any way paralleled what we are experiencing. It's more than just a movement from one village to the next, and it's quite different from the expansion of empires through conquest and colonization. Immigration and integration are common experiences, and a job transfer can easily mean moving to another country.

When everyone in the community looks just like you, it is not difficult to justify isolation and exclusivity.

In Los Angeles, migration has created the world's second largest Mexican city, the second largest Salvadorian city, and the largest Korean city. For churches locked into homogenous paradigms, migration creates friction. In our pre-global society, our churches were filled with people just like us. When everyone in the community looks just like you, it is not difficult to justify isolation and exclusivity.

Migration, though global, is most dramatically felt locally. What has become known as the phenomenon of transitional communities is simply the local expression of radical migration. People move all the time, and, of course, what that means on a communal level is that neighborhoods are constantly changing. And so we find white churches in new black communities, black congregations in immigrant Latino communities, and Latino congregations in emerging Korean communities. But again, what creates friction for the church can also be traction: The nations are at our front door, we have an opportunity to love our neighbors as ourselves, and the practical application of reconciliation is right across the street.

For years the bulk of American Christians who were committed to "missions" could only participate through giving and praying. Today the call to crosscultural ministry doesn't even require going; it just requires staying with a purpose.

URBANIZATION: SETTING OUR GLOBAL CLOCKS

The second significant global shift is urbanization. If you walked into my office, you would see seven clocks on the wall, all set to different times. Underneath each clock there is the name of a different city: New York, London, Paris, Berlin, Tokyo-Yokohama, Buenos Aires, and Shanghai.

These seven clocks represent the first seven cities to gain a population of five million people. In 1950 they were the sole members of this exclusive group. Today there are more than seventy cities with more than five million people. Mexico City, which was not even among the first seven, is perhaps the largest city in the world, with somewhere around thirty million people. Next to those seven clocks is a giant clock. Underneath that clock the name reads "Los Angeles," reminding me every day that, in many ways, Los Angeles is the capital of this new world.

Like many cities across the world, Los Angeles inhales the nations and has the potential of exhaling the gospel. In recent years, Ralph Winter has proposed that the last great frontier for the gospel is the cities. It is impossible to talk about the future without mentioning the cities. While human history began in a garden, it ends in the city. The rural beginnings of humanity have succumbed to the urban future. This is a planet of great cities.

This phenomenon creates great friction for the contemporary church. The church has been informed and formed by rural ethos. Even the suburban church is in many ways the natural development of the county-seat church, maintaining its focus on family, community, and rural values. Again, there is nothing inherently wrong with these focuses and expressions of the Christian faith, but they certainly find themselves in crisis when surrounded by the urban world.

It's ironic that the word *pagan* finds its roots in a word meaning "country dweller." Where once the pagan lived in the country and the danger of the city was to be Christianized, now Christians tend to live away from the cities and view the urban dweller as the true pagan.

THE CONCRETE JUNGLE

The impact of urbanization goes far beyond inner cities, ghettos, and poverty. The urban world encompasses the most dramatic expressions of what many call postmodernism. Urbanites tend to be more liberal and culturally progressive. Urban centers and mega-cities are often microcosms of the entire planet. They have a disproportionate influence and impact on human development and culture. What happens in the city seeps out of the concrete streets and shapes the minds and lives of suburban youth and, often, even those who live in the most isolated regions of our country.

While urbanization has created tremendous friction for the contemporary church, it can also generate extraordinary traction. Many times in the rural or suburban community, the real issues of human poverty are camouflaged and overlooked. That's rarely possible in the urban world. When masses of people are pressed together, the society begins to reflect—on a societal level—the realities that are true within each human being's heart. Everything seems accentuated in the city. Poverty is accentuated; entertainment is accentuated; loneliness is accentuated. Lust for power, wealth, status, prestige, and all those things that are often overlooked in the suburban world are exposed in the urban world.

> **From crimes to acts of kindness, the actions humans choose are not lost in the city, but in fact the exact opposite is true.**

Please don't misunderstand: These very things exist in the country and in the suburbs, as well as in the city. But the city is a context in which these things are magnified and intensified. From crimes to acts of kindness, the actions humans choose are not lost in the city, but in fact the exact opposite is true.

The church has, for far too long, yearned for a return to nature's serenity and safety. It is no small matter that places like Colorado Springs are the new Meccas of the Christian faith. It seems that every year we watch major Christian organizations flee the urban challenge of Los Angeles.

FROM URBANITIS TO URBAN EYES

Years ago Kim and I were driving through the rolling hills of Arkansas. I have to admit that the surroundings were beautiful, even to an urbanite. The radio was turned off, and we were enjoying a time of complete quiet. I don't remember how long it lasted, but I was the one who made the mistake of breaking that silence. After soaking it all in, I turned to Kim and I said, "Look at all this undeveloped land."

My wife is normally rational and only occasionally violent, but she began beating me mercilessly as I drove the car, shouting some theological construct such as, "Erwin, those are trees! God created trees! God created trees! Man created cities! Those are trees! This is not undeveloped land!"

I'm not always the picture of a sensitive man, but I was astute enough to know that I had said the wrong thing. To this day I still wonder how many of us have urban eyes and how many of us have urbanitis.

Urban eyes see the potential of the future mega-cities. They are inspired by the latent possibilities where millions of people are within walking distance and within hearing range. Urban eyes are opened by the burden of the masses and believe that every city can be renamed, even as Ezekiel renamed the city "The Lord Is There."

Urbanitis is an acute allergic reaction to any urban environment; any proximity to this environment is avoided at any and all cost. The inconveniences of highways that turn into parking lots during rush hour, of air that you can see but not breathe, of buildings that keep replacing trees, of sprawling masses absent of genuine community are justification enough to stay away. However, urbanization creates traction when we see that God is scooping the masses and placing them carefully together, making it easier for the gospel to get to them.

POPULATION EXPLOSION: LOOK AT ALL THE LONELY PEOPLE

The third friction traction is the population explosion. About sixty years ago, the global population finally reached its first billion. It took the entire history of mankind to accumulate that many people walking this earth. Since that time, a billion people have been added almost every decade. The global population today stands at almost 6.2 billion.

This creates tremendous friction for any church that is seriously attempting to embrace the great commission. If we couldn't effectively reach the nations when there were one billion people on this earth, what chance do we have when there are six times that many? The present strategies of the contemporary church are at best incremental, while the world population has exploded exponentially.

If we were predicting the future health and viability of a nation, and we could see that for every hundred adults only one new baby was born, we would know that we were committing a national or

"Those of us who live in this window of history must consider ourselves uniquely appointed by God."

ethnic suicide. We know from basic arithmetic that, to maintain the population, you must be able to at least replace yourself. To increase a population, you must not only replace yourself, but also add at least one. While the human population has gone far beyond this minimal growth, the American church has not in any way maintained pace with this explosion of humanity. The friction is that the church in America has been declining, while the world around us has been increasing. While there are growing churches, it would be difficult to describe the American church as thriving. The friction is that our strategies for incremental growth are inadequate for a time of exponential growth.

Entire people groups (ranging in the millions) have only one disciple of Jesus Christ committed to reach them. For other people groups the situation is bleaker. The task can seem so overwhelming that it would be difficult not to give up. But the traction of this population explosion can be tremendous. We live in a unique time of human expansion. Most likely the human population will never again grow at so fast a rate, and certainly never before has this phenomenon taken place. Those of us who live in this window of history must consider ourselves uniquely appointed by God.

God chooses not only the places but also the times in which we live. He has privileged us to live not only in the greatest expansion of human population but also with the greatest opportunity for the spread of the gospel. No previous generation, even maximizing its potential, could ever have considered reaching six billion people for Christ. If the church a hundred years ago had reached everyone on the face of the earth, they wouldn't even have begun to touch the possibilities facing us. I am convinced and inspired that God would not allow us to live in a time of such great opportunity if he did not have on his heart the desire to pour out the greatest movement of his Spirit in human history.

We must take the friction of this massive challenge and create traction. We must consider strategies for incremental or nominal growth as inadequate, and we must re-examine our assumptions of how the Spirit of God desires to work through the church. We must not be satisfied until we enter into an explosion of global transformation that matches the challenge that has been entrusted to us.

TECHNOLOGICAL REVOLUTION: THE END OF REALITY

The fourth friction traction is technology. When Jesus addressed the Samaritan woman's question about where she should worship, in the temple or on the mountain, he told her that the Father is looking for those who worship him "in spirit and in truth" (John 4:23-24). In every culture and generation, the church has tried to flesh out what this means in its particular context. The church is foremost about Spirit. She must, at her core, be shaped and defined by the work of God in her midst. This doesn't eliminate the value of effort or tradition, but it does make it clear that the fuel of the church must be the Spirit.

In the same way, the church is to be reflective and responsive to truth. The essence of the church forms out of the very person of God. God's character informs the Christian community. To say that the church is built on a person beyond propositions is not an understatement. Truth exists because God is trustworthy. Anything born out of God would have to be, in its essence, spirit, and truth. But then there's the world around us. Truth would be easy to apply if the church was called to a monastic existence. Truth might be easier to understand if our faith was essentially private and expressed without relationship to people or culture.

The technological revolution has created tremendous friction. While the study of how things work has brought tremendous advances and benefits, it has also been like performing an autopsy on a living being. For a people who should be clearly identified as an authentic and real community, the ways in which we engage in a world of technology raise very serious questions. From Quakers to Baptists, Christian communities have struggled to address a crucial question: What is the appropriate relationship between the church and this technological world? The friction increases as we feel the church surrendering Spirit to technique.

TECHNICALLY SPEAKING

Is the church just a big "how to"? Does the church find her legitimacy in simply knowing how to do things better? At the same time, can the church even be meaningful without addressing "how to's"? Will the church have anything to say, or will the church even be heard if we cannot speak to the practical issues of life?

Then there's the whole arena related to practical technologies. Does the church sell out to culture when she begins to utilize the inventions of contemporary society? Does the church lose authenticity when she picks up innovation? There are very few contemporary thinkers who see the technological revolution through childlike eyes.

> **Our resolution to be discomforted with technology will ensure that we remain at least fifty years behind.**

August 6, 1945 changed our romance with technology forever—the day the bomb dropped on Hiroshima. All the promises that the scientific and technological revolution would create a better world were now found to be empty. The hope that an advanced society would bring an end to violence, poverty, and senseless human suffering was now replaced with cynicism and despair; yet the conveniences and luxuries that technology brought us maintain their power to mesmerize and captivate us.

Out of this context comes the friction that so many of us feel. We reject technology and at the same time depend on it. We bring our cell phones into church and want the music to be unplugged. Our resolution to be discomforted with technology will ensure that we remain at least fifty years behind. Even the most culturally conservative churches have no problem turning the lights on, using the microphone to preach against technology, or enjoying having running water and good plumbing. Ironically, we tend to accept technologies that bring us comfort and convenience, while rejecting the technologies that can produce creativity and innovation. And of course, this is where friction can turn to traction.

Being authentic doesn't inherently eliminate accessing technology. In fact, the best use of technology takes the focus off the technology. It accentuates humanity in the same way that spotlights should—not getting people to look at the light but helping people to see the speaker clearly. The best use of technology is to enhance the power of worship that is an expression of spirit and truth. If we can move beyond the question of whether technology is our friend or enemy and realize that it is nothing more than a tool, we can begin to see the possibilities for the Christian revolution being catalyzed by the technological revolution.

The nations that were once considered "closed access" now have Internet access. For the first time in history, we actually have the technology to speak to the planet. Without question, Hollywood's influence far surpasses that of any political leader or nation. The possibility of spreading the gospel through film, videos, television, live feed, and the World Wide Web—not to mention the continuous influence of print media and radio—gives us the real potential of saturating the planet with the message of Christ.

INFORMATION EXPLOSION: MORE THAN YOU WANTED TO KNOW

A subset of the technological revolution is the information explosion. Not only can you transmit information to almost anywhere on the planet, but now information is also available to anyone who wants it. The days of information being available only to the elite are gone. Everyone who wants to know can know. But this extraordinary access to information brings us to two new places.

The first is an era of global responsibility. I was sitting in my living room, going through a periodical. On the second page I saw a full-page photograph of a little Somalian boy whose body was ravaged by famine. His head was swollen, and his body was nothing more than skin and bone. The backdrop was clearly a desert, barren and lifeless, and standing directly behind him as he staggered to the ground was a vulture waiting for him to die.

"Our access to information, made possible by the technological revolution, places us at the epicenter of global responsibility."

This photograph incensed me. I was overwhelmed with anger. As my wife, Kim, looked at it, she began to weep. After looking at the picture time and time again, I finally grabbed the magazine and closed it as if it were pornography. I felt that my home had been invaded, that my consciousness had been violated. Kim asked me why I was so angry, and frankly, I was uncertain at the time. But soon it became clear: I didn't want to know. I didn't want to know that somewhere on this planet there was a little boy who didn't have the strength to make it to the water station. I didn't want to know that famine has a face and that suffering has a name. That one photograph robbed me of my peace of mind. It robbed me of my ignorance. It robbed me of any innocence I could hold onto.

James says that if you know what is right and you don't do it, it is sin. Our access to information, made possible by the technological revolution, places us at the epicenter of global responsibility. In some ways we know too much. We know when there's a war in the Middle East, a famine in Central Africa, a massacre in South America, or an act of violence across the street.

TOO MUCH OF A GOOD THING

The second thing that the information explosion has placed in us has been defined as "information overload," or "information anxiety." We have access to too much information. Unending data can overwhelm our memories. In some ways we know so much that we don't know what to know.

Several years ago a pastor from Arkansas called my office. I had been working with him and his church for several months, helping them address the issues of culture shifts and how to transition his congregation for an effective ministry. The moment I said hello, he blurted out, "Please don't tell me anything new. I don't want to know anything. I am overwhelmed with information. I just need some advice."

That was a turning point for me. I love information. I'm a compulsive human databank. But I had forgotten that what people need is not unlimited access to information; they need interpretation. One can reach a point where he has so much information that he doesn't know anything at all. Somehow, we have to work our way to the place where we are able to know what we need to know. If we're not careful, we can end up like a fly trapped in the World Wide Web.

It is important to keep asking ourselves the question, "What am I supposed to do with this?" The information junkie is as helpless to bring about significant change as the one who is paralyzed by the deluge of information. The information explosion creates friction for the spread of the gospel by making the church one voice among a trillion megabytes, but it generates traction when we realize that the world is only a click away.

THE GLOBAL MOSAIC: WHEN WORLDS COLLIDE

The next friction traction the church will face is the challenge of a multicultural, pluralistic world. The two most significant cities in the United States—New York and Los Angeles—are vivid expressions of a global mosaic. For the first time since cultures emerged from the Tower of Babel, the nations have begun to come back together to begin a global dialogue. This multiculturalism has created tremendous friction for the contemporary church because the church has fashioned itself around monocultural ministry—not simply in its style and texture, but also in its message.

The gospel, as presented in our time, has been crafted in a way that would only win Christians to Christ. Our religious diversity has tended to exist within the confines of a Christian worldview. We often preach to convert sinners who already believe in the God of the Bible. And our most extreme antagonists have been "Christian" atheists who adamantly reject the existence of the God of the Bible. Even with unbelievers our presentation of the gospel has been built on the assumed authority of the Scriptures.

Our most basic presentations of the good news of Jesus have been filled with assumptions. When we would eagerly tell the unchurched that God loved them and had wonderful plans for their lives, we *knew* that the word *God* would evoke the same image that we had. When we would ask an unbeliever, "If you died tonight, do you know for certain that you will be in heaven with God?" we *knew* it was unnecessary to build an argument for the existence of heaven. But we were wrong.

The idea that people without Jesus are going to hell went down far too easily for Christians who only knew Christians.

A NEW SPIRITUALITY

Evangelism for much of the church has not been among unbelievers but focused on receivers—people who already accepted our worldview. And then the Buddhist moved in across the street. He was different than the atheist. He had a value for spirituality and mysticism that surpassed the religious fervor of many church attendees. Spirituality was sometimes more central to his life than ours, and we wanted to explain to him how believing in Jesus was right.

What we began to describe as a New Age movement was the first wave of multicultural influence. For the first time we had access to multiple systems of belief. This global mosaic advocated pluralism from both a theological and relational perspective. It was easier to be certain you were right when you had never even heard of an opposing position. It was easier to be sure you were right when you felt you were in the majority position. It was easier to believe everyone else was wrong when you didn't know him or her personally. The idea that people without Jesus are going to hell went down far too easily for Christians who only knew Christians.

Everything begins to change when the world becomes your friend, when the nations become your neighbors. For many American churchgoers, pluralism ended an age of certainty. It became arrogant to think we were right and everyone else was wrong. It was presumptive to believe that our American convictions could also be imposed on a Chinese colleague or especially on someone who had never heard.

The global religious banquet-table created a buffet-line approach toward faith. People suddenly had greater options and choices of religious expression, and the blanket dismissal of other cultural values and faiths seemed to only validate how wrong fundamental Christian thinking had been. These new neighbors were not supposed to be nice people. It wasn't supposed to be so easy to like them. The fact that they were so intelligent, thoughtful, and spiritual caught many off guard. Many aspects of spiritual expression such as Zen, yoga, meditation, and discipline appear to be superior to the average experience of the American churchgoer.

If the global mosaic gives us the context for a growing pluralism, then pluralism has undoubtedly influenced a generation of Christian universalism. Unfortunately, the church was unprepared for this cultural challenge. There are intelligent answers to the questions raised out of pluralism. There are healthy and meaningful responses to the challenges and opportunities found in this new diversity. The complexities created by colliding cultures are not insurmountable to the church of Jesus Christ. In fact, the things

> If a spiritual expression wants to be considered as legitimate in the emerging culture, it must be able to cross the barrier of racism and isolation.

that have created tremendous friction give us our greatest opportunity for generating traction and moving fast-forward to lead the way in the emerging world.

WHAT'S IT GONNA TAKE?

The "great sociologist" Rodney King once said, "Can't we all just get along?" The answer, of course, is no. We can't all just get along. We've proven it time and time again in history. And it's often not because of our extreme differences. One of the peculiar realities of crime and violence is that there is far more white on white, black on black, and brown on brown crime than there is across colors and cultures. People who outsiders view as similar, whether it's the Hutus and Tutsis or the Bosnians versus Serbians or the North against the South, often carry out the greatest conflicts. Civil war is as difficult to stop as international war. Multiculturalism has only accentuated the human inability to bring peace on earth.

Former President Clinton at one time banked his legacy on the issue of diversity. It is not unreasonable to say that issues related to diversity, reconciliation, and multiculturalism are the forefront issues of our time. This creates tremendous friction for the church. We live in a society that openly wonders why eleven o'clock on Sunday morning is the most segregated hour in America.

If a spiritual expression wants to be considered as legitimate in the emerging culture, it must be able to cross the barrier of racism and isolation. The friction felt by the homogenous church can produce tremendous momentum as it gains traction. Every step the church of Jesus Christ takes to bring peoples of different cultures and colors together, no matter how incremental or insignificant it seems, will be like a light in the midst of darkness. The church has an opportunity to reverse this integration of Babel and—as at Pentecost—to become an expression of the nations coming together and hearing the gospel in their own languages.

Cornerstone was my first multicultural community. We watched the Spirit of God bring together African Americans, Latin Americans, and Caucasians to worship as one people. Many times, seekers who were visiting would come up and tell me that, though they were not Christians, this is how they imagined heaven would be. They knew intrinsically that, if there was a God, he would bring people together and erase the walls that divide us.

Jesus came and destroyed the dividing wall that not only separated man from God but also Jew from Gentile. God is about destroying walls that divide. The church will gain traction in the multicultural environment when she begins to dismantle the walls created not by the hands of God but by our own hands. Sometimes this will require nothing less than confession of the sin of racism and prejudice and the kind of repentance that leads to change. It isn't enough to go to church with a diverse world; God calls us to embrace those who are different as brothers and sisters.

WHEN THE MANY BECOME ONE

I was consulting with a church of more than five thousand in attendance. Though it was in Southern California, the church was extraordinarily homogenous. The leaders asked me what they needed to do to move from being an exclusively white congregation to becoming ethnically diverse. I simply posed one question to the fifty or so leaders in the room, "How many of you have a friend who's an ethnic minority?" The answer wasn't encouraging.

The beginning point was simple. If your goal is a diverse church, then you need to ask God to give you love for people who are different from you. People go to church where they have friends or make friends. You can't expect people who

> If the church embraces the challenge of reaching the nations through Jesus Christ, it will stand at the forefront of the emerging cultural dilemma.

are different from you to come to church simply because you want to paint a picture of diversity. This only happens when love actually brings people together.

Often when people visit Mosaic, they will ask me what I think of a homogenous principle. Donald McGavern's description in *Perspectives on the World Christian Movement* of how people socialize with people who are similar to them has become the church growth movement's prescription for how to evangelize. It would be foolish for me to deny the realities of McGavern's observations, and so I quickly acknowledge them to be true.

It's also important to acknowledge that the radical ethnic diversity at Mosaic has most likely slowed our rate of growth or at least made the process of assimilation far more complex and challenging. Nevertheless, every week I reflect on the incredible privilege I have of not only leading this congregation but also living in the middle of a miracle. To step into a community each week in which at least a third of the congregation is of Asian descent; a third is of Latino descent; and the other third is a mix of Caucasian, African American, Middle Eastern, Indian, and other ethnicities is indescribable if you have not experienced it.

Mosaic represents the nations. At times I've tried to count how many countries are represented in our midst. I know there are at least fifty, perhaps more. I can't help but imagine what it would be like if there were at least one person from every country on the planet worshipping together in this community of faith, hope, and love. The global mosaic gives us tremendous potential for generating momentum. It gives us the opportunity to move beyond keeping pace with culture. If the church embraces the challenge of reaching the nations through Jesus Christ, it will stand at the forefront of the emerging cultural dilemma. I guarantee you that any community that can answer Rodney King's question, "Can't we all just get along?" with a "yes" will have the ear of every significant organization in our society.

HYPERMODERNISM: FAST-FORWARDING MODERN HISTORY

One more friction traction that is creating significant turmoil for the church is hypermodernism. As I mentioned earlier, one of the more common descriptions of the changing philosophical construct in Western thinking is known as postmodernism. There are many effective treatments of postmodernism and even of its relationship to the Christian faith. I only mention it here to address the relationship of postmodernism to the dynamic of friction traction. Many who are addressing postmodernity speak of it in terms of the dangers that lie within it, and certainly there are serious concerns that need to be addressed. However, here I would like to unwrap some of the dynamic implications from a human rather than a philosophical perspective.

CATEGORICAL MELTDOWN

I was sitting in east L.A. in a Chinese restaurant owned by Korean Christians. Around the table were a young woman from the Midwest, an Arab from Lebanon, and a Salvadorian and two Persians from Iran. The purpose of our gathering was to meet one of the two Persians for the first time. Abe had recently come to faith in Jesus Christ, which is fairly dramatic for a Muslim man over forty years old. It was through the witness of Nabil, the Lebanese man, and Mimi, his American wife, that Abe had come to faith. Abe was now hoping that his childhood friend would also find a similar relationship to Jesus Christ.

As we began our conversation, Abe began to explain to me his beliefs in Allah and shared his thoughts as guided by the Koran. Over the next twenty or thirty minutes, I began addressing the issues of who God is from a Muslim perspective. He explained to me that liars and murderers would never be allowed to enter the presence of a holy God, so we focused our time on the judgment of murderers.

I asked him if he affirmed the teachings of Jesus, and as a good Muslim, he said, "Of course." I showed him that Jesus said if you hate someone, you have as much as committed murder. I asked him if he had ever hated anyone.

He said, "That's not fair. The criteria is too high." But it wasn't long before he had concluded that he, too, was a murderer, and, as he had earlier pointed out, murderers will never escape the judgment and wrath of God.

I have to tell you that I thought, "This is the perfect moment. He now sees his need for Jesus." But he looked at me and said, "Well, I'm truly not Muslim. I'm Bahai. I believe that all roads lead to God."

In my frustration I said, "But you told me you were Muslim when we began." He explained to me that this was his first time engaging a conversation with a Christian and that I needed to be patient with him.

We live in a world where people feel perfectly comfortable shifting and flowing from one worldview to another. Constructs are both temporary and disposable, and when one no longer seems to work, it requires very little to shift to another. It is important to note that this gentleman was over forty years old, highly educated, and had lived across the globe.

> **We don't just live in a world where Muslim and Hindu live side by side; we live in a world where the Muslim and Hindu both live inside one person.**

Too many people confuse postmodernism with what it means to be a Gen-Xer. We have superficially attributed to generational trends what are in fact worldview shifts. On a practical level, postmodernism often describes the end of categories and the beginning of fluidity. We come by this honestly. It is one thing to be raised with one view of reality and to then, perhaps, in adulthood discard that view as parochial and embrace a new view that you see as more refined and precise. It is another thing to then discard that view and embrace another and then once again go through the same process of examination, deconstruction, and reconstruction. If you change your view of reality enough times, you simply become less committed, even to the view you presently hold.

We don't just live in a world where Muslim and Hindu live side by side; we live in a world where the Muslim and Hindu both live inside one person. If we are to engage in a conversation about the gospel, we need to be aware that the people we're talking to may in no way have a cohesive view of reality. Individuals may hold multiple views of what's real or true. And as you engage them in an apologetic, you may effectively respond to one of their arenas of reality and never touch an entirely contradictory view. In practice this could be described as cynicism.

THE FANS OF TRUTH

Here in L.A., even though we don't have a football team, we have avid football fans—die-hards. Most of them are either huge Oakland Raiders fans or Dallas Cowboys fans. It's always entertaining to watch a game with one of these fans. Some are forty-year-old men who act like fourteen-year-old kids. They celebrate uncontrollably when their team wins, or they sulk and become angry when their team loses. They seem absolutely unaware that they're not on the field and had absolutely nothing to do with the outcome.

I love harassing them when their team loses, but the tables inevitably turn when they ask me which team I root for. I always tell them the truth: "I don't know yet. I have to see who wins." I explain to them that I have a perfect system for experiencing ultimate satisfaction as a fan. During the season I'm emotionally detached. I don't pick a team; I let the team pick me. As a team begins to win, I hear it calling me out. When the playoffs get here, I've narrowed down my favorite team to fewer than a dozen. After the first series of games, half of those teams have been eliminated as my potential favorite team. With each playoff game, I eagerly watch to discover which team I like better. When it comes to the Super Bowl, the choices have been narrowed down to two.

I have to admit that I'm not always certain which one of the teams is my favorite team. Sometimes I get a little confused. One team begins to win in the first and second quarter, and I enthusiastically begin to support it, believing that it is my favorite team. But then in the third or fourth quarter, information is gathered that changes this position, and that team begins to lose. Sometimes it takes longer than other times for me to decide. Sometimes I'm certain by the first quarter, and other times not until the closing minutes of the game. But in the end my team wins every season.

Those who consider themselves lifelong, die-hard, loyal fans have absolute disdain toward my approach. They want me to pick a team. They tell me it is absolutely essential. They don't understand how I can be so loose and fickle with my affections, but then I tell them that I grew up a Minnesota Vikings fan. Four Super Bowl losses changed my view of reality. I no longer believe I know who's going to win and don't want to invest emotional energy to care enough to let it hurt. So I let the team pick me.

> **If people are observing your Christianity and reserving their allegiance to see what team actually wins, is there evidence enough in your life to cause a person to see Jesus as sufficient?**

My approach to football is a better parallel than that of the avid fan for how contemporary Americans relate to truth. Fewer and fewer people are embracing truth up front and holding on to it with the belief that, in the end, their team will win. They're simply traveling through the season, observing as dispassionately as possible, and allowing different claims to truth to eliminate themselves. And so a Christian becomes an agnostic; a Buddhist, a naturalist; a Freudian, a Christian. It's not so much about what is true but what guarantees the win.

The friction, of course, is obvious. Our approach to apologetics assumes that we are engaging an individual who has a cohesive view of truth and reality. When a person freely and often contradicts himself without regard to continuity and does not see that contradiction as evidence or proof that he is wrong, it leaves Christians frustrated and paralyzed in the work of evangelism.

Opportunities for traction are exciting. For too long we have hidden behind the rightness of propositional truth and have ignored the question of whether or not it works. Does the faith you advocate get you to God? If people are observing your Christianity and reserving their allegiance to see what team actually wins, is there enough evidence in your life to cause a person to see Jesus as sufficient? What an incredible opportunity we have in a world of uncertainty! We know that God is and that Jesus is his name. There are many things that we don't know, but what we know is enough.

THE WORLD OF THE MAYBE

He seemed so uncomfortable in the middle of our celebration, and I knew up front that I was taking a risk by walking up to him and saying hello, but I had a fairly strong feeling that I might never see him again. As I approached him and introduced myself, I asked him if this was his first experience within the Christian faith. He quickly explained to me that it wasn't his "deal." I asked him whether he was talking about church or God, and he said "both." He went on to tell me that he was an existentialist and that he saw religion as nothing more than a myth and a delusion.

A small crowd gathered around, and I could feel that they were waiting for my response. For some reason I knew what I had to say. I looked him in the eyes and simply said, "You must have been really hurt sometime in your life." His head dropped down, and his eyes turned away. A few long and uncomfortable seconds passed, and then he looked up and said, "Maybe."

What a strange answer to that particular question! If I had asked him, "Don't you know that God exists and that you are created in his image and likeness?" I could understand him saying, "Maybe." If I had said, "Don't you get it? There's a heaven and a hell, and those without Christ get the worst of the two options," I could understand him saying, "Maybe." If I had said a countless number of different things, "maybe" would have seemed appropriate. But my question was about his experience, about something locked away inside of him.

He could have said, "No, this has nothing to do with the hurt in my life." He could have said, "Yes, I have been hurt. What's that to you?" Or he could have looked at me and said, "It's really none of your business." But his answer was "Maybe."

Hypermodernism is the world of the *maybe.* Not just the objective *maybe,* but the subjective *maybe.* Not the *maybe* of the outside world, but the *maybe* of the inside world.

Too many of us have subdivided the world into what exists outside of us and what exists within us. So many of the philosophical discussions around postmodernism address the issue of objective truth and reality. Is it noble? But I think that in some ways we've been naive. The objective *maybe* is born out of the subjective *maybe.* The loss of confidence in knowing the outside world is a result of a loss of connection to our inside world. We don't simply see the *maybe;* we live the *maybe.*

For those whose lives are secured in a sense of absolute truth, whose most comforting metaphor is that God is our rock and our foundation, this can be extremely frustrating. And frankly, the church sounds so certain about everything. There seem to be no *maybes* at all. We act as if we have it all down. We've got all the answers. If you're confused, just come to us because we have it all mapped out. Sometimes it's as if there is no mystery to God or the gospel, yet Paul speaks of it as a mystery. And last time I checked, the God of the Bible was still the invisible God.

> **Where once modernity was seen as the enemy of the church, today it seems that Christian thinkers run to modernity's side to find protection from what is hidden behind the shadows of the postmodern world.**

FINDING ANSWERS IN QUESTIONING

The friction comes through a loss of credibility when we refuse to admit that we don't have all the answers. If we seem to never struggle with the *maybes,* there is serious doubt about whether we truly know anything at all.

The traction comes when we become honest with ourselves and others—when we become cheerleaders for inquiry and seeking rather than simply knowing and finding. Traction comes when outsiders experience the church as a place where honest questions can be asked when people journey together to discover God and find the answers in him. We are well-positioned to move this dilemma from friction to traction, for in Jesus we find the perfect model to engage this paradox. Jesus is the truth and at the same time reveals truth. He is truth incarnate—neither subjective nor objective; inside nor outside; but pervasive, organic, and relational.

While the foundations of the modern world have melted into the fluidity of the postmodern world, the church has been eagerly modernizing. We built up an armory of defense against the modern argument. We debated scientists, while making empirical conclusions that God created the heavens and the earth. We applied logic and rational apologetics to defend the faith in the realm of intellectualism. And we re-examined and redefined the Bible in an attempt to be taken seriously in the arenas of anthropology and philosophy. But while we were occupied in those efforts, the modern world began spiraling out of control into what we now describe as postmodernism.

Where once modernity was seen as the enemy of the church, today it seems that Christian thinkers run to modernity's side to find protection from what is hidden behind the shadows of the postmodern world. We seem blind to the tremendous opportunities that await us. The search for the experiential, the desire to connect to those things primal and natural, the cynicism toward commercialism and even materialism, the extraordinary openness toward spirituality and mystery, the value and longing for community, and the reawakening inevitably of the aesthetics and the search for beauty are all hidden in the postmodern journey.

SEEING THE BOARD DIFFERENTLY

Years ago, Aron Nimzovich became the defining personality at the heart of a revolutionary and unconventional form of chess. It was called Hypermodern. It was a response to what is commonly known as classical chess. In classical chess, you control the middle, protect your pieces, and, by all means possible, leave yourself with no weak spaces. Hypermodern chess saw the board differently. You relinquish the center, you send your bishops to the edges, and you allow perceived and present weaknesses in exchange for the opportunity to return with greater strength.

I think there is much for the church to learn from this innovation. I am convinced that the friction of postmodernism can create tremendous traction for the church if we will do much the same. Concede the center—the church is supposed to live on the edge anyway. Send the bishops to the edges—the leaders of the church need to be apostles, prophets, and evangelists, not simply pastors/teachers. And embrace positional sacrifice—no longer hide our weaknesses, but stand in them so that, through them, God can be revealed as our strength.

While the church was intended never to accommodate culture, much of the friction that we have been experiencing is due to the fact that we've been driving on square tires. It's time to turn friction into traction and gain momentum.

> **❝I am not an Athenian or a Greek, but a citizen of the world.❞**
> —SOCRATES, FROM PLUTARCH, OF BANISHMENT

FUEL FOR THOUGHT

1. What is something worth attempting, even if we fail?
2. Read Deuteronomy 2:24-36. What battles have we been avoiding?
3. What best summarizes our church's attitude toward the world: antagonistic, apathetic, or apostolic?
4. What arenas of our church have responded to change by isolation and/or irrelevance? What must be done to engage a lost and broken world?
5. Does a church lose authenticity when it picks up innovation?
6. How can we incorporate new technology for accelerating and accentuating creativity and innovation?
7. How fully do we embrace the opportunity to shape worldviews?
8. How can we begin to reorganize our ministry to address the realities of our new world?

CHAPTER TWO

MOMENTUM

W hen I was around ten years old, I went to a carnival and got on one of those rides (called something like The Polar Express), that spins around and around, faster and faster, sometimes backward but mostly forward. It was one of the most traumatic events of my life. I distinctly remember the moment my seat belt broke. I was holding on for dear life. I was on the inside, watching helplessly as the engine below sucked me in. The announcer kept yelling into the microphone, "Do you want to go faster?" Everyone kept screaming, "Yes! Yes! Yes!" I'm sure I was the only kid desperately screaming, "No! No! No!" Every time he asked, I screamed, "No!" but all the cheers of affirmation overwhelmed my desperate cry for help. When the ride finally came to an end, I peeled myself out of the seat, staggered off the ride onto secure ground, and vowed I'd never get on a roller coaster or carnival ride again.

For the next five years of my life, I was grounded. I was afraid of everything that moved fast. I was terrified of speed. I would still go to the carnivals and watch as my friends got on the rides. I always thought it was odd that they would actually be laughing in what I considered to be a house of terror. It wasn't until I was a teenager that I finally endeavored to get on another ride, just to see if I could handle the pressure of speed. It was Space Mountain at Disney World. It was more than a roller coaster; it was an experience. It was an invitation to go on a journey that I couldn't resist. Since that time, I've become an addict. I love speed. I love anything that moves fast. I love the feeling of being, essentially, out of control: the pounding of my heart against my chest, the rush of fear, and the wind blowing against my face. Call me crazy, but I was born again.

WELCOME TO FAST COMPANY

Wanting my children to have a different experience than I'd had, I made it my personal responsibility to have them face the roller coaster challenge early on. My son took to it as if he were born for speed. My little girl was a little different. I put her on the Log Flume, and she loved the little boats. She thought it was going to be an enjoyable little ride. But the dramatic drop at the end took her breath, and she began to cry. It took me several years to help her overcome that experience. It was too fast. Too fast.

It was such a joy for me later when I took her to a "roller coaster clinic" in Minneapolis, Minnesota, called the Mall of America. I took her to Camp Snoopy and convinced her to trust me. We got on the roller coaster. She had the time of her life and rode it over thirty times in a row.

Speed can be a frightening thing, but it can also be exhilarating. Now I suffer from an unusual malady. Strangely enough, my son has the same illness. We both get carsickness, seasickness, and motion sickness if we're moving too slowly. We're fine in fast cars, fast boats, fast planes—anything that moves fast. But if it moves slowly, both of us become nauseated.

Like many in our culture, we have become addicted to speed. Everything is moving faster. We live in a world defined by speed. We get there faster, get it faster, and want it faster. We've shifted from good food to fast food, but now we want good food fast. We've left slow cook and gone to microwave. The national pastime of baseball has been overtaken by the fast game of basketball. Football is giving way to hockey. The slow pace of our old American pastimes, in which you spend too much time standing around huddling, is giving way to the fluid movements of sports in which instantaneous decisions must be made. We've shifted from epics to edits.

> We live in a world defined by speed. We get there faster, get it faster, and want it faster.

MTV has changed our visual capacity. We are a nation that is ADD and ADHD. What once was considered fast is now normal. Communication has gone through the journey from Pony Express to Federal Express, from telegraph to wireless communication, from post office to cyberspace.

GENERATING CHANGE

Everything is moving faster. Generations change faster than they've ever changed. At one time you could talk of three generations in one breath: Abraham, Isaac, and Jacob. How strange that this combination of names would be in our culture! It carries far more implications than we could ever imagine. Abraham, Isaac, and Jacob: three generations that wore the same kind of clothes; ate the same kind of food; listened to the same kind of music; and shared the same values, beliefs, and worldview. Abraham, Isaac, and Jacob saw eye to eye and understood each other.

Can you imagine three generations being described in the same breath today? Can you imagine wearing the same clothes that your father or grandfather, or your mother or grandmother, wore? Of course, you may do that in a brief window called "retro," but only because it's a declaration of the past, not the present. Can you imagine listening to the same music that your father or grandfather listened to? At three generations apart, we don't even share the same views of reality.

Not long ago, those who study generations evaluated a generation as changing every forty years. But in this last century, we began to see the acceleration of generational changes from World War II, post World War II, the baby boomers, the baby busters, Gen-X, Gen-Y, Millennials, and whatever else people want to describe the emerging generations as. The point is that people are changing rapidly and radically in the way they understand and express themselves.

All these generational labels are nothing more than an attempt to describe the dramatic changes that are visible in the emerging culture. The church is living in the middle of this radical change. We're living in what many call an age of discontinuity, an age of cultural turbulence.

Change isn't new. There has always been change. What's new is how fast and how dramatically things are changing. The pace of change is simply different. In many ways the church was unprepared for the acceleration that has hit us. As the church was building on values that affirmed stability, security, predictability, and standardization, the era of change seemed to catch us by surprise. This is ironic when you consider that the church was intended to be a revolution—a movement, not an institution.

MONUMENTS, MONASTERIES, AND MOMENTS WITH MONET

While we must always endeavor to be relevant to the culture in which we live, we must also remember that we are strangers, out of town guests, in this world. We are to pitch tents, not to build cathedrals. The church must always be ready to move. But sometimes we choose to build monuments rather than create movement.

In some ways monuments are important. Monuments are part of giving honor where honor is due. They are a part of remembering the very best of history, of people. Monuments allow us to reflect and remember the gifts we've been given and the legacy we've received. I remember when I stood in front of the Vietnam Memorial. Although I didn't have any family mentioned there or personal attachment to anyone in that conflict, seeing that memorial was still stirring and profoundly meaningful to me.

Monuments have a tremendously positive impact on us all, but the church was never intended to be a monument. We must be careful not to attempt to build tributes to God. God always wants us to remember what he has done, but he demands that we not live in the past. In Isaiah 43:18-19 the Lord says, "Forget the former things; do not dwell on the past. See, I am doing a new thing! Now it springs up; do you not perceive it? I am making a way in the desert and streams in the wasteland."

This is an unusual statement for a God who continuously told his people to remember, remember, remember. He always called them to remember what he had done in the past. One of the great stories of the people of Israel is how God, through Moses, had delivered them out of slavery in Egypt. The Lord often called his people to remember what he had done, that their faith might be increased. In Isaiah he clearly declares that, while we are to remember the past, we are not to remain in the past. Our memories of God's activity in our lives are to move us into the future. Our experiences from the past are to give us the confidence to face the challenges of tomorrow. We are not to build monuments but to join the movement. Sometimes we choose instead to build monasteries. Too often, the church becomes our secure place, our haven from the outside world.

> **Too often, the church becomes our secure place, our haven from the outside world.**

A REFUGE FOR THE WORLD, NOT FROM IT

It isn't hard to understand why people look to the church as a refuge from the realities of the world around them. The world can seem like a scary place. It's like getting on a roller coaster and having your seat belt break. While someone else may scream, "Do you want to go faster?" you're begging to get off and move to stable ground.

A lot of us have felt like the seat belt broke, and we didn't know if we were going to make it. So we turned our churches into monasteries—places that became spiritual havens for us, focusing on our spiritual life, caring for our spiritual needs, and nurturing our spiritual health. The church was the one place where an unbelieving world could not get to us. We were protected. But the church was never intended to be a monastery. In fact, God intends that there be no place that we can hide, except in his presence. When the church becomes our shelter from a radically changing world, we fail to turn to God and make him our hiding place and our shelter.

When the church is a movement, it becomes a place of refuge for an unbelieving world. The church becomes the place where the seekers finally find the God they were searching for. The church becomes the place for the broken and the weary to finally find the healing and the help they've cried for. The church becomes the place where the lonely and outcast are finally embraced and loved in the community of Christ. When the church becomes a movement and not a monastery, she becomes a place of transformation for the very culture from which we run in fear.

MOVING MOMENTS

Sometimes I think we need to spend a day with Monet. He had a clear sense of what was hidden in a moment. Most of us think of a moment as something that's stationary, stagnant, and unchanging. We want to capture the moment and stand in the moment. If there's a moment you want to preserve or remember, you take a snapshot.

The genius of Monet is that he saw the moment for what it really was. It was as if he actually read the dictionary and realized that the essence of the words *moment* and *motion* are the same. Monet was a master of light and movement. His paintings were blurred and obscure and yet beautiful and full of insight. If we could somehow see life through his eyes, we would begin to see life as it really is. Our ability to see the world as it really is has been corrupted by the camera. With a turn of the lens or a push of a button, we are able to take the blur out. We've come to see the world through still frames, when in reality life is in constant motion.

The church was never intended to be a monolith but a movement creating moments that change history. Change is an inescapable reality in this era of speed. And though I'm advocating our need to become a movement, I would like to encourage you to give up on keeping up. In many ways, we've been trying to solve the problem the wrong way. We feel culture leaving us behind. We sense that we're out of touch with society. The church is singing songs that were written two hundred years ago or sometimes, at best, twenty years ago. We're locked into architecture that wasn't cutting edge when it was designed.

> **The key to dealing with this rapidly changing world, to dealing with this culture addicted to speed, is not to catch up but to give up on keeping up.**

To enter the church experience is to take a step back to some treasured period in history. Each denomination chooses its own century of preference. And yet the key to dealing with this rapidly changing world, to dealing with this culture addicted to speed, is not to catch up but to give up on keeping up and to discover that there is something more significant than going fast, and it is the power of force. It is what is gained when there is genuine apostolic momentum.

FASTER THAN A SPEEDING CULTURE

The first-century church didn't keep up with its time, didn't spend its energy keeping up with its time. The first-century church changed time. It rewrote history. It radically impacted culture. The church was the forerunner, not the runner up. And out of the church's influence came the greatest art, the greatest music, and the greatest thinkers. Out of the church's influence were born the cultures from which came Voltaire, Nietzsche, Einstein, Newton, and Hawking, not to mention Jefferson, Franklin, and Edison. The Michelangelos and the da Vincis came right out of a context that Christ had radically shaped. I am not saying that they all were followers of Jesus Christ, but I am saying that they were all indebted to him.

How do we regain the kind of momentum that ignited the first-century church? How can we give up on speed without falling behind? Does nature have something to say about this? Science tells us that the cosmos has a great deal to teach us. The formula for momentum is $P=MV^2$. P being momentum, M equaling mass, and V equaling velocity. Science understands momentum as the combination of mass and velocity squared.

One of the interesting nuances to this formula is that velocity without mass does not produce momentum. In the same way, mass without velocity does not produce momentum. In other words, if you're missing either mass or velocity, the equation ends at zero. There's zero momentum. But any mass and any velocity joined together begin to create momentum.

MASS CAN BE A MESS

Whenever we talk about church growth, the dominant part of the conversation is really about mass. Conferences and seminars are jampacked with church leaders who come with one simple question, "How can my church grow?" Only after we begin to deal with the complexities and challenges of growth do we tune in to issues such as assimilation and discipleship. Anyone who has experienced significant growth in a congregation knows that assimilation and discipleship are integral to growth and, in many ways, impossible to separate from that dynamic. But when you're standing at the front end of the challenge of leading a congregation to grow, you're just asking the simple question, "How do I get more people here?" It doesn't take that much intuition to figure out that if you don't have any people, you're not pastoring a congregation.

Mass equals people. Without people there is no momentum. When people move together with common purpose, momentum happens. And while most Christians would quickly acknowledge that it is important to reach people for Christ, an

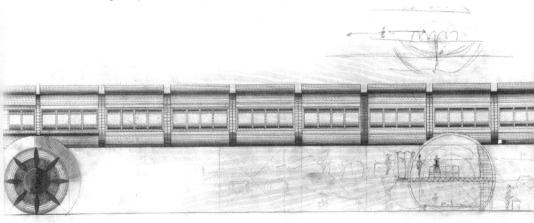

underlying comfort level is often threatened when growth actually happens.

In today's environment we have a tentative relationship with mass. There is a growing sense among many that small is always better than big. In fact, we could go as far as to say that, many times, big is equated with evil and small with good. While we like what big can provide for us, we want to access it in small ways. We have created an unconscious dichotomy between quantity and quality. Our experience equates quantity with assembly line and conformity, while quality accentuates the unique and the authentic. Our conflict is that we hate the mono-lithic texture of our mall society and still want everything convenient and easily accessible. In the same way, there seems to be a growing disdain for large churches.

> **While most Christians would quickly acknowledge that it is important to reach people for Christ, an underlying comfort level is often threatened when growth actually happens.**

I cannot tell you how many times I have been asked if Mosaic is going to be a *mega-church*. Yet that has never been asked as a positive question. The word mega-church is more of a derogatory term, and the question is always motivated by fear or concern. It's easy to understand where that concern comes from. Mega-churches are often seen as large, corporate, religious organizations that are im-personal, non-responsive, and monolithic. I am not saying that this is true but that more than one person carries this concern and perspective.

However, the very same people who abhor the idea of a church getting large are the same ones who are both connected, inspired, and mobilized by the unique ministries that emerge through critical mass. There are things that only a large church can do. Mosaic has mobilized over four hundred people to serve the underprivileged communities of Ensenada, Mexico. It's really hard to do that if you're a congregation of fifty. Over one hundred actors, dancers, set designers, producers, directors, and writers mobilized to create a theatrical pro-duction in the heart of Los Angeles that touched thousands. It would be really tough to do that with seventy-five people in the entire congregation. Both the human and financial resources to accomplish this kind of vision require signif-icant critical mass.

We cannot underestimate the importance of mass in the acceleration of momentum, but the warnings should not be taken lightly. We must listen carefully to the characterizations that exist so that we do not miss the warnings that we need to embrace. Bigger is not *always* better.

The size of the mass does not equal the degree of momentum. There are extremely large things that have no momentum at all. A hundred thousand people can go watch the Cleveland Browns play football. You have mass, but you do not have movement. The Rolling Stones had six million people come to their live concerts; that doesn't mean that the mass generates momentum—insanity, enthusiasm, and energy, maybe, but not momentum. *Who Wants to Be a Millionaire* has developed a mass viewership of twenty million people but is not a generator of momentum. A church may have five thousand attendees every single week, but that does not mean that there is genuine momentum.

> **"Mass does not equal momentum."**

Mass does not equal momentum. It doesn't in nature, and it doesn't for God. Judges 7:1-8a reads: "Early in the morning, Jerub-Baal (that is, Gideon) and all his men camped at the spring of Harod. The camp of Midian was north of them in the valley near the hill of Moreh. The Lord said to Gideon, 'You have too many men for me to deliver Midian into their hands. In order that Israel may not boast against me that her own strength has saved her, announce now to the people, "Anyone who trembles with fear may turn back and leave Mount Gilead." ' So twenty-two thousand men left, while ten thousand remained.

"But the Lord said to Gideon, 'There are still too many men. Take them down to the water, and I will sift them for you there. If I say, "This one shall go with you," he shall go; but if I say, "This one shall not go with you," he shall not go.'

"So Gideon took the men down to the water. There the Lord told him, 'Separate those who lap the water with their tongues like a dog from those who kneel down to drink.' Three hundred men lapped with their hands to their mouths. All the rest got down on their knees to drink.

"The Lord said to Gideon, 'With the three hundred men that lapped I will save you and give the Midianites into your hands. Let all the other men go, each to his own place.' So Gideon sent the rest of the Israelites to their tents but kept the three hundred, who took over the provisions and trumpets of the others."

Gideon was focused on mass. God was focused on momentum. You can only imagine how Gideon felt when he saw twenty thousand men leave and only ten thousand remain. All too often, we are infatuated with numbers that do not carry behind them the weight of genuine force. In the end, God chose three hundred rather than thirty thousand. As God spoke to Gideon and said, "You have too many men for me to deliver Midian into their hands," could it be that, in our times, God would say the very same thing to us?

In my experience, I have seen that, before churches grow, they often first decline. I know that's been the case in my own life. Jesus speaks of pruning the tree before it bears fruit. It's hard for us to believe that, before you can grow larger in a way that honors God, you may actually have to grow smaller. But growing smaller is not the goal. You don't prune the tree to kill it but to thicken it and allow healthy growth to take place. Sometimes we act like God is against growth, and certainly the context in which the church exists affects the rate of growth. But God does not believe that big is bad.

In Genesis 13:1-17, we find what we could describe as an Old Testament Church split that resulted in growth. Abram and Lot lived in community together along with their families and people, but their families grew so large that they found it difficult to stay together. It is interesting that their situation is described as a conflict born out of having many possessions. The solution was to divide the land and go their own ways. Abram let Lot choose whether he would go to the right or the left, and in response, Abram would go in the other direction. His point was that there was no need for them to fight. There was enough room for everyone to keep growing.

> **You don't prune the tree to kill it but to thicken it and allow healthy growth to take place.**

After their division was complete, God took Abram outside and said to him, "Lift up your eyes from where you are and look north and south, east and west. All the land that you see I will give to you and your offspring forever. I will make your offspring like the dust of the earth, so that if anyone could count the dust, then your offspring could be counted. Go, walk through the length and breadth of the land, for I am giving it to you."

If you haven't had the time to do the research, there is a lot of dust on this earth. God was saying to Abram, "Your people are going to grow." If this were not enough, in Genesis 15 God did it again. He took a walk with Abram, and in verse five, God said, " 'Look up at the heavens and count the stars—if indeed you can count them.' Then he said to him, 'So shall your offspring be.' "

Again, if your nights have been too busy and you haven't taken a look, there are a lot of stars out there. God was saying to him, "Your people are going to grow." We can't move on without remembering verse six: "Abram believed the Lord, and he credited it to him as righteousness."

God did not see a conflict between quality and quantity, between expansion and genuineness. For God, the more good there can be, the better. We see the same pattern in the eruption of the church. Peter preached one message, and three thousand people were added to the church. That's three thousand people who were baptized in that one day. That doesn't even describe how many people listened and rejected the message, or how many people listened and were intrigued but needed a little more time to process the information. You would think three thousand a day was good enough.

Certainly if God had been worried about quantity affecting quality, he wouldn't have added one more person for several years. Yet Acts 2:47b tells us that "The Lord added to their number daily those who were being saved." It is without question that mass can be a mess, but without mass, you have no movement.

Proverbs tells us, "Where no oxen are, the manger is clean, but much revenue *comes* by the strength of the ox" (Proverbs 14:4, New American Standard Bible). In other words, the church would be the perfect place if there were no people. Wherever there are lots of people, you will also find a big mess. Lives are messy; sin is messy; ministry is messy. When the ox messes up the manger, it accomplishes the purpose for which it was created. We are not called to have clean mangers.

The same people who make the church messy also make the church meaningful. After all, people are what God is about. We must never come to the place where there is not room for one more person. We must be willing to make a mess to save a life.

Revelation 5:9-12 says, "And they sang a new song: 'You are worthy to take the scroll and to open its seals, because you were slain, and with your blood you purchased men for God from every tribe and language and people and nation. You have made them to be a kingdom and priests to serve our God, and they will reign on the earth.' Then I looked and heard the voice of many angels, numbering thousands upon thousands, and ten thousand times ten thousand. They encircled the throne and the living creatures and the elders. In a loud voice they sang: 'Worthy is the Lamb, who was slain, to receive power and wealth and wisdom and strength and honor and glory and praise!' "

> **We must never come to the place where there is not room for one more person.**

Sounds like a lot of people to me.

INTELLIGENT SPEED

For mass to become momentum, there must be velocity. Just as momentum is dependent upon mass, if there's no velocity, there's no momentum either. So you can have a substantial mass without velocity and miss the objective God has for the church. Velocity is the church's answer for speed. Speed contains less information than velocity. Speed is used only to express how fast something is moving, but it contains no directional or coordinate information.

Velocity is different. It always specifies a direction. So while speed is about motion, velocity is about movement. Velocity is speed with somewhere to go. Velocity is speed with a purpose, speed with intentionality. Velocity made human is action with direction. It is speed focused around a goal. So velocity has several critical components. The first is obviously speed. Direction without movement is not velocity. This concept translates into a powerful, practical reality for the Christian faith. God never intended the Bible to be studied for information or knowledge alone. The Bible was written so that we might respond to the truth and voice of God.

Biblical interpretation must be missiological, not theological. A theological construct for interpretation finds success in the attainment of knowledge. The more you know, the more mature a Christian you are thought to be. And yet knowledge of the Bible does not guarantee application of the Bible. To know is not necessarily to do. When the construct applied to the Bible is missiological, you engage the Bible to discover the response required of your life. It is significant that the history of the first-century church is called the book of Acts, not the book of Truths.

> **It is significant that the history of the first-century church is called the book of Acts, not the book of Truths.**

Speed is determined by one's level of responsiveness to God's commands. Obedience is the spiritual equivalent of speed. Light speed is immediate obedience to the voice of God. When you bring together the willingness to obey and the wisdom to know what God is saying, velocity emerges. It is a synergy between direction and decision. As God brings light into your life through his Word, you accelerate.

Paul says it like this in 1 Corinthians 9:24-27: "Do you not know that in a race all the runners run, but only one gets the prize? Run in such a way as to get the prize. Everyone who competes in the games goes into strict training. They do it to get a crown that will not last; but we do it to get a crown that will last forever. Therefore I do not run like a man running aimlessly; I do not fight like a man beating the air. No, I beat my body and make it my slave so that after I have preached to others, I myself will not be disqualified for the prize."

IT'S ABOUT GETTING THERE

"Therefore, since we are surrounded by such a great cloud of witnesses, let us throw off everything that hinders and the sin that so easily entangles, and let us run with perseverance the race marked out for us. Let us fix our eyes on Jesus, the author and perfecter of our faith, who for the joy set before him endured the cross, scorning its shame, and sat down at the right hand of the throne of God. Consider him who endured such opposition from sinful men, so that you will not grow weary and lose heart" (Hebrews 12:1-3).

The writer to the Hebrews describes us as runners engaged in a race that we are supposed to win. Victory comes to the one who has both the strength of speed and a clear focus on the goal. Velocity is the result of speed and direction. And sometimes the fastest way to get somewhere isn't the straight line.

Several years ago, I was scheduled to speak in Ames, Iowa. Coming from Los Angeles, I can tell you that getting to Ames was not an easy task. I arrived late at the airport and stood at my gate pleading with the attendants to let me on the plane. They insisted that, though the door was still open, for me the door was closed. I had to run and find another airline that would transport me to

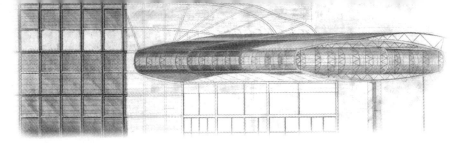

Ames. I couldn't find a single airline going to Des Moines, Iowa, the closest big city. But eventually I found an airline that would fly me from Los Angeles to Phoenix, another airline that would fly me from Phoenix to Denver, and a third airline that would fly me from Denver to Des Moines. And although they required almost seamless connections at each airport, I decided it was worth the risk since it was, after all, the only way to get to Ames on time.

I caught the flight to Phoenix, but I didn't have time to grab my bags in the baggage claim before I left for Denver, so I had to leave them behind for several days. At my Denver stop, I called my friend in Des Moines and requested that someone pick me up. Once I arrived in Des Moines, I was promptly picked up and driven straight to Ames. I arrived at the conference facility literally less than a minute before I was to speak. I walked on stage and proceeded to share with the participants my journey in getting there.

Many times the only way to get to our destination requires ingenuity, innovation, loss, and patience. For me, this was no small miracle. Only God could connect Southwest Airlines to America West Airlines to Northwest Airlines and get me where I had to be when I had to be there! We cannot be so anxious to accomplish the vision that God has placed in our hearts that we only see the straight line. The journey is full of unexpected twists and turns—the very context for God's miraculous surprises.

GAINING THE LEAD

Remember that velocity is speed with direction. This translates into intentionality. When the church is moving on mission with God, velocity and mass together can increase momentum. Velocity is critical to apostolic leadership. The leader must have a clear direction and must move with intentionality in that direction. I know that it's been said many times before, but the leader actually does need to be in front.

I was talking to my son one day, and he was watching cartoons. I think it was *X-Men*. I asked him to explain the characters and tell me what was going on. With delight, he began to tell me all about his cartoon heroes. I thought I'd ask him a simple question, "Who is the leader?" and he gave me an astonishing explanation. He

> **We cannot be so anxious to accomplish the vision that God has placed in our hearts that we only see the straight line.**

said, "Well, that's the leader," and he pointed to one of the characters. I said, "How do you know?" He said, "The leader always stays in the back and only gets involved when everyone else is about to die." He was developing a Marvel Comics theory of leadership, which is, more often than I'd like to admit, on target.

Too many times we see leadership as our right to tell people what to do. We direct from the back and only get involved when people are desperate or dying on the vine. Revolutionaries do not lead from behind a desk. There are some things that you cannot delegate if you're not the one in front. You may hold the title, but you're not the leader.

> **The way not to be overwhelmed by the radical changes and speed in our world is to know where you're going, to know why you're going there, and to do it with urgency.**

Leadership is not simply about setting the course or steering the course; it's about running the course. To attempt to lead without speed is simply to stand in line. Something mystical happens when you get over your motion sickness and begin to move with God. Remember that momentum equals mass multiplied by velocity squared. Momentum increases proportionately to mass but exponentially to velocity.

BLINDING SPEED

We've looked at two components that will increase your velocity. One is intentionality—always moving toward the goal—and the second is acceleration—increasing the force of your actions. The leader learns to thrive in a world of what others consider to be blinding speed. But it is in this context that the apostolic leader sees most clearly.

This was illustrated in an extraordinary way in the movie *The Matrix*. The agents pursuing Neo and his colleagues could move at superhuman speed. They could literally dodge bullets. If Neo was to survive and fulfill his destiny as the deliverer of his people, he would have to learn how to move at the same rate of speed. What we discovered is that what others experienced at blinding speed, Neo experienced in slow motion. He could dodge bullets because they looked as if they were simply floating.

When you move with spiritual velocity, with a clear sense of God's calling, with clarity of vision, and with a heart that moves with immediate obedience to the Spirit, the environment that once overwhelmed you with its rate of speed can now be experienced in slow motion. The way not to be overwhelmed by the radical changes and speed in our world is to know where you're going, to know why you're going there, and to do it with urgency.

I used to be an information junkie, but now I'm an information connoisseur. I don't have to know everything, but I'd better know what I need to know. My goal is not to keep up with the changing world, but to be standing there waiting for it when it arrives. People are going to need someone to show them the way.

Speed is an important leadership dynamic because it helps the leader identify emerging leaders, as well as helping others identify him or her as a leader. When the pace of the church is unusually slow, those individuals who desire to get somewhere quickly will be naturally filtered out. If the person who stands in the role of leadership or in the position of leadership moves slowly, or even cautiously, he will only be seen by those who appreciate that pace. At the same time, the leader who values a slow rate of change often perceives those who try to move faster as rebellious, insubordinate, undisciplined, and adversarial.

The tragedy is that many who are perhaps crafted by God to become apostolic leaders become invisible to those who see velocity as the enemy of the church. By the same token, the leader who moves at an accelerated speed with intention and a God-given direction can more effectively identify those who have apostolic gifts. Such a leader literally begins to see certain people more clearly. It is almost as if we live in a different space-time continuum.

For those who choose to move slowly, those who move too fast are a blur. And for those who move rapidly, those who move slowly can be virtually invisible. It is as if we're moving at a blinding speed. The rate at which you lead determines who remains in your field of vision. The practical result of this is that, many times, revolutionary leaders are seen as indifferent and perhaps uncaring. They don't stop long enough to check the wounded.

Apostolic leaders understand that what God is creating is a community with a cause. Both the needs of the community and the sacrifice necessary to accomplish the cause are clearly before them. It is through such leadership that movement is initiated. Fueled by faith, these leaders move forward to accomplish the purpose of God. They personify velocity: speed with a purpose.

However, this is only one aspect of apostolic leadership. Just as significant is the ability to move others. Remember that velocity without mass equals zero momentum. Momentum requires both speed with direction and people actually going along. The apostolic leader is more than a spiritual entrepreneur; he is a spiritual catalyst. The first moves quickly; the second moves others quickly with him.

> **Movement will not happen if people do not move together in common mission.**

The entrepreneur can find total satisfaction in the uniqueness of his own endeavor. If he accomplishes his personal dream, there's a sense of contentedness and satisfaction. The catalyst on the other hand begins with a knowledge that what God is calling him to accomplish cannot be done alone. It is critical that he win the hearts and capture the imagination of others. He doesn't see people as a hindrance to accomplishing his goals. He doesn't find a way to go around people because they slow him down. His entire calling is wrapped up in the calling out of God's people to fulfill God's purpose.

The focus of the catalyst could be broken down to four distinct areas: two related to mass and two related to velocity. The first is understanding the critical importance of both the volume and the density of mass. To catalyze a movement, you have to have mass. In practical terms, this means the more people, the greater the mass (volume), and the deeper the people, the greater the mass (density). Both are of equal importance in the shaping of a movement.

Volume is pretty easy to figure out. A hundred people are more than ten. That's quantity. Density is more about the depth of spiritual maturity. That's quality.

In relationship to velocity, the catalyst's first focus is calling people out to the purpose of God. Movement will not happen if people do not move together in common mission. The catalyst takes seriously the description of the first-century church being of one heart and mind. He would rather have ten people on common mission than a hundred who are simply curious. He understands that, in the long run, the ten will impact far more people than the hundred would.

The second focus is the need to accelerate the group's response to the Spirit of God. The spiritual catalyst experiences God as the wind of his spirit and recognizes that momentum remains fragile in the time between understanding and commitment. Momentum is both powerful and fragile at the same time: powerful in that, once it is obtained, its force can be unstoppable; fragile in that it can be easily lost.

The church that learns to celebrate the spontaneous movement of God's spirit and even the unexpected invitation to follow him increases the force of its movement. The catalyst not only calls God's people to move toward intentionality, but continually inspires and motivates God's people to accelerate their rate of spiritual response.

SEEING AT BLINDING SPEED

I want to make clear that what focuses the speed of the church is not a plan but a purpose and a passion. This may sound strange, but you can focus the energy of a movement without knowing where you're going. You do this by knowing why you're going. We see this in the life of the Apostle Paul as described in Acts 16:6-10.

The apostolic leader finds his direction from the compass of the purpose of God, is fueled by the passions of God, and, while he's moving to do what he knows, God clarifies and directs.

"Paul and his companions traveled throughout the region of Phrygia and Galatia, having been kept by the Holy Spirit from preaching the word in the province of Asia. When they came to the border of Mysia, they tried to enter Bithynia, but the Spirit of Jesus would not allow them to. So they passed by Mysia and went down to Troas. During the night Paul had a vision of a man of Macedonia standing and begging him, 'Come over to Macedonia and help us.' After Paul had seen the vision, we got ready at once to leave for Macedonia, concluding that God had called us to preach the gospel to them."

You would think that if anyone had ever known the will of God, it was the Apostle Paul, evidenced by the incredible impact of his life. You would assume that he always knew exactly what he should do. After all, he was the Apostle Paul. He met Jesus face to face on the Damascus Road. If anyone had inside information or intimate knowledge, it would be him. Yet we find that Paul had no idea where he was going. He tried to go to Asia, and the Holy Spirit wouldn't let him. He tried to go to Bythinia, and the Spirit of Jesus would not allow him to. The entire Trinity got involved in keeping Paul from going to the wrong place. He was going for the right reasons: He went to take Jesus to those who had never heard his name. But he didn't have any idea where his actual destination was.

So he went to sleep. He was exhausted from trying to figure out where God wanted him to go. And while he slept, he had a dream. In that dream a man from Macedonia called to him, "Come over to Macedonia and help us." I can relate to the humor in this passage. While Paul was conscious, he couldn't understand the word of God. God had to get him unconscious to make it clear. He woke up and concluded he should leave for Macedonia.

Too many times as leaders we feel pressure to tell people things we don't know. In other words, we make them up. Spiritual leadership is not the ability to define everything the future holds. It is the willingness to move forward when all you know is God. The apostolic leader finds his direction from the compass of the purpose of God, is fueled by the passions of God, and, while he's moving to do what he knows, God clarifies and directs.

I was sitting in the car with a friend of mine, talking about his future. We had already shared over twenty years of friendship and ministry. He had resigned his church and had come to Mosaic for a time of restoration and renewal. As he shared with me his confusion about his future, he summarized everything we are talking about here. He said, "I don't know the path, so I'm choosing the environment." More times than we care to admit, we simply don't know what the next step is. But if our hearts are bound to the heart of God, we are never lost.

SPIRITUAL MAGNETISM

There is one other interesting element to this formula for momentum. It's gravity.

Everything that has mass has gravity. And when gravity is exerted, it pulls other objects toward it. In other words, people who have mass are magnetic.

If you're committed to velocity—to focused speed—but you're all alone and have no mass, you might wonder how you can be a part of creating movement. You may not be able to immediately affect volume, but you can affect density. The beginning point is always ourselves. We must submit our lives to Jesus Christ, let him change our hearts and character, become servants, and model a life of humility and sacrifice. Then our spiritual density will make us magnetic. The more Christ reigns in our lives, the more people will be drawn to the Jesus in us.

It must be more than a coincidence that the word *glory* literally means "density." There's no one thicker than God, no one deeper or more profound. The density of God makes him magnetic, compelling. And God is always moving. Creation begins with the spirit of God moving over the surface of the earth.

God has both density and velocity. He is the great mover. Jesus described his spirit as coming and going from directions and to places that no one knows. The church erupted from a rushing wind. It should not be of any surprise to us that Jesus is the greatest revolutionary who ever lived or that the church is the greatest movement that has ever existed on the face of the earth.

When you move with Christ, you are never alone. His velocity and his density—his glory—begins to surround you. And with your first step toward Christ, you are brought into his movement. Your life now has divine momentum, and those who are seeking after him will be magnetized to your life.

> ❝We have to understand that the world can only be grasped by action, not by contemplation. The hand is more important than the eye... The hand is the cutting edge of the mind.❞ —JACOB BRONOWSKI

FUEL FOR THOUGHT

1. Is our church a refuge <u>for</u> the world or <u>from</u> the world? Explain.
2. How fully does our church share the attitude that there is always room for one more person?
3. How can we quicken the pace of obedience within our church?

Answer the next three questions as an individual leader:

4. Are you fueled by the passions of God?
5. What will you do, starting today, to gain confidence and skills in winning people's hearts and capturing their imagination for God's movement?
6. How can you build density among other leaders: being submitted to Christ, exercising servanthood, practicing humility, being committed to sacrifice?
7. Read Isaiah 43:18-19. What new things is God wanting to do through our congregation?

CHAPTER THREE
CHANGE THEOLOGY

Within the word *momentum*, we find the inescapable reality of change. Remember our definitions of speed, velocity, and momentum: They are all in relationship to time—more specifically to the distance covered in a certain period of time. The movement of the church is really no different. And if we're going to address the real issues related to regaining movement in the church, we have to deal with the realities of change in relation to time.

We have become engaged in this conversation about momentum because things are changing so rapidly. If the church were advancing at a faster rate than culture, there would be little reason to sound an alarm. If the church were advancing at an equal pace to culture, even if we sounded an alarm, most would not consider it significant. The reason so many of us are becoming more aware of the need for the church to regain its essence as a movement is that we can feel history, and our relevance to it, slipping away from us.

So much of the church growth movement's emphasis on relevance to culture is a response to the fact that the world has changed while the church has stayed the same. But at the root of this problem is nothing more than the utilitarian reality of either changing what we do or facing an inevitable death of the movement. Yet in my experience, churches are not highly motivated by utilitarian realities. We are first and foremost a community brought together by God. If God is not an advocate of change, we rightfully conclude that we shouldn't change. For many sincere followers of Christ, the reaction against what they would consider worldliness or accommodation is rooted in a conviction that we must be a biblical people.

AN UNCHANGED GOD WHO CHANGES EVERYTHING

The only real text or context for dealing with change that many Christians have been exposed to is the promise that God is an unchanging God—the same yesterday, today, and forever. The metaphors of God as our rock, our fortress, our stronghold, and our foundation dominate our view of God and how he works.

> Although change is rarely taught or extracted from the Scriptures, the Scriptures are a document about change.

But if we are going to effectively regain momentum, we must go beyond accepting changes of reality and become agents of change.

To do that in a manner that is both pleasing to God and grounded in his Word, we must establish a proper theology of change. Although change is rarely taught or extracted from the Scriptures, the Scriptures are a document about change. You can never properly understand biblical theology without accepting that change is one of the most significant dynamics that God instigates in the church. It is often easier for us to see on a more personal level. If a person is to become a part of God's kingdom, radical personal change must take place. We call this conversion.

Paul says it like this in 2 Corinthians 5:17: "Therefore, if anyone is in Christ, he is a new creation; the old has gone, the new has come!" The Greek word used for "new creation" means metamorphosis. Many of us know metamorphosis through the image of a caterpillar becoming a butterfly or a tadpole becoming a bullfrog. It describes a radical and irreversible change in the very essence of the object of that metamorphosis.

When a person becomes a disciple of Jesus Christ, she is not simply accepting a new view of reality; she is not simply accepting new patterns of thinking; she is not simply accepting new habits for living; she is being radically and irreversibly changed.

A CHANGE OF HEART

In Ezekiel 36:26, God unwraps this concept with his new covenant: He will not fix our old heart but take out our old heart and give us a new heart. He will take our heart of stone and replace it with a heart in which his spirit lives. God makes the same point in Jeremiah 31:31-33: In his new covenant there will be a transformation of the human spirit. Again using the metaphor of the heart, he promises that to those who turn to him, he will put his law in their minds and write it on their hearts.

For those who understand the Gospel, we understand that it is a promise of transformation. Transformation is just another word for change. If you don't like change, you'd better not become a Christian. Once you belong to Jesus, change is inevitable. Our whole Christian experience is an experience of change. It is an experience of putting off the old and putting on the new. It is an experience of no longer being conformed to the pattern of this world but being transformed by the renewing of our minds.

The whole theological concept of sanctification is rooted in the reality that God changes people. Repentance is change, conversion is change, regeneration is change, transformation is change, and sanctification is change. All of the deeply theological constructs that we have embraced and understand to be true cannot exist outside of a theology of change.

We describe repentance as a radical change of heart and mind, a total reversal of life in actions, a 180-degree turn from one's present course to a divine call. These are, by their very nature, processes of change. Repentance was never understood to be an incremental decision or action; it is the complete surrender of the heart and will to the heart and will of God.

When it comes to personal change, I think we get it. But when we move into the arena of the church, we seem to lose our handle on this construct. We tend only to think of the need to change the outside. Our communities need to change; our city needs to change; our nation needs to change; the world needs to change. Everybody needs to change except the church. The church is just fine the way she is. In fact, the church becomes the last bastion of protection against change; the reminder of what the world looked like before it changed; the preserver of tradition and ritual, rather than the catalyst and advancer of the kingdom of God.

> **While not many churches perform their services in Latin today, our language, style, music, and methods are pretty much Latin to the unchurched population.**

My most poignant memory of this was as a child attending Mass. Everything was in Latin. It sounded beautiful and spiritual, yet I couldn't understand a word. It might have been the right message, but I never knew. While not many churches perform their services in Latin today, our language, style, music, and methods are pretty much Latin to the unchurched population.

A HISTORY OF CHANGE

The most practical application of change should be the corporate life of the church. The local church is to be God's expression of his radical commitment to change. God is about changing history, or perhaps better said, about making history. His ultimate goal for the church is not to follow cultural change, like a water skier behind a boat, but to be the dynamic, catalytic community that brings change in a world that so desperately needs the God of change.

We must never forget that we serve the changeless God of change. God is not satisfied with the status quo. He is not trying to keep up with culture. His greatest ambition is not for the church to become a great imitator of generational trends. He is the God of creativity, the God of imagination, and the God that chose—through his Son—to ignite a revolution. The implications that begin on a personal level always extend to the whole of the people of God.

Paul summarized it like this: "The righteous will live by faith" (Romans 1:17b). We could easily retranslate this to "the righteous thrive in the midst of unpredictable change." The classic example of this in the Scriptures is when God called Abraham to leave everything he knew and follow him on his promise of a better future. He was required to uproot himself and his family, to risk everything for the privilege of being a part of God's ultimate plan in history.

Abraham was called into a life of radical change. The same can be said for all the pillars of our faith. From Moses to David and Elijah to Jeremiah, a fundamental requirement of following God has been leaving the secure and predictable in order to follow God into a world where only he is unchanging.

GENERATIONAL SHIFTS

There are endless texts from which a theology of change can and must be constructed, but some stand out as pivotal. One critical passage dealing both with the reality and the theology of change is found in Ezra 3, which was written after the first Temple had been destroyed. For a generation, Israel had lived without a temple in which to worship God. Now they were about to build a new Temple. Ezra 3:10-13 gives us a description of this event: "When the builders laid the foundation of the temple of the Lord, the priests in their investments and with trumpets, and the Levites (the sons of Asaph) with cymbals, took their places to praise the Lord, as prescribed

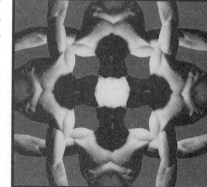

by David king of Israel. With praise and thanksgiving they sang to the Lord: 'He is good; his love to Israel endures forever.' And all the people gave a great shout of praise to the Lord, because the foundation of the house of the Lord was laid. But many of the older priests and Levites and family heads, who had seen the former temple, wept aloud when they saw the foundation of this temple being laid, while many others shouted for joy. No one could distinguish the sound of the shouts of joy from the sound of weeping, because the people made so much noise. And the sound was heard far away."

This passage describes a significant generational shift and cultural crisis. The older priests and Levites and family heads wept when they saw the foundation of the Temple, but the others began to shout with joy.

When we lived outside of Dallas in a new community, we lived in one of the first five or six houses in the whole residential area, so our little boy, Aaron, spent a few years watching houses go up. I would love taking him and our foster daughter, Patty, to the lots that were being developed. We would stand in the middle of the foundation, and I would describe to them what the house was going to look like: where the garage would be, where the bedrooms were, whether it would be a one- or two-story house. They would look at me in disbelief. They thought there was no way I could possibly know what the house was going to look like. But as the house was built and the frame established, what was at one time a ruin began to take form. I would show them that my predictions were accurate. The foundation is the blueprint for the rest of the house. Once you've seen the foundation, you know what the house is going to look like.

The reason the older priests and family heads wept when they saw the foundation was that they knew that this Temple was not going to be like the former Temple. They had seen and experienced the splendor of the first Temple, built by Solomon. This was the Temple that caused kings to stand in awe. It was an architectural marvel built from the wealth of Israel. The new Temple would pale in its shadow, and those who could remember it could only weep.

In contrast, the younger generation had never seen the first Temple and had never stood in the middle of this majestic structure. All they knew were the stories. Their lack of tears could be seen as an act of disrespect toward a loss of something so sacred. But in actuality, their celebration was sincere. They were celebrating because the foundation was a promise of a new place to meet with God. It didn't matter to them that it did not look like the first Temple. It didn't matter to them that it paled in regard to any human measure. The purpose of the Temple was to establish a place where God would meet the representative of the nation of Israel. The purpose of the Temple was to offer sacrifices for the forgiveness of sin, to worship the one true and living God. The purpose of the Temple was to meet God face to face, and they shouted with joy.

LIVING IN THE PAST

If there was a tragedy, it lay in the fact that the former priests and family leaders could not overcome their own sense of loss to celebrate what was now being passed on to their children. Sometimes the most painful reality of change is that we have to leave behind things that were of great value to us. If only change left alone those places that were sacred to us and just touched the worst part of us. But many times the most difficult things to give up are those things that we have identified with God's blessing and presence in our lives. For us the crisis of our Bethel is the place where we meet God; the context in which God becomes real to us; the songs we sang when God's presence filled our hearts; the very best of our experience with God. Yet God calls us to take the memories with us but to leave the memorabilia behind.

It would be difficult enough if our inclination to hold on to the past was only rooted in our sacred experiences, but the reality is that, many times, we would rather have Godless security than spirit-led change. I am reminded of the people of Israel being delivered out of Egypt and how they cried out to God, begging him to respond and deliver and then their greatest nightmare came true: God answered their prayers and delivered them. As soon as they were free from the hands of Egypt, from the grip of their oppressors, the people of Israel had their first opportunity to smell the fresh air of freedom and get their first clear look at the implications of living by faith in the living God.

> **God calls us to take the memories with us but to leave the memorabilia behind.**

Their response shouldn't surprise us. It has been relived from generation to generation, from people to people, from local church to local church. They became angry with Moses and blamed him for their plight. They begged him to let them return to the slavery of Egypt. Israel's conclusion was that it was better to be slaves in the land of Egypt than to be free and be forced to live by faith in the context of radical change. How many of us have not done the same thing?

FUTURE PEOPLE

We can learn many things from this experience in the history of God's people, but what is important is that, as he did with Moses, God regularly chose an individual to be an agent of change as he called his people to be a people of change. When describing the armies of King David, the Scriptures not only unwrap for us the tremendous military force that was at David's disposal but also the essential and critical need for changed leadership. In 1 Chronicles 12:32 we read that among the warriors of David, which numbered over 300,000, there was an important faction of two hundred chiefs called the men of Issachar. The key function or contribution of these two hundred chiefs (and the relatives under their command) was to understand the times and to know what decisions needed to be made.

It is significant that Webster's defines *vision* as "the power of seeing." Webster's breaks down this perceptivity as the ability to foresee and perceive. If you simply flip that around, you have a description of the tribe of Issachar. The tribe of Issachar could perceive and foresee. They understood the times, and they knew what they should do.

The prophets were also voices of change. Whenever God's people moved into the stagnant waters of religion, God raised up voices that would call them to become, once again, followers of the living God.

From the beginning, God has raised up men and women who have had the power of seeing. They understood the times in which they lived. They understood the context to which they were called. They had the ability to understand change and create change. They could both perceive and foresee.

THE REVOLUTIONARY MOVER

And then there's Jesus. As a religious teacher, he was expected to be an advocate of the status quo. His orthodoxy was measured by his willingness to conform to the established religion. Any expression or application of the Scriptures that did not conform to the already established policies and procedures was considered heresy. According to Jesus' assessment, the Word of God had been turned into an instrument of death, rather than life. His reminder that the written word is death but the Spirit brings life both explains and informs us about all of Jesus' actions. For Jesus, the Word of God was living and active. When approached with a heart of humility, God's Word creates a dynamic interaction between God and man.

> **Simply stated, if the Bible doesn't bring change, it is not being engaged.**

Obedience to the Scriptures unlocks their mystery. Jesus was establishing a missiological interpretation while the religionists of his time had taken on a theological interpretation. Simply stated, if the Bible doesn't bring change, it is not being engaged. Jesus was merciless in exposing this reality. He condemned the people of God for forsaking the Word of God for the traditions of men. Through his life, he systematically negated their most sacred interpretations. He was accused of defiling the Sabbath by healing on it. He became a glutton by celebrating life. He was accused of being a friend of sinners simply because he actually was their friend. He treated tax collectors as if they could access the mercy of God. And he chastised the temple-goers as an abomination to God.

Jesus deconstructed the religion of Israel and ushered in the religion of God. Why would anyone be surprised that the core of the New Testament church is radical change? From the very beginning, the church was born out of radical change.

CHANGING CULTURE

The entire nation of Israel operated on a Sunday to Friday calendar. Saturday was the Sabbath—no work, no play, and no good works. Saturday was the holy day, and all who would give homage and honor to God would keep the Sabbath holy. Right out of the gate, the church moved the holy day to Sunday. On the Sabbath, Jesus was still dead. On Sunday he rose from the dead. I have to imagine that this timing was important to God. The church started meeting when Jesus showed up. This is an excellent process to follow.

All who were followers of Jesus Christ began to supercede the Sabbath and make holy the Lord's day. Talk about a radical religious and cultural shift! Can you imagine if today we began to make Monday our day of worship? How many of our employers would give us Monday off? How many companies would suddenly open up on Sunday because we were available and wouldn't work on Monday? What real possibility is there that the weekend would move from Saturday and Sunday to Sunday and Monday? Can you imagine the resistance we would receive if we were not only establishing a new faith but also demanding that the entire culture reorient itself around our particular religious preferences? Yet that is exactly what happened two thousand years ago. In a society in which you worked six days and worshipped on the seventh, the weekend was born. Thousands of years later, thousands of miles away, generations and cultures separating us, we enjoy the weekends because Christianity reshaped not only the spiritual center of this new Israel but also the cultural and social patterns of a nation and of the world.

From the beginning, the church was a symbol of radical change. When you see the pace of the book of Acts and realize that this new emerging movement was without established patterns, methods, or even a common address, it makes sense that the disciples had to stay connected on a daily basis just to know where the church was going. The issues of change for the first-century church ranged from practical logistics—they met in houses—to the very philosophy of ministry, relating to the church's culture itself.

> The first major council was not, as we often understand it, about theology. It was not about issues of morality or even a primary doctrinal position. It was about how the church would engage culture.

NEVER THE SAME AGAIN

In Acts 15, at the Council at Jerusalem, a question of change brought together Paul, Barnabus, Peter, and James. The question was whether the church would adapt itself to the new cultures she was engaging or the new cultures had to reform themselves to match the culture of the first converts of the church, which was Judaism. The first major council was not, as we often understand it, about theology. It was not about issues of morality or even a primary doctrinal position. It was about how the church would engage culture.

Was the church required by God to preserve the Jewish culture? Was the gospel properly expressed in the transformation of Gentiles into Jews? Was there a sacred culture for the Christian faith that would solidify the church's expression for generations to come and nations to come? The answer was an emphatic "no."

In Acts 15:10-11 Peter asked the question, "Now then, why do you try to test God by putting on the necks of the disciples a yoke that neither we nor our fathers have been able to bear? No! We believe it is through the grace of our Lord Jesus that we are saved, just as they are."

Those known as the Judaizers were demanding that everyone become like them. They genuinely believed that for non-Jews to be pleasing to God, they had to reject their own culture and embrace the culture of the Jewish Christians. James' response to this position is significant not only for that one crisis but also as a pattern for the church to establish its ministry upon. In Acts 15:19 he says, "It is my judgment, therefore, that we should not make it difficult for the Gentiles who are turning to God."

This was his foundational statement for the recommendation that followed. In everything that is negotiable, we should not make it difficult for those who do not know God to come to him. The Gentiles would in fact be Gentile Christians. They would not have to first become Jewish to become Christian. The basis of this decision was the acceptance of the Gentiles by the Holy Spirit, evidenced in the outpouring of the Spirit into their hearts. In everything that is about style and preference, the church must be willing to change for the sake of those who are lost. It is difficult enough for a sinful man to deal with the realities of repentance and humility without the church establishing unnecessary boundaries between man and God. We must remove every nonessential barrier facing those who seek God but have not yet found him.

James' judgment was that the church was not to remain the same. In fact, it was not allowed to remain the same. The ultimate desire of the legalists who demanded that everyone submit to their pattern of worship was to preserve one form of Christian expression. James not only said this was not required, but he also concluded it was in contradiction to the mission of the church. This council unleashed the church to become the pliable and adaptive movement that has radically impacted the world in the last two thousand years. The church is a paradox of unchanging convictions grounded in

God's truth and the incarnational expression of every culture and people who respond to the God of grace.

A CHANGE OF DISPOSITION

Without question, the church was established on the promise of change. Hearts would be changed, families would be changed, marriages would be changed, communities would be changed, cities would be changed, and, yes, even the entire history of humanity and the earth itself would be changed by those swept up in this movement of God. This should be seen as cause for celebration, not consternation. The reality of change is rooted in God's promise that he will work in and through our lives. What would happen if we began to hear the words of God in the context of a promise for change?

In Jeremiah 33:3 he invites us into a journey of radical change: "Call to me and I will answer you and tell you great and unsearchable things you do not know." The prophets understood the inseparable nature of miracle and change.

> **For too long the church has longed for the good old days, has hoped that the future would simply be a detour to the past.**

Habakkuk cried out, "Lord, I have heard of your fame; I stand in awe of your deeds, O Lord. Renew them in our day, in our time make them known; in wrath remember mercy" (Habakkuk 3:2).

To cry out to God and ask him to act is an invitation for God to bring radical change in our lives. God promises Haggai that he will act and change history. "This is what the Lord Almighty says: 'In a little while I will once more shake the heavens and the earth, the sea and the dry land. I will shake all nations, and the desired of all nations will come, and I will fill this house with glory,' says the Lord Almighty. 'The silver is mine and the gold is mine,' declares the Lord Almighty. 'The glory of this present house will be greater than the glory of the former house,' says the Lord Almighty. 'And in this place I will grant peace,' declares the Lord Almighty" (Haggai 2:6-9).

God is continuously inviting us to believe that his future is better than any past we have experienced with him. Can you believe that the glory of this present moment can be greater than the glory of your best memory? For too long the church has longed for the good old days, has hoped that the future would simply be a detour to the past. This has never been God's promise, and it is not God's desire for us. He wants to shake heaven and earth and shake us loose from all that holds us back from entering his future. This future cannot be experienced without embracing and experiencing change.

WHAT ARE YOU DOING HERE?

We should not think that by ignoring the Lord we will secure safety and stability.

The Lord says in Zechariah 7:11-14a, "But they refused to pay attention; stubbornly they turned their backs and stopped up their ears. They made their hearts as hard as flint and would not listen to the law or to the words that the Lord Almighty had sent by his Spirit through the earlier prophets. So the Lord Almighty was very angry.

" 'When I called, they did not listen; so when they called, I would not listen,' said the Lord Almighty. 'I scattered them with a whirlwind among all the nations, where they were strangers.' "

It appears that, if we are unwilling to move with the wind of God, we will be moved by the whirlwind of God. One type of movement is a journey into God's future; another uproots us from all the securities we refuse to relinquish.

Remember how fear of the world around him paralyzed the great prophet Elijah? He'd seen so many victories. He, above all others, knew the power and authority of God. He had seen fire come down from heaven, the altars consumed by the holy presence of God. And yet, because of the rumors of Jezebel's intent to kill him, he lost faith, ran to the desert, and wished to die. God caught his attention by sending a great and powerful wind that tore the mountain apart and shattered the rocks. God then sent an earthquake to shake the earth underneath Elijah's feet. God then sent a fire as a demonstration of his power. But as Elijah stood on the mountain in the presence of the Lord, he was reminded of God's gentleness, not his power. For in that moment, God spoke in a gentle whisper and asked the question that he always asks his people when they are hiding from the world around them: What are you doing here?

The church was never meant to hide. She was never supposed to pull the cloak over her face and hide within the darkness of a cave. We must hear the Lord say to us what he said to Elijah: "Go back the way you came" (1 Kings 19:15b). We must return to the world from which we ran. We must face the dangers and challenges that filled our hearts with fear and realize that God has called us to stand in the midst and call sinners to God.

The reality of change is the promise of miracle. The same God that changes our hearts and changes the world around us calls the church to change. When the church refuses to change, she refuses to obey. It is essential that we do not water down what is really going on. The church is God's agent of change through which his power is revealed.

> **We are not only called to be changed and to embrace change but to be the catalysts of change.**

EXCHANGING FEAR FOR A DIVINE FUTURE

God's purpose for the church is nothing less than how Paul described it: "Now, through the church, the manifold wisdom of God should be made known to the rulers and authorities in the heavenly realms, according to his eternal purpose which he accomplished in Christ Jesus our Lord" (Ephesians 3:10a-11).

If embracing change for the purpose of obeying God is not reason enough to change, consider how thrilling it is to become an agent of divine change and the human embodiment of the wisdom of God! Our obedience not only changes individuals and history itself; it impacts the heavens. We are not only called to be changed and to embrace change but to be the catalysts of change. We can go beyond fearing and resisting change. We can go beyond changing for the sole purpose of being relevant to culture. We can be free of the trappings of this world and unleash the imagination of God. Paul invites us to nothing less: "Now to him who is able to do immeasurably more than all we ask or imagine, according to his power  that is at work within us, to him be glory in the church and in Christ Jesus throughout all generations, for ever and ever! Amen" (Ephesians 3:20-21).

God wants to do more for us than we could ever ask. We can never say that our dreams are too big. It is God's desire to take us where our imaginations can soar. Sometimes we forget that dreams require change. If you are not willing to change, you are not willing to venture to the place where your dreams can come true. People who do not change in the end become people without dreams. When the church refuses to change, she becomes a terribly unimaginative place.

Traditions are not only roadblocks for change; they can become roadblocks for dreams. Traditions that become treasured memories can be the catalyst for new dreams and new experiences. But when they trap us in the past, they stifle the imagination, bring an end to creativity, and make innovation impossible. Where there are no dreams, there is no hope. And when there is no hope, there is no future.

Everywhere God moves, there is change. Everywhere God moves, he creates the future. Everywhere God moves, hope is alive and well. The church must be grounded in a proper theology of change, not simply to address the radically changing world in which we live, but to advance the cause of Christ in a world that cannot produce the real change that has to take place.

Remember that momentum is related to the distance covered in a certain period of time. For the church, momentum is more about time than distance. When we do not change, we actually distance ourselves from the world around us. When we cling to the past, we create distance between ourselves and what God is doing in the present.

SOMEWHERE IN TIME

Look in the mirror. What do you see? Who do you see? Look again—more closely. Focus on the details. Look for the wrinkles you've never noticed before. Pay attention to the texture of your skin. See the blemishes? Any new gray hairs on your head? A few pounds there you've never noticed before? If you look close enough, a new person will begin to appear. Someone you've never seen before. It's who you are today. Welcome to the present.

Most of us never really see our present selves. We look in the mirror, but only see the image of who we were. In many ways we spend our lives looking at a version of the real thing. We know one day we'll be older, but right now we miraculously stay the same. Nowhere do we continuously look at the present but see the past more often than in our own mirrors. Rarely do we ascribe to the future what already exists in the present more than in our own self-perception. Yet this isn't the only place we do this. In fact, this isn't the exception; it's the rule.

We're all chronologically challenged. With all the experience we have with time, we still lose track of it. Though it always moves at the same rate of speed, time still flies and sometimes stands still. Even with the major distinctions—past, present, and future—we seem unable to keep things in their proper place. We live in the past, miss the moment, and go back to the future. The real problem with time isn't that it's relative but that it's elusive.

> The further we are from the past, the better we remember it—but not the clearer. Soon the details are lost to the dream. In the end what we remember never existed.

Most of us are captured by the past. We create our own *Truman Show*. What we call the present is really a mental construct formed out of our memories. We choose not only a place to live, but also a time. Most often it trails behind reality. Living in the past can be intoxicating. The further we are from the past, the better we remember it—but not the clearer. Soon the details are lost to the dream. In the end what we remember never existed. History is lost to nostalgia. Like a seductress, the past can tempt us to leave the present and forfeit our future.

The paralyzing fear for many who are clinging to the past is moving into an unknown future. There's an irony in this. While we think we're moving into an elusive future, all we're actually doing is moving into the already existent present. The great leap of faith isn't from the present to the future but from the past to the present! All we have to do to discover the future is unwrap the present.

IDENTIFYING THE RIGHT "TIME-PLACE"

When we try to keep others in our own time-place, it becomes a source of tremendous conflict. There can also be great conflict when the development of another person is moving him or her out of our view of the present. It can be equally challenging when it's critical to move others out of their time-place in order to effectively engage reality. These experiences are the result of our view of time. We see the past as the present. We see the present as the future. We see the future as the past. So we wait for the good old days to return.

Our children grow faster than we hope they would. We want to keep them as we remember them, yet they're convinced that they're more mature than their age. We're in a time war! The battle to define what really is the present is fundamental to good presenting. Often our children's determination to move into the future forces us to relinquish the past and step into the present. It's a sobering realization when we finally see that our little babies have grown up.

Our congregations change more slowly than we know they should. We want them to become what we see for them, and all too often they want to preserve who they've been. The battle over relevance and worldliness is often really more about time. How in the world can you move together in unity when you can't even agree upon the era in which you're living? Often spiritual leadership is calling God's people to relinquish the past and move into what God's already doing!

When I came to L.A. eight years ago, I discovered that a journey of twenty years is as treacherous as a journey of two hundred. While we weren't trapped in the traditional era of hymns and robes, we had settled into a 1970s groove. The church had been a forerunner in so many areas and was known for its innovation. Yet the journey from The Church on Brady to our future as Mosaic was a difficult one. The best way to describe it is that we traveled at the speed of sound to get to the present. The speed of light would have killed us!

Many of the changes were either methodological or technological. We went from an overhead projector to a slide projector to a video projector, making up thirty years in three years. In other words, we went from words to picture to images. Why? So that our people could receive in their own context and language the most powerful message on earth! After all, isn't moving into the future really all about people? Yet with these changes come the accusations of becoming like the world. That happens when you stop looking like the past and start looking like the present.

> **This is the danger of nostalgia: In the comfort of a safe and warm time-place, we become blind not only to the real world we are called to engage but also to the movement of God's Spirit in our day.**

While God instructs his people over and over again to remember all his great deeds, he doesn't call us to live in the past. Memories are intended to be fuel for future faith. They aren't intended to become an alternative reality in which we choose to hide from the present challenges. God's promise is that he's doing something worth living for right now. And it's happening in front of our very eyes. The tragedy is that we may not even see it.

ENVISIONING THE FUTURE

This is the danger of nostalgia: In the comfort of a safe and warm time-place, we become blind not only to the real world we are called to engage but also to the movement of God's Spirit in our day. If we don't see the present for what it is, we'll miss the God moment. Fear of the future causes present blindness. The scripture warns us that without vision, the people will perish. Webster's defines *vision* as "the power of seeing." This power must first be exercised to see the present clearly. Only then can we begin to foresee. If we are going to see the future, we must step boldly into the present.

It is critical as God's people that we keep looking forward to the future. This is where God is going! When Jesus calls us to follow him, time is as important as place. Trusting him with our tomorrow may be more difficult than trusting him with our possessions. Yet his invitation to us is full of promise. " 'For I know the plans I have for you,' declares the Lord. 'plans to prosper you and not to harm you, plans to give you hope and a future. Then you will call upon me and come and pray to me, and I will listen to you. You will seek me and find me when you seek me with all your heart. I will be found by you,' declares the Lord" (Jeremiah 29:11-14a).

The future is full of hope. God has placed it there for those who will follow him into it. Yet the only way we'll ever receive so great a gift as the future is by unwrapping the present.

My wife, Kim, and I were driving to San Diego from Los Angeles. About halfway there she asked me where we were. I told her, "I can tell you where we've been. I can tell you where we're going. But when in motion, where we are is constantly changing and becomes elusive." She looked at me and said, "Shut up and tell me where we are!" As difficult as the now is to define, spiritual leadership understands the times and knows what to do. We must leave the past, engage the present, and create the future.

We're all time travelers. We must never forget this. Our perception that the world is standing still is wrong on every count. The reason we can never go home again is that we're trying to return to a time and not a place. We're in constant motion. And time stands still for no one.

H.G. Wells dreamed of a machine that would allow us to travel through time. Most of us dream instead of a machine that would cause time to stand still. Time moves forward—without prejudice or regard to the quality of the moment. Tomorrow is always its destination. We must stop resisting history's relentless pursuit of the future and instead capture the present opportunity.

❝When you're through changing, you're through.❞ —BRUCE BARTON

FUEL FOR THOUGHT

1. Have we invited God to bring his change into our church?
2. What would build a change mentality into our congregation?
3. How is change fundamental to being a follower of Jesus? to personal leadership? to the movement of the church through history?
4. What distinguishes a missiological view of the Scriptures?
5. Do we interpret the Scriptures theologically or missiologically? Explain.
6. How would our church change if we sought to follow more fully a missiological view of the Scriptures?

"This is the covenant I will make with the house of Israel after that time, declares the Lord. I will put my laws in their minds and write them on their hearts. I will be their God, and they will be my people. No longer will a man teach his neighbor, or a man his brother, saying, 'Know the Lord,' because they will all know me, from the least of them to the greatest" (Hebrews 8:10-11).

GOD'S PURPOSE HAS ALWAYS BEEN ABOUT REDEEMING A PEOPLE. But the modern church has reduced it to the conversion of individuals. And there is a radical difference between leading one person to faith and leading a people to faith. The former produces a follower of Jesus Christ; the latter produces a movement of Jesus Christ. The first requires one heart bound to God. The second requires many hearts bound together in God. We know that there is a mystical connection between man and God, but we seem to have forgotten that mankind was created to live in a mystical relationship to each other. It takes on many shapes: family, clan, tribe, village, commune, gang, sect, community, society, nation, people. At the center of each expression is a culture born out of cult. People are bound together by an ethos that shapes not simply actions but minds and hearts. God sent his Son not only to call individuals to himself, but also to transform culture. And he prays for us that we would be one even as he and the Father are one.

"All the believers were one in heart and mind. No one claimed that any of his possessions was his own, but they shared everything they had" (Acts 4:32).

E-motion

SECOND MOVEMENT

C H A P T E R   F O U R

E-MOTION

Emotions are those unusual, inside-out experiences and feelings that cannot be explained in absolute, concrete terms; and yet they are common experiences that we all share. Webster's definition that an emotion is an "intense mental state that arises subjectively" expresses the power of ethos on an individual level. Emotions move us. They swell from within and, if intense enough, overwhelm us.

Like individuals, communities feel deeply. Cultures share a common heart. We often speak of that heart as shared values. They bind us together. They unify us without force or coercion. Hidden beneath our communal beliefs are mutually held convictions, common concerns, and shared experiences. If a worldview is the way a community *sees* reality, then an ethos is the way a community *feels* reality. Ethos is what happens when many individuals make autonomous choices that create a unified movement. Ethos moves us when nothing else will and like nothing else will. Ethos can be described as a tribal emotion. Like emotions fire us up, ethos is the tribal fire. Ethos is the fuel of our caring and the fire of our passions. Ethos is the e-motion of a community.

Ethos (n.) The fundamental character or spirit of a culture; the underlying sentiment that informs the beliefs, customs, and practices of a group or society. The distinguishing character or disposition of a community, group, or person. To simplify, an ethos is expressed through spontaneous, recurring patterns.

Ethos is a corporate-intense mental state that arises subjectively, not only in an individual, but also in the entire community. When something happens, everyone feels it the same way. When something is violated, everyone is offended. When something is obtained, everyone celebrates. In many ways an ethos is an e-motion that doesn't have to be prompted, but everyone feels it equally in response to an event.

HEART TRANSPLANTS

There is something extraordinary about the invisible influence of ethos. It is fundamental to understanding how values are transferred, even from generation to generation.

My wife, Kim, and I are first-generation Christians. Our parenting has been a step-by-step learning process. We don't really know how to raise kids in a Christian home through experience. When my son was three years old, his older sister brought him to me so that he could tell me something important: He told me that he was a Christian. I have to be honest with you: I didn't believe three-year-olds could become Christians. I even grilled Patty to make sure she didn't coerce him into praying some sinner's prayer. I discovered that his decision was genuinely the result of his own initiative, but I still didn't believe him.

About six months later he told me he wanted to be baptized. I was sure that was the only reason he had told me he was a Christian. Now I knew his real motivation: He wanted to get in the water. I told him that before he could be baptized, he needed to be a Christian, and he reminded me that he was one. I thought that was a pretty good memory for a three-year-old.

When he was four, he began to ask me when he could begin teaching about Jesus. I began to think that maybe he really was a Christian. Every night I would pray for Aaron before he went to sleep. So we were sitting by his bed one night, and I said to him that since he was now a Christian, he should pray and not just me. I'll never forget Aaron's first prayer. We were holding hands, and I expected him to repeat the prayers that I had prayed for him over the past four years, but he didn't. He prayed something that I had never prayed for him. His first words were, "Jesus, make me a leader of men." I have to tell you that I was in shock, and I squished his hands. He thought he did something wrong and said, "I know I'm too little right now."

When I left the room that night, my eyes were filled with tears. I was overwhelmed with an incredible sense of both pride and disbelief. I went to Kim and said, "You won't believe what Aaron prayed." I shared with her his prayer. Without even blinking an eye, she looked at me and said, "Of course that's what he's going to pray. That's all he ever hears about." It struck me that, even though I had never intentionally taught Aaron about leadership, the environment we had created had a powerful impact on him.

I'm also reminded of Mariah's school open house in the second grade. All the parents walked into the room to enjoy their children's artwork and scholastic achievements. As I walked up to one of the walls, I noticed that my little seven-year-old girl had written that when she grew up, she wanted to be a singer. She listed six or seven countries she intended to visit to perform concerts—from Indonesia to Australia to New Zealand. Beneath that, she had listed the titles of about ten songs she had already written. I realized that I was staring at ethos made manifest. She was growing up in an environment that was both global and creative. She not only felt that she had permission, but she felt it natural to see herself traveling the world, using her creative gifts and talents.

ENVIRONMENTAL SPONGES

This is the power of ethos. Human beings are sponges that draw in whatever is around them. We know, all too well, that children are radically affected by their environments. Negative environments raise negative and broken children. Healthy environments give children their best opportunity to become everything they were created to be.

> **When our children grow up, they mirror what we've really cared about.**

In the same way, values are transferred through relational environments. When our children grow up, they mirror what we've really cared about. If our children do not do what we say, they do what we do. And often they don't become what we'd like them to become; they become a response to who we are.

The power that a given environment has over our lives doesn't end when we become adults. It affects us throughout our lives here on earth. Healthy environments move individuals toward health. Unhealthy environments accentuate brokenness and dysfunction.

Many of us grew up under the influence of *Star Wars*, with the concept of "the Force." In the movies, this invisible, spiritual energy can be tapped from either the side of good or the side of evil. As Christians, we immediately reject both the impersonal and dualistic view of God, but we need to realize that there are significant, invisible forces that shape our lives. Some of them relate to our connection to the invisible kingdoms. Others are part of an invisible force, which we call culture, ethos, and environment. For too long we have underestimated the power of this invisible force.

READING THE INVISIBLE SIGNS

We can see the power of ethos through experiences in everyday life. I live in Los Angeles. Going to the beach and taking your shirt off is no big deal. It's an everyday experience for beachcombers. Yet in the summertime, when our building can be swelteringly hot, not one guy takes off his shirt. We have no rule against taking off your shirt in our church building. It is not unethical, immoral, or unbiblical; yet I've never witnessed anyone even attempting to do it. I can say pretty confidently that not one guy has even thought about it. But every guy who comes to our church will drive to the beach and, without any instructions or posted signs, know exactly when it's appropriate for him to take off his shirt. When he leaves, he will also know exactly when to put it back on.

I was recently speaking with some Christian leaders in the Midwest when the issue of the appropriateness of wearing sandals—rather than shoes—came up. In that particular culture, wearing dress shoes was considered nonnego-

tiable. But a new team member had come from a culture in which wearing sandals was perfectly OK. He had gotten himself in trouble because he hadn't picked up on the cultural cues that were being sent out.

Maybe you can remember a time when you didn't like brushing your teeth. In my experience, many children do not like brushing their teeth, or at least they forget a lot. As parents, one of our common questions is, "Did you brush your teeth?" It's OK to remind them when they're five, but if you still have to tell them when they're fifteen, you have not accomplished the task.

Somewhere between five and fifteen, brushing moves from what was once an irritation to a discipline to, eventually, a value. At some point in between, kids do it because they know it's required. One day they don't even think about it anymore. They don't wake up and say, "I need to brush my teeth." They do it from a subconscious, automatic response. One day it just becomes a part of who they are. They're not brushing their teeth because their parents told them to. They're not even brushing their teeth because other people appreciate it. They're doing it simply because it's what one does.

WHEN LAWLESSNESS IS GOOD

Remember when seat belt laws were implemented? If you are in any way like me, it was an absolute invasion of privacy! I did not want to buckle up. It was uncomfortable; it was irritating; it wrinkled my clothes; it was uncool. It really hampered the entire style and essence of dating.

At first I only buckled up when I saw police, and for the first several months there was a grace period. The police would pull you over and give you a warning, but there was no ticket or penalty involved. When that grace period expired, you were required to buckle up at the risk of penalty. Many of us reluctantly conformed to the law. We were not necessarily convinced that we would be safer or even that the government had a right to invade this area of our privacy. In those days, any parent who would let us jump in the back of a truck and carry ten of us down the freeway to the baseball game was the coolest parent in town.

> **Laws cannot control unsupervised activity. Only ethos has this kind of affect on our decision-making.**

Look how the world has changed. Today if you see an unbuckled child in a car, your thoughts immediately turn to his negligent parents. Children tell their parents to buckle up, not because eight-year-old kids are concerned about the law or the ticket. They believe it's immoral not to be buckled. It's simply wrong.

Our seat belt experience as a society is an example of a successful transition from law to value. What we were once required to do—even though we felt it was an invasion—we now do because we believe it's right. In fact many of us don't even realize that we're buckling up. We just get in the car, strap the belt across us, and turn the key without any conscious thought.

Other attempts have not worked as well. Prohibition, the attempt to legislate sobriety, was a miserable failure in changing cultural values. If anything, it created a context for the development and strengthening of the Mafia, rather than the development and strengthening of a moral position against drinking. For many of us, driving the speed limit is now on the bubble. How many of us drive the speed limit because we really have an emotion that tells us it's right, rather than a deep desire to keep our license?

One of the limitations of laws is that they cannot tell you what to do; they can only inform you of the consequences associated with certain actions and activities. If you don't agree with a law, you can commit the offense and try to avoid getting caught. Laws cannot control unsupervised activity. Only ethos has this kind of affect on our decision-making. When we combine all those things that shape ethos—beliefs, values, worldview—we find something far more powerful than laws.

Ethos has the capacity to influence and shape everything in our lives—from activities such as personal hygiene to dramatic shifts in cultural values, beliefs, and understandings of reality. In fact, when a culture begins to lose the power of its ethos, it begins to become overdependent on its laws. Laws are born out of values. They attempt to enforce cultural values, but they themselves are not the source of ethos. If the laws do not express the genuine ethos of a society, the laws will remain powerless in the end. It is far more important to shape the values of a community than to set the rules.

UNCOMMON COMMONALITY

When we sense the dissipation of our ethos, we begin to undergird it by establishing more laws and more rules. And that has been the experience of the church. In seeking to keep people moving in a common direction, the church has become far too dependent on rules, guidelines, and laws.

One of the unusual things about a commonly held belief or value is that the law or the rule isn't necessary to keep people within its boundaries. If you have to try to *make* someone do something, then you have a real problem. As long as you're *making* people do things, it implies that they don't want to. This may work with children, but it is destined to fail with adults.

When the church neglects the development of ethos, legalism rules. After ethos has long disappeared, only rules are left. So this leaves us with a critical question: Can the church create and shape culture? I am convinced that the answer is yes. In fact, this entire book is built upon the conviction that, more than anything else, this is what the church must do.

Acts 2:44 says, "All the believers were together and had everything in common." We often refer to this description to highlight the unity that existed in the first-century church. That alone is an extraordinary achievement! But the description that surrounds it is just as inspiring. It's the development of the first-century community: "Every day they continued to meet together in the temple courts. They broke bread in their homes and ate together with glad and sincere hearts, praising God and enjoying the favor of all the people. And the Lord added to their number daily those who were being saved" (Acts 2:46-47).

> **"No empire is more powerful than ethos."**

Acts 4:32 describes the binding together of the hearts of the new believers. It says, "All the believers were one in heart and mind." The idea fleshed itself out because no one claimed that any of his possessions were his own. Instead they shared everything they had.

One of the mysteries of the first-century movement was that it was both unifying and expanding at the same time. Every single day the church expanded. It grew outwardly, reaching new people and bringing new complexity to the situation. And at the same time, the church is described as growing together with common purpose, common values, common vision, and common movement. They had a common e-motion. Their hearts were wrapped around the heart and values of God. Their minds were being shaped by the mind and perspective of God. Everything else recorded in the book of Acts is the outcome and overflow of this apostolic ethos.

No empire is more powerful than ethos. The force of this embryonic movement would soon turn Rome upside down. Jesus Christ began a revolution that transformed individuals and created a transformational community.

THE EVOLUTION OF A REVOLUTION

Nothing is more dangerous to a revolution than winning. When a revolution wins, it must face the prospect of becoming an institution. No better example of this exists than when Constantine began mandating national baptisms. Christianity changed from a movement to an institution, from a global revolution to a world religion. You could now become a Christian without ever having met Jesus Christ personally. This was a bad thing—like keeping the shell and tossing the egg.

> **The ultimate goal of American Christianity should not be to make us good citizens but to make us revolutionaries in the cause of Jesus Christ.**

The irony in this is that the force of Christianity first changed the Roman world and then relinquished its power in the name of accommodation. It's easy to see the difference between Christianity as a religion and Christianity as a revolution when we look back to the days of Constantine and the Dark Ages that followed. It's more difficult to see that difference in our contemporary environment because we are standing in the middle of it. Our great awakenings were born through men and women who could see that the church had lost her way. They led the church back to the third day: from death to resurrection. They called God's people out of the apathetic to the passionate.

America has been known as a Christian nation due to the tremendous impact that the Christian faith has had on our society. At the same time, the Christian faith has become delusional, over-identifying itself with the society as a whole. A Christian revolution must live in tension with human societies and cultures. We want to see an authentic Christian expression in every culture on this planet—in fact we are called to make it so. But there must never be a moment when we perceive Christianity as equal to the culture itself. When we begin to see being Christian and being American as indistinguishable, we lose the transforming essence of our faith. The ultimate goal of American Christianity should not be to make us good citizens but to make us revolutionaries in the cause of Jesus Christ.

We need to recognize that the Christian expression in this nation is far more institution than revolution. We'll never discover the inspiration or desperation it requires to awaken the apostolic ethos if we do not first recognize the serious condition of the American church. It is critical that we regain the power of ethos. In doing this, we will not only be able to restore the evangelistic focus of the local church, but we will also be able to produce the transformational influence that shapes and reshapes culture.

Real, sustainable change occurs when actions are in response to values. But helping a community based on legalism change to one based on ethos can be terrifying. A community really can't be based on both. You can either invest your energy in attempting to control people's actions and thereby lose their hearts, or you can focus on winning their hearts so that, in the end, their actions will represent the values that are important to you.

A PENNY FOR YOUR THOUGHTS

Although it's popular to reconstruct American history and claim that this nation was founded without any influence from the Christian faith, any honest appraisal of this nation's beginning would have to acknowledge the power of Christian culture in shaping our national ethos. It doesn't take a genius to flip a coin over and read the statement "In God We Trust." If this nation was not in any way affected, influenced, or shaped by Christian culture, how exactly did that get there? If it was an accident, I'm sure it would have been removed by now. It's one thing to say it's not appropriate for Christianity to have a dominant influence over American society, but it's another thing to reconstruct history and say that it was never so. Arguments over whether Jefferson or Washington or any of the founding fathers were Christians are irrelevant to this conversation. It's not about whether individuals were Christians, but whether as a whole, the source of their information came from a Christian worldview.

I remember the first time I visited Washington, D.C. One of my highlights was traveling to the Jefferson Memorial and reading the words engraved there. Jefferson wrote all of the following quotes: "Can the liberties of a nation be thought secure when we have removed their only firm basis, a conviction in the minds of the people that these liberties are of the gift of God?"

"I tremble for my country when I reflect that God is just; that his justice cannot sleep forever."

"We hold these truths to be self-evident, that all men are created equal; that they are endowed by their Creator with inherent and inalienable rights; that among these, are life, liberty, and the pursuit of happiness; that to secure these rights, governments are instituted among men."

"Almighty God has created the mind free...All attempts to influence it by temporal punishments or burthens…are a departure from the plan of the Holy Author of our religion."

"No man shall be compelled to frequent or support any religious worship, place, or ministry…otherwise suffer on account of his religious opinions or belief…All men shall be free to profess and by argument to maintain their opinions in matters of religion."

The argument that Jefferson was a deist and therefore was not shaped by a Christian worldview is absurd. He was a good Christian deist. His conclusions came out of a mind formed by Christian values, beliefs, and worldview. Even his conviction that every individual has the right to worship as he so chooses emerges from the construct that Almighty God has created the mind free.

> **On a national level, Jefferson appeals to the power of ethos as greater than the highest form of institutional or governmental authority.**

Jefferson's commitment to establishing a form of government that insured these kinds of liberties was not the result of a non-Christian or anti-Christian bias, but more accurately the result of his thinking being shaped by the values affirmed in the Scriptures. At the same time, Jefferson raises a concern that security of the liberties he has given his life to establish could be lost if we lose the conviction that these same liberties are a gift from God.

Jefferson expresses greater confidence in the power of beliefs and values than in the establishment of constitutional laws and guidelines. On a national level, Jefferson appeals to the power of ethos as greater than the highest form of institutional or governmental authority. Jefferson was a pioneer in the establishment and preservation of our national e-motion, that powerful ethos that has come to be known as the pioneer spirit of Americans.

A MEANING-FULL CULTURE

T.S. Eliot addresses the same issue in *Christianity and Culture*. Eliot contends that only a Christian culture could have produced a Voltaire or Nietzsche. To explain this he writes, "The dominant force in creating a common culture between peoples each of which has its distinct culture, is religion. Please do not, at this point, make a mistake in anticipating my meaning. This is not a religious talk, and I am not setting out to convert anybody. I am simply stating a fact. I am not so much concerned with the communion of Christian believers today; I am talking about the common tradition of Christianity which has made Europe what it is, and about the common cultural elements which this common Christianity has brought with it."

He goes on to say, "It is in Christianity that our arts have developed; it is in Christianity that the laws of Europe have—until recently—been rooted. It is against a backdrop of Christianity that all our thought has significance. An individual European may not believe that the Christian Faith is true, and yet what he says, and makes, and does, will all spring out of his heritage of Christian culture and depend upon that culture for its meaning."

One of the curiosities of secular thinkers in our society is that they love the benefit that has developed out of a Christian worldview in the formation of this nation, but at the same time they desire to liberate themselves from the very constructs that shape their thinking. It is in a nation shaped by the Christian mind that values such as freedom, truth, autonomy, and choice are held as priceless. This environment is ideal for the atheist, the secularist, the philosopher, the antagonist, and even the God-hater. Each person's personal freedom to choose and live his or her life as he or she determines appropriate is protected in this context. I just don't see that kind of intellectual liberty emerging out of communism or any other world religion. In fact, an argument can be made that quite the opposite is true: that the power of the ethos—born out of the Christian faith—has dramatically impacted cultures around the world in a positive way.

WHEN LOSING IS THE BEST THING FOR YOU

I once heard Tom Wolf speak about the unique way in which America treats its conquered. Historically, when a nation is conquered, the consequence is devastation and brutality. At best, the conquered people are allowed to live within the context of slavery and oppression. Yet the American response to victory, in the modern world, has been quite different.

Both Japan and Germany were the defeated foes of American military might. Japan experienced the devastation of two bombs that dropped on Hiroshima and Nagasaki. Germany became a divided nation with the infamous Berlin Wall, a reminder of its crimes against the world. Yet today both those nations stand as economic powers and peers to the United States. Rather than resulting in continued domination, being conquered by the United States created an opportunity for economic and social revitalization.

Japan is arguably the jewel of Asia, surpassing nations with far greater natural and human resources. One of the curiosities of Japan's success is that there are no natural resources on the entire island, and yet, in isolation from the rest of Asia, it has emerged as a global economic power under the nurture and tutelage of its conqueror.

The same is true for Germany. Here the contrast is more personal. A wall divides a people whose culture is identical. And over a span of about forty years, two nations are shaped that become dramatically different. One nation, East Germany, is a reflection of the Soviet Union; the other, West Germany, is a reflection of Western and specifically American values. East Germany soon took on the appearance of a nation defeated by a harsh conqueror. West Germany,

in contrast, flourished as a result of its defeat.

When the Berlin Wall came down, the economic and social contrast between the two nations related by flesh and blood was dramatic. Two nations that were once separated by a wall were faced with forming a national ethos from two distinct ethos.

Capitalism cannot explain the American view of conquest. Something more deeply rooted in the American spirit causes us to see ourselves as the healers of nations. On a national scale, we have seen the result of loving our neighbors as ourselves and the extraordinary admonition not to hate but love our enemies. The foreign policy that shaped our response to World War II was largely formed by a Christian ethos. Again, it's not that the shapers of these policies were themselves Christians. I am not arguing that those who held office were followers of Christ or even believed in God, but the core beliefs and values that shaped their worldview and their understanding of reality and right and wrong were drawn from a Christian context.

Christianity affected and shaped their thinking, and in the end, their decisions have to be considered extraordinary and aberrant in relationship to the history of war and power.

THE FREE WORLD

The ability of an ethos, specifically a Christian worldview, to permeate other cultures can be seen in other national political arenas as well.

I was on a Southwest Airlines flight from Los Angeles to Dallas, sitting in the first row where the seats face each other. After the plane had taken off, the person across from me initiated a conversation. She was a political science major at the University of Texas in Austin.

"Ethos has the power to create momentum, and that momentum can create and shape a culture."

Early on in the conversation, I shared with her that I was a Christian, and she began to freely share with me her disdain for the Christian faith. I asked her why she felt the way she did, and she responded that she had no tolerance for the way Christianity treated women. I asked her if her conclusions were the result of global studies related to women's rights issues. I also asked her what nations or cultures she had found to be most effective at empowering women, in terms of education and economic status. She acknowledged that she lacked research and familiarity with the subjects.

We took a few minutes and reflected together on the condition and the role of women around the world. At the forefront of recent news headlines were reports that women in India were being set on fire for having insufficient dowries.

It was not difficult to assess that the Christian context was more liberating for women than Hinduism. She was quick to affirm that the Muslim world was certainly not a better alternative. In fact, even her questions would be considered intolerable in that environment. And, of course, the once popular view that communism was the great cultural savior of the common person and the oppressed is rarely advocated in today's context.

In our conversation, I mentioned two individuals that I felt would certainly serve as sources of inspiration and hope. One being Aun San Su Chi, the courageous political dissonant within the fundamentalist Buddhist country Miramar (formerly Burma) and the other being Indira Gandhi of Hindu India. I reminded my new acquaintance of the curious connection between their elevation to national leadership and the fact that both of their fathers were educated through a Christian-founded university. On top of that, both Aun San Su Chi and Indira Gandhi were educated in the same university at Oxford, England. It is not a coincidence that two of the most significant women leaders who have emerged out of cultures in which women are not considered either capable or qualified to hold such roles emerged through the influence of a Christian context.

All this is to say that ethos has the power to create momentum, and that momentum can create and shape a culture. In many ways nations are movements that worked. Nations are the integration of beliefs and values and a worldview that unite people with a common identity.

IMAGINE-NATIONS

Lawrence E. Harrison, after twenty years of working on Latin America's development problems, began to draw some unusual conclusions about the economic condition of Latin America. He put his research conclusions into a book entitled *Underdevelopment Is a State of Mind*.

In his introduction, Harrison writes that "it is culture that principally explains, in most cases, why some countries develop more rapidly and equitably than others. By 'culture' I mean the values and attitudes a society inculcates in its people through various socializing mechanisms, e.g., the home, the school, the church."

Later he summarizes the basic message of his book: that culture is the principle determinant of development. By comparing various parallel nations whose economic, political, and social progress are dramatically different, he builds his argument, comparing Nicaragua and Costa Rica, Argentina and Australia, the Dominican Republic and Haiti. He paints a picture that demonstrates that it is not access to resources or the capacity for progress that determines the development of a nation. His argument is that a culture or ethos that realizes the creative potential within the society will progress the fastest. In other words, he makes an argument for a culture that breeds and encourages human creativity and entrepreneurialism.

Harrison writes, "I believe that the creative capacity of human beings is at the heart of the development process. What makes development happen is our ability to imagine, theorize, conceptualize, experiment, invent, articulate, organize, manage, solve problems and do a hundred other things with our minds and hands that contribute to the progress of the individual and of humankind...the engine is human creative capacity."

He goes on to describe this creative environment as something that is not localized in one person but permeates the entire community. He explains, "It is not just the entrepreneur who creates progress." Harrison follows the creative process from the entrepreneur to the inventor, to the scientist, to the engineer, to the farmer, to the machine operator, to the salesman, to the teacher who taught them all.

What Harrison is advocating is the core of e-motion—that ethos is more important than laws and that a cultural environment can nurture and develop human potential. In a certain sense, some cultures can be better than others. Some cultures are healthier than others.

NURTURING A HEALTHY ENVIRONMENT

I know this is not a popular view, and certainly my last two statements are far from politically correct. However, I am convinced that, just as some cultures regard human potential as their greatest value, in other cultures even the human being himself is considered to have no value at all.

> The problem in many of our congregations is not that we've chosen a wrong strategy or have an irrelevant style but that we have an unhealthy culture.

In the same way, churches span the continuum of healthy cultures. The problem in many of our congregations is not that we've chosen a wrong strategy or have an irrelevant style but that we have an unhealthy culture. It should not be a surprise that if we were to enter many congregations, we could see how the uniqueness of the human spirit and the potential God has placed in each individual is being wasted.

In many churches compliance and conformity are the greatest values. There is rarely a rumor, much less a reality, of a church being the center point of imagination, invention, and innovation. If we are teaching sound theology but neglecting to create an environment in which people fulfill their God-given purpose, are we not, by definition, an unhealthy culture?

I am convinced that, beyond the eruption of human potential empowered by the Holy Spirit, a healthy culture also produces healthy people. The apostolic ethos not only empowers us to make manifest the imagination of God, but it also creates an environment for spiritual health. And spiritual health is expressed substantially in and through emotional, relational, intellectual, and physical well-being.

A person who is growing in spiritual maturity is developing emotional health. A person who is growing in spiritual maturity is healing broken relationships and building healthy ones. A person who is growing in spiritual maturity begins to take every thought captive to the obedience of Christ and no longer allows the imaginations of the heart to run riot. A person who is growing in spiritual health begins to treat his or her body as the temple of the Lord and establish personal disciplines that result in overcoming such vices as gluttony. A person who is growing in spiritual health dreams great dreams with God.

Again, the momentum of an apostolic ethos is both outward and inward. It is expressed both externally and internally. The momentum changes the world around us, while at the same time it changes the world within us. The tragedy of the church without an apostolic ethos is that we've allowed ourselves to be captured by the cultural ethos around us, rather than to be an ethos that shapes culture. And if this were not bad enough, we have seen at least three generations reject the community of the church in pursuit of an ethos that would value their uniqueness and creativity. This has been true in both the intellectual and artistic arenas.

A CULTURE OF GREATNESS

There's an old joke about the Sunday school teacher who asks his students, "What has four legs, is furry, climbs trees, and eats nuts?" One student hesitantly raises his hand and says, "I think it's a squirrel, but I'm going to go ahead and say Jesus."

The implication is that in the church, we're not allowed to think. We're forced to swallow simplistic answers to complex issues. If our answer for everything doesn't begin with Jesus, then we're heretics. A church must raise a generation that can identify a squirrel and, at the same time, thank Jesus for creating it.

As a philosophy student in college, my view of Christians was that they were against intellectual and philosophic pursuits. It came as both a great joy and surprise when I discovered that a thinking Christian was not an oxymoron. At the same time, the church has been at best aesthetically challenged, if not in fact an enemy of the arts. Somewhere on the road, we seem to have lost our love of beauty for beauty's sake, as if somehow God did not indulge in this kind of triviality. Those who worship the God of creation must never forget how beauty both reflects God and his values.

Artistry matters to God. The building of the Temple of Solomon was not simply assigned to good-hearted people who wanted to give God their best; it was assigned to the most skilled artisans and carpenters. The ministry of worship that was not entrusted to people who just loved to sing or who worshipped with all their hearts; it was actually given to those who were skilled in playing musical instruments and gifted with voice.

In every discipline, from the intellectual to the artistic, the church should be the envy of nations, much like the way Jewish culture has maintained an ethos that has nurtured the intellect of some of the world's most renowned scientists and the artistry of some of the world's most gifted filmmakers. The church's birthright is to be the fountainhead of creativity and human potential.

For centuries the church has struggled between giving God glory and unleashing human potential. It seems like we either magnify the greatness of God and minimize the contribution of man or deify human potential and demean the image and greatness of God.

The apostolic ethos fuses together a belief in the awesome nature of God and a stewardship of the God-given potential within every human being. One of the most misunderstood verses in the Bible is one in which Paul tells us that it is in our weakness that God is shown strong. For too long we have not only implied that God working through our weaknesses is an encouragement but have, in fact, implied that when we operate in our strengths, we are dishonoring God. The truth is that if we operated solely on our greatest strengths, we would still find ourselves inadequate in reaching the goals that only God can accomplish through us.

You don't have to look to your weaknesses to find yourself weak in the face of God. Even in the context of our greatest strengths, we can learn how God's strength works through our weakness. Through his death and resurrection, Jesus ignited an ethos that could be infused into every cultural expression on this planet. Each culture has different styles and rhythms; each has different languages and histories; yet within each one, the power of an apostolic ethos can potentially be fully awakened and energized. And when this happens, we will begin to gain e-motion.

> I know it may sound like heresy, but it is more important to change what people care about than to change what they believe!

THE FIRE THAT MOVES US

Jeremiah, when faced with the reality of walking in obedience to God's Word, got fed up. For a moment he contemplated choosing another way. Not a road of blatant rebellion, just silence. Not anger, just apathy. But what he discovered changed his life. He confessed, "But if I say, 'I will not mention him or speak any more in his name,' his word is in my heart like a fire, a fire shut up in my bones. I am weary of holding it in; indeed, I cannot' " (Jeremiah 20:9).

Jeremiah discovered that he didn't just believe; he cared! It wasn't just a truth but a passion! The light placed within him was not just a bulb but a fire! It is not enough to be enlightened; we must be inflamed. For too long we have focused on making sure people believe the right things and have left their concerns alone. I know it may sound like heresy, but it is more important to change what people care about than to change what they believe! You can believe without caring, but you can't care without believing. We cannot afford to fill our churches with members who have biblical beliefs and worldly concerns. When we awaken the apostolic ethos, the heart of God begins to pulsate throughout the church of Jesus Christ. The Christian faith is to be a *moving* experience!

> ❝We are what we repeatedly do. Excellence, then, is not an act, but a habit.❞ —ARISTOTLE

FUEL FOR THOUGHT

1. What is the ethos of our church?
2. What significant events have shaped our church's ethos?
3. Is our leadership more concerned with rules, doctrine, or spiritual culture?
4. What are we doing today to nurture our environment?
5. What are we doing to encourage the use of God-given potential within our congregation?
6. How are we developing the God-given potential within every human being?
7. What significant events could be created to shape the future of our church's ethos?

CHAPTER FIVE

CULTURAL ARCHITECTURE

Cultures sing their own songs, tell their own stories, and carry their own aromas. A culture is a beautiful art piece that uses people as its canvas. A culture's formation is both spiritual and natural. Uniting a crowd into a community requires spiritual leadership, and what emerges in the process is the generation of a common culture built upon commonly held beliefs, values, and worldviews.

There is no more significant reason to be a pastoral leader than to awaken an apostolic ethos. To embrace the God-given task of connecting the local church to the first-century church is an extraordinary responsibility. But God has already placed within the body of Christ everything we need to ignite the flames of spiritual revival and revolution. If local churches are essentially spiritual subcultures waiting to become cultural revolutions, then we as spiritual leaders need to engage our environment as cultural architects.

In every culture you'll find essential metaphors that define and shape its ethos. Your symbols hold your secret stories. The metaphor causes an eruption of images, ideas, dreams, beliefs, and convictions all at one time. The story of an entire people can be contained in one symbol. A culture often has two or three symbols that are fundamental to the identity of the people.

METAPHORICALLY SPEAKING

I love looking at nations and trying to figure out which metaphors reflect their values and culture. When I think of the precision, discipline, and orderliness of the British culture, it comes as no surprise that their cultural icon is Big Ben. The world keeps its time on England's clock. Lined up precisely behind that metaphor is the nation's most symbolic activity, the changing of the guard. Being a citizen of El Salvador, I find it hard to imagine that Big Ben and the changing of the guard would ever be selected as cultural expressions of Latin America.

Metaphors are not foreign to our own culture. In fact, if you look carefully enough, you'll see that we're a culture packed with metaphors. Our team sports are built around metaphors. You have the Oakland Raiders, the bad boys of the NFL. The Miami Dolphins could never

> We live in a world of commerce where one symbol says everything necessary.

achieve that level of badness. Dolphins are too nice. The 49ers are hard workers, and the Bears are in the black and blue division of grunt-it-out type football teams. The New York Jets may best be remembered for Joe Namath wearing pantyhose. If you had to pick a bird as a metaphor, being a Cardinal is much better than being a Robin. It would be hard to evoke fear in your opponent if you were the Robins, the Hummingbirds, or the Doves!

We live in a world of commerce in which one symbol says everything necessary. For Nike it's the swoosh. For Starbucks, it's the two-tailed siren. For Apple it's a...you guessed it. Branding has become the consummate integration of artistry and marketing. The same culture that rejects the meta-narrative embraces the metaphor.

My brother, Alex, is married to a Brazilian, Adriana. The national metaphor for Brazil would be contained not in a clock but in a festival. To think of Brazil is to think of the Mardi Gras. The cultural metaphor for this passionate South American country is the biggest party on the planet. Dancing somewhere behind that metaphor is the other cultural icon of Brazil, Pelé—perhaps the greatest and most beautiful athlete in the world. If you can discover and unwrap a culture's metaphors, you can begin to understand the essence of that culture.

THE IMAGES OF THE INVISIBLE GOD

God has placed as a center point in the Christian movement metaphors that, once unwrapped, begin to transform not only the hearts of its constituency, but the entire ethos of the community.

The central metaphor of the Christian faith is the cross. Rich with passion and purpose, the cross evokes the kind of e-motion that transforms a church into a movement. For followers of Jesus Christ, the cross becomes more than a reminder of his sacrifice, death, and resurrection. It also serves as an invitation to deny ourselves, take up our crosses, and follow him. This central metaphor of the church demands sacrifice and servanthood: The only way to live in the kingdom of God is to first die to yourself.

If this were not enough, the essence of this metaphor is reinforced with another Christian metaphor, baptism. Baptism is a water grave. It is yet another reminder of Jesus Christ's death, burial, and resurrection. Every individual who becomes a part of the Christian community must personally declare his or her own death, burial, and resurrection in a very peculiar and extraordinary way. Every follower of Jesus Christ goes to his or her grave and then lives.

And there is even a third metaphor in the movement of Jesus Christ. It is the Lord's Supper—the ongoing ordinance of the church. We revisit this metaphor over and over again. Should we be surprised that when we unwrap this third metaphor, it goes back to the same essence, passion, and purpose of the first two? The Lord's Supper is done in memory of Jesus' suffering, death, and resurrection. The bread being his body broken for us; the cup, his blood shed on our behalf. Jesus commanded us to do this in remembrance of him. And in the same way we are called to die to ourselves. Paul said it like this: "To live is Christ and to die is gain" (Philippians 1:21b).

Many times the names of our churches become our metaphors.

In Galatians 2:20-21 he explains: "I have been crucified with Christ and I no longer live, but Christ lives in me. The life I live in the body, I live by faith in the Son of God, who loved me and gave himself for me. I do not set aside the grace of God, for if righteousness could be gained through the law, Christ died for nothing!"

It is inescapable that the ethos of the New Testament church is wrapped around the concepts of sacrifice and conquest. It is a call to life through death. The apostolic leader unwraps these three metaphors and reignites the fire that burned in the first-century church. Their church erupted under the shadow of the cross. One by one, Jesus' first followers joined Jesus in his death. Church by church, they celebrated at his table. And generation by generation, through dying to themselves, Christians brought the life of Christ to the nations.

As powerful as these metaphors are, it is not enough to simply uphold them in memory of what Jesus did. It is absolutely essential to understand these metaphors if we are to shape the heart and values of the contemporary church. The metaphors not only root us in the past, but they also guide and shape our future.

LOCAL IMPRESSION OF FAITH

While every local church uses central metaphors from the culture of *the* Church, we need to be acutely aware of the sub-metaphors that we create in our local churches. Many times the names of our churches become our metaphors. An icon in our worship or structure can become a metaphor. Designations such as Family Church, Bible Church, Community Church, or Baptist Church often have more power in shaping the ethos of our local churches than even the metaphors given to us by our Lord.

In south Dallas we worked with individuals and families to establish a foundation for a church based on Jesus Christ and his Word in a community that was impoverished and economically depressed. We chose the name Cornerstone to communicate that, in a world where everything seemed unstable and uncertain and where violence was commonplace, there was someone or something that you could build your life on that was sure, unchanging, and worthy of your trust.

When we planted a Spanish-speaking community in east Dallas, we knew

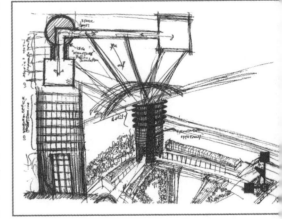

we would attract many that came from an institutionally Catholic background. We named that congregation *El Pueblo de Diós* (The People of God) to build a sub-metaphor which expressed that people are more important than the building or material possessions.

The church I came to in Los Angeles had a sub-metaphor for the church that was rather obvious. The name of the church was The Church on Brady. The name evolved naturally as the founding members invited the community to build a church on a street called Brady. Originally, the name of the church was The First Southern Baptist Church of East Los Angeles. But due to the fact that it was located in a dominantly Catholic community—not exactly in the South—where being a First Baptist Church was not prestigious, they found the name to be a liability. Those with a heart for evangelism instinctively started calling it The Church on Brady. This was a beautiful response born out of sensitivity to those without Christ.

CRAFTING A NEW METAPHOR

When I arrived nearly fifteen years later, the new challenges we faced required us to consider relocation. If we moved, the sub-metaphor of The Church on Brady changed from being a tremendous asset to a tremendous liability. When I proposed the idea of relocation, the question that was asked of me was literally, "What's going to happen to the people on this street?" not, "What's going to happen to the people in this community?" (Though I'm sure that's what the questioners meant.) But it was the street that became the focal point in our talks of relocation.

This experience led us not only to renaming the congregation, but also to carefully selecting a new central sub-metaphor. There was so much we wanted to wrap around a new metaphor describing our community of faith. We wanted to capture the uniqueness of our congregation in its multi-ethnic expression, even though at that time we were not nearly as diverse as we are today. We were a congregation consisting predominantly of Mexican-Americans with perhaps 30 percent Caucasians, a handful of Asian-Americans, and one African-American—who was on staff leading worship. We wanted to make central to our message that in Jesus Christ the many are made one. We had the seed of a church that reflected the nations.

This is a wonderful example of how a metaphor can not only define you, but also create and shape your future. Today at Mosaic we are closer to 40 percent Asian; 30 percent Latino; and 30 percent Caucasian, African-American, and other.

We also wanted our metaphor to communicate that we were a community of broken people who were—together—finding healing and wholeness in Jesus Christ. Another significant aspect of who we had become was a people who understood God as the master artist, the creator who placed within each human being the spirit of creativity.

For months we searched for a metaphor, an image, a word that would adequately describe the heart and vision of our congregation. We prayed and thought and dreamed, but nothing seemed to stick. One day I was walking to the Coke machine with two of the staff members, and one of them threw out this outlandish idea that he wanted to invent a soft drink which, every time you drank it, turned into a different flavor. The other staff

> **Every culture has stories that are wrapped up in their religion, their mythology, or their folklore.**

member said, "Oh, I have a perfect name for your soft drink. You should call it Mosaic."

When I heard that response, I knew instantly that this was going to be the name of our congregation. I looked at them and said, "That's not the name of a soft drink, that's the name of our church." They looked at me like I was out of my mind.

"Mosaic" is the perfect metaphor not only for who we are, but also for who we long to become. A mosaic is an art form of broken and fragmented pieces brought together to reflect the glory of God, especially when light strikes it. It took us a while, but soon the entire body accepted and celebrated the imagery that we are the Mosaic of God, reflecting his beauty through the light of Christ.

THE ART OF STORY

Wrapped up in the metaphors of a community are the stories. Every culture has stories that are wrapped up in their religion, their mythology, or their folklore. Stories retell the lives and experiences of gods or heroes. These stories do more than entertain; they inform. They are interwoven with the beliefs and ideals of the society. Stories both define and direct. In many ways, a culture's story is the story of everyone in that culture. It's the story that describes the life of the society. It's the story that describes the desired life of each individual.

Leaders must choose their stories carefully. Of course, in this we Christians have an advantage. The Bible is full of great stories, and locked within those stories are the core values that God desires to pass on to his people. Ultimately, the Bible is one great story. It is the story of God's activity in human history, both of his creation of all that exists and of his redemption of his people. This story is so big, so rich, and so profound that it requires many stories to be wrapped around it to give it proper texture and depth.

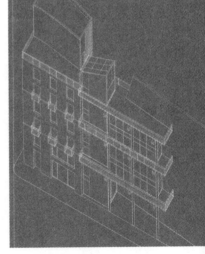

Apostolic leaders are great storytellers, and they make sure that the great story is central in shaping the ethos of the community. One of the dangers in telling the individual stories in the Bible is to lose the ultimate purpose that drives the whole of God's story. The story of the Bible is God's intention to bring the nations to himself. Genesis gives us the context of the problem; Revelation gives us the hope of the ultimate resolution. The Old Testament shows God's determination to reach the nations through a nation; the New Testament begins with God's intervention in human history through the person of Jesus Christ. Jesus' story unfolds as he pursues his purpose to seek and to save that which is lost (Luke 19:11), and then ushers in the revolutionary movement known as the church to be his witnesses in Jerusalem, Judea, Samaria, and to the very ends of the earth.

The church was born out of stories. The first-century church was driven by the narrative. There was no New Testament; there were no Gospels to transmit the story of Jesus. His story was entrusted to storytellers. The Christian faith grew through story—not text. Only later did the stories become Scripture. While the Scripture must be held in the highest regard, we must not neglect the power of story.

THE WHOLE STORY

The church is a part of God's story, but our chapter is not meant to be read from beginning to end. To live out the chapters intended for us, we must begin with the end in mind. The story is that God will not be stopped and history will not come to a close until the church accomplishes Jesus' purpose of redeeming people from every tribe and nation. We read in Revelation 7:9-10, "After this I looked and there before me was a great multitude that no one could count, from every nation, tribe, people and language, standing before the throne and in front of the Lamb. They were wearing white robes and were holding palm branches in their hands. And they cried out in a loud voice: 'Salvation belongs to our God, who sits on the thrown, and to the Lamb.' "

Our chapter of the story only makes sense when we tell the whole story. There are many subplots in this great story: lives are changed, marriages are healed, relationships are restored, broken hearts are healed, and shattered dreams are reborn. But it all happens in the context of God calling us out to become fishers of men and conquerors of nations.

LIVING A GREAT STORY

Other great stories are equally significant in the shaping of ethos. These stories are the stories of those within the culture whose names have faces and who not only bring the mythology of heroes and legends, but demonstrate the humanity of everyday people who are neighbors, family, and friends.

> **If people do not believe a leader has a true story of God, no other stories he tells will have a meaningful impact.**

First of all, there are stories that shape the leader and stories that develop deep within core beliefs and values that result in unwavering conviction, even in the face of disaster or conflict. Every leader has to stand in his story—the story of God in his life. And in that story, there may be many stories that explain an intimate knowledge of God. If people do not believe a leader has a true story of God, no other stories he tells will have a meaningful impact. You can remember the stories that have shaped your life—the stories that people tease you about because you tell them over and over again. These stories are more than a memory; they explain who you are and why you are going in the direction you're headed. They're stories of prayers answered, of obstacles overcome, of dreams fulfilled, and of sacrifices that realized the miraculous.

Apostolic leaders are not only great storytellers; in many ways their lives tell a great story. The themes are consistent with our faith's core metaphors of sacrifice, death, and life.

For Kim and me, many of our God stories are born out of the context of working among the urban poor for ten years. Although our context has changed, the God that we met and have come to know remains the same and carries us into the stories ahead. The stories we have lived only inspire us to call others to a similar journey, that they too may have their own stories of God.

Paul describes Christians as epistles, or letters of God, written on human hearts. With each story lived, the church becomes a place that is rich with God's stories; and with each story, faith increases and deepens. What then happens is that those without similar stories begin to search for their stories. They begin where those who have traveled their journey recommend they start. The Christian experience becomes a journey of discovery and experience with God, and with each added story, the momentum of this life-transforming movement exponentially increases.

WHEN A STORY COMES TO LIFE

One of the arts that leaders must craft is the selection of great stories. Preaching must be more than moving toward doctrinal soundness, more than simply calling people toward life application. Preaching must elevate the stories of God that draw a picture of what life can be like for everyone. God's promise is that he will be found by those who seek him and will be known by those who long to walk humbly with him.

If all your stories come from outside your local culture, you'll end up with a diluted result. Almost nothing is more powerful than telling a story of transformation and then pointing to the person whose story it is, especially when everyone knows the person. One thing that *is* even more powerful is having him or her stand up and tell his or her own story.

REBECCA'S STORY

I remember the week that Rebecca Catalan was in a hospital on the verge of dying. Her blood platelet level had dropped to a critical, even lethal, low. And the only procedure available to reverse the terminal process failed to take effect. By Thursday her situation was hopeless from a medical standpoint. But when we gathered to pray for

> 66 When your son has died, and God has brought him back to life, it isn't hard to understand the message of the cross. 99

her, we all sensed a divine moment—God's gracious and powerful response. Within thirty minutes, the doctors informed Rebecca's parents that she was miraculously recovering. And on that Sunday, only three days after the doctors had given up hope, she sat with us in worship. You can imagine the response when I told her story and then pointed her out, sitting among those worshipping the Lord. The power of prayer became more real through Rebecca's life and story.

JOSIAH'S STORY

On Tuesday morning Cyndi and Paul Richardson were preparing to leave for Indonesia to invest their lives in a Muslim nation that so desperately needed the love of God. They were already packed and preparing to go to the airport. They had already said their goodbyes and wanted nothing more than to leave everything they valued behind and please God in their service.

Moments later, they found their ten-month-old son, Josiah, at the bottom of a pool. He had wandered through an open gate and fallen in. Some estimate that he had been unconscious up to five minutes. After receiving CPR, Josiah was transported via helicopter to Children's Hospital, where nearly a hundred people, including myself, joined Cyndi and Paul to pray for their son as they grieved amidst this tragedy.

I'll never forget walking through the hospital parking lot with Paul as he sobbed, trying to absorb the information that his son might remain a vegetable for as long as he lived, if he lived at all. We interceded on Josiah's behalf, laying our hands on his small body and begging God to restore his life. Unbelievably to most, he was spared a death or severe disability that seemed certain. Imagine what it was like for our congregation when they heard Josiah's story and saw him there in worship only a few days later, sitting with his father, mother, and sister!

Though their journey was delayed a few months, Paul and Cyndi went on to Indonesia to live in the midst of an unstable environment in which the Christian faith is not looked upon favorably. When your son has died, and God has brought him back to life, it isn't hard to understand the message of the cross.

DAVE'S STORY

Dave Auda was a truck driver for UPS for nineteen years, working fifty-five to sixty hours a week, while being a husband and a father to four daughters. Dave started what we call a life group with two other families, and within six months, the high attendance of the group was over sixty. And the group had seen thirty-three people come to Christ, as well as eighteen be baptized. This all happened during Dave's limited spare time. The story of this busy layperson growing a small group faster than most full-time pastors grow their congregations had a tremendous impact on our congregation. It was amazing how many people were encouraged to greater faith and involvement when this church member of twenty-one years joined our pastoral staff.

Frankly, we could never have afforded him (remember, he worked for UPS). But God worked another miracle. As a result of fatigue and serving endlessly at the church, Dave fell asleep behind the wheel and drove his tractor-trailer off a 19-foot embankment. God spared his life, but his injuries ended his career with UPS. Operating out of my gift of mercy, I went to Dave and told him, "Now that you're unemployed, we can afford you. Let me offer you a raise from unemployment." Dave is a natural catalyst, but telling his story and affirming his life multiplied the impact of his personal ministry and helped reshape the ethos of our body.

MARI'S STORY

Mari Takashima was born in Japan and connected to our church when she and her husband, Ross, were struggling in their marriage. They began attending Mosaic through the invitation of a friend and joined us on a service trip to Ensenada, Mexico to help us work in an impoverished community. Mari and Ross were both working with a mural team, transforming a local athletic center in one of the *colonias*. They were painting three words in Spanish, words they did not understand. Those words were *believe, belong, become.* Another guest on the Ensenada team, who had not yet received Christ, read the mural and was so touched that she received Christ shortly after with one of the team members.

That night in our wrap-up session, the Mexican-American woman who had come to faith because of the mural shared how it expressed exactly what she had longed for in her heart and helped bring her to faith. Mari was sitting there, hearing how her own work had brought someone to Christ while she hadn't 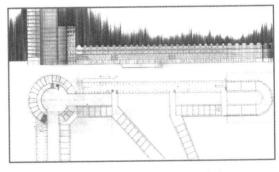 yet chosen to follow him. That night, in that same room, as a result of the woman's sharing her story, Mari gave her life to Christ. Evangelism through the arts takes on a whole new meaning through Mari's portrait.

ERIC'S STORY

I noticed Eric Bryant while I was coming to church early one day. He was wearing an orange vest and directing

> **The stories you choose to tell inform the emerging culture.**

traffic. Every time I saw this guy, he was doing some kind of service. I kept hearing stories about this guy named Eric. Whatever the task, he seemed to volunteer. Nothing seemed to be too humble, insignificant, or unrewarding. I talked to him for the first time at a beach party. I asked him to tell me a little bit about himself and what his interests and passions were. And before the conversation was over, I had asked him if he would be our youth pastor. I never looked at a resume and didn't call for references. But as I explained to him, I'm a sucker for servanthood. His servant's heart was a story we wanted to tell and a pattern we wanted to reproduce.

UNWRAPPING GOD'S POWER

Stories contain within them the essence of ethos. You can either talk to people about God's power or tell them the stories that unwrap the power of God. You can talk to them about the power of a small group community in the work of evangelism, or you can tell them a story that fleshes it out. You can tell people that creativity is not only the natural result of spirituality, but also an extraordinary tool for evangelism in the post-Western environment; or you can let them be the product of that reality. You can talk all day long about the importance of servanthood and service; or you can work from the pattern of Jesus and exalt those who humble themselves, giving positions of greatness to those who are willing to be the least in the kingdom.

The stories you choose to tell inform the emerging culture. Stories that are rooted in the life of the congregation breathe life into the congregation. Great leaders are great storytellers. Great churches have great stories. Great stories create a great future.

YOUR WORDS DEFINE YOU

Another significant way that ethos is culturally transmitted is through language. You can discover what's important to a culture by how many words that culture has to describe something. As a child in El Salvador, I only learned one word for snow, and that was the word *nieve*. *Nieve* covered both ice cream, which we knew very well, and snow, which we had never seen.

When we lived in Miami, I was a huge Minnesota Vikings fan. Because of that, I became enthralled with snow. I loved watching Joe Kapp and then Fran Tarkenton lead these Norsemen onto the frozen tundra of Minnesota as they would engage lesser opponents on their battlefield. It made me always long for the snow.

As you can imagine, when it came to snow, my decade in Miami left me wanting; but then we moved to North Carolina. I couldn't wait for my first snow experience. Of course, I hadn't really factored in how cold it had to be for it to snow, but that's another story. And then it came. It was wetter than I thought it would be and didn't look quite as thick and textured as I had imagined. In fact, it was pretty uncomfortable.

That first snow was a real disappointment, but then someone explained to me that it was sleet, not snow. It was sort of like an atmospheric slushy. Then later I experienced what I thought was snow, but I was again corrected. These were only flurries. Once I even had a somewhat dangerous experience with snow. Snow was coming down hard and fast and in golf ball size and shape. It was like snow motivated by rage, but I soon learned that this was hail.

The more you step into the world of snow, the more you discover it's far more complex than you ever imagined. There are more than snowballs and snowmen. There are snowdrifts, snowstorms, snowplows, and of course, to every student's delight, snow days. It's my understanding that some cultures have literally dozens of different words for snow due to the continuous experience of this phenomenon.

IN OTHER WORDS...

Language is an important transmitter of culture, not only because it helps you describe your experience, but also because it helps you gain tools to survive and thrive in your particular environment. The same is true in the church environment. The more words you have for something, the more likely it is a genuine part of your ethos. If you did a brief study of your cultural dictionary, what would emerge? How many words for evangel-

> **It should concern us if we never move beyond the Christian language found on bumper stickers and T-shirts.**

ism would you have? How many words for servanthood? How many different ways of expressing and defining love? Do words like *risk, sacrifice, catalyze, innovate, create,* and *fail* surround the language of faith? Remember that the more nuanced the description, the more dominant the experience is in the culture. How

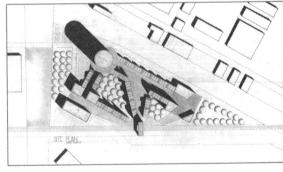

many adjectives surround the word *love* in your context or illustrate the importance of hope in your community?

There is a difference between language that describes ethos and jargon or cliché. In fact, whenever you hear or find a great many clichés to describe a certain value or experience, you can almost be certain that the genuine value or experience does not exist. At the same time, while unique cultures will develop their own unique or distinct dialects, jargon is different than this. Jargon is the use of superficial and even meaningless language in an attempt to describe something that is more profound and substantive.

It should concern us if we never move beyond the Christian language found on bumper stickers and T-shirts. In the transmission of an ethos, it is essential that people can describe the genuineness of their own experience in their own words. For this reason, the language a leader chooses to use has tremendous impact on the shaping of a culture. At the same time, the ability of members of the community to clearly articulate and explain their values as their own is an essential evidence that an ethos is genuinely emerging.

One of the starkest examples of the influence of words in our culture is the emergence of the language of dysfunction. It may be hard to believe, but not that long ago the word *dysfunctional* wasn't part of our vocabulary. Only those highly trained in a particular school of psychiatry would use or even understand the language of psychosis and neurosis. It may be even more difficult to believe, but before the list of descriptions of human brokenness grew to what it is today, people could have generally been described as functional and even healthy. The few who were placed in asylums were simply understood to be insane or to have gone mad.

In a span of barely fifty years, we have gone from minimal cultural experience of psychological distress to a culture well-schooled in human fragmentation. Today it's common to speak of people as psychotic or neurotic, manic-depressive or bipolar, schizophrenic or suffering from multiple personality disorder. What was once saved for courses on abnormal psychology has now become the language describing ordinary Americans. If language is an indicator of a cultural ethos, then we can only begin to imagine what the implications are. Our fragmentation is so profoundly experienced that our definitions simply take on initials such as ADD and ADHD.

CHOOSE YOUR WORDS CAREFULLY

One of my most interesting experiences with the connection between language and culture occurred while I was sitting in a small Spanish-speaking congregation. We were a blend of immigrant Mexican, Central American, Caribbean, and South American. To the outside observer, we would have appeared to be of the same culture and ethnicity. Although all of us spoke what would be described as Spanish, there were huge language barriers between us.

> **When we use language that is not substantiated by action, the words diminish in value and lose their power.**

I had invited a Puerto Rican pastor to speak to our dominantly Mexican audience. He began to explain in his testimony that before he was a follower of Christ, he had *chavos* everywhere and that he lived for *chavos*. In every city he made *chavos*. He had *chavos* here and *chavos* there, and the most difficult thing for him to give up as he was confronted with the message of Christ was his love for making *chavos*.

I didn't understand what he meant. I had never heard the word *chavos* before in my life. But the Mexican women in the room grew more shocked and astonished with every word he spoke. Their surprise soon turned to anger. The speaker didn't know what was happening, but another one of our Puerto Rican pastors quickly intervened. He helped us all understand that in Puerto Rico, *chavos* means "money," while in Mexico it means "babies." As the guest speaker was explaining that he had loved making money and made money in every city, here and there and everywhere, the Mexican women heard him say he loved making babies, here and there and everywhere. And on top of that, he said it was the most difficult thing for him to give up in becoming a follower of Christ! One word made all the difference in the world.

RECLAIMING LANGUAGE

The meaning contained in the words we use is more significant than the words themselves. Two churches can use the same words and have dramatically different meanings. Every church uses the language of faith, love, and hope, but the meaning can be dramatically different. Every church uses some kind of language around servanthood and ministry, but the meaning won't be the same everywhere.

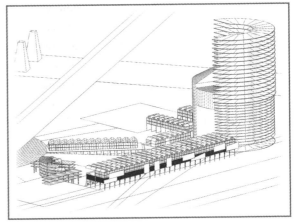

To examine the power of language to shape ethos, we must go beyond the words that are spoken and evaluate honestly the meaning behind those words. What does *fellowship* mean in your church? I have yet to meet a dying congregation that does not describe itself as having a great fellowship. Such a definition of fellowship is extraordinarily inclusive and without question exclusive of those outside of the church.

What does your church mean when it uses the word *missions?* It has always astonished me that so many churches and individuals who are "missions minded" rarely engage in the mission of Christ that requires them to come face to face with an unbeliever and love that person into God's kingdom.

Language can powerfully influence ethos and our actions, but our actions can also demean the power of words. When we use language that is not substantiated by action, the words diminish in value and lose their power. When this happens, we either have to find new language to describe an old value or reclaim the old language by establishing what will appear to be a new definition.

There may be no more important word for us to evaluate in this area than the word *church*. What does it mean to be the church of Jesus Christ? What is an acceptable definition of a local church? When does a local church cease to be a church of Jesus Christ? One of my greatest hopes in writing this book is that our cultural language about the church will be elevated and we will, at the same time, capture new language that inspires us to believe great things for the local church. Then we'll be able to recapture the power of the biblical language that informs us about who we are and who we are to become as God's people.

A MAN OF ACTION WORDS

One other nuance in relationship to language and ethos is the use of nouns and verbs. While descriptive language is important in the defining of an ethos, perhaps even more important is the creation of language that promotes action. Some words wait for definition. They hang in the balance between noun and verb.

> "From the Beatles to the Rolling Stones to Radiohead, our generation has seen the emergence of what could perhaps best be described as secular worship."

Faith is like that. It can either dominate our culture as "the faith" or catalyze movement as we live by faith. While both the "noun" and the "verb" are part of establishing a culture, the noun without the verb may result in description without application. A momentum ethos takes words like faith, love, and hope and moves them from noun to verb, creating a language of action, movement, and application.

It is not incidental that some of the most effective communicators in our culture, both Christian and non-Christian, focus on the application of the idea they are advocating. This is the basis of all felt-need preaching—to move people toward application and obedience and to teach the doctrine but call people to action.

The power of theology is in the mission that it produces. Language that directs people toward information rather than action may educate, but it does not create movement. Communication has the capacity to both form and inform.

THE ART OF ART

Another significant tool in the process of cultural architecture is aesthetics. In any culture the expression of beauty is a significant shaper of the cultural ethos. In many ways aesthetics are an expression of what a culture holds true through the abstract medium of images and sounds.

Music, poetry, and dance are not simply extraneous expressions of culture.

They are the soul of a culture. When a culture holds certain values and ideals as true, the expression of those truths goes beyond words. Art uses a canvas as a medium for communicating the soul of people. Dance brings physicality and rhythm to the beliefs and values of a culture. The musician and the poet are the voices of the culture and not simply the cultured.

When a culture neglects the expression of aesthetics, that culture neglects its own health and vitality. In many ways a famine in the area of aesthetics will result in the starvation of that culture. Art expresses culture; art transmits culture; art creates culture. The rhythms of each culture's dance speak to the emotional texture of that culture. The myths and folklore that affirm and support the culture's values are immersed, submerged, and then emerge from the music and poetry to the hearts of those who hear and read them.

Whether you're talking about the Grateful Dead, Megadeath, or the Dead Kennedys, those who gather in masses around their song and story identify and reflect the culture. It can be unlocked in their lyrics. The music both speaks and feels the heart of the culture. From the Beatles to the Rolling Stones to Radiohead, our generation has seen the emergence of what could perhaps best be described as secular worship. It is in the heart of all people to worship. And while for many a concert is nothing more than a concert, for more people than we would imagine, it is the closest thing to a spiritual experience that they know.

We cannot underestimate the significance of the Scripture's mandate that we be a worshipping people. It is not incidental that the book of Psalms, with 150 chapters, has been preserved by God for us in the Bible. The people of God are a people of sounds and rhythms and percussion and dance. In fact, the Psalms incite us to sing a new song to the Lord and to praise him with dancing.

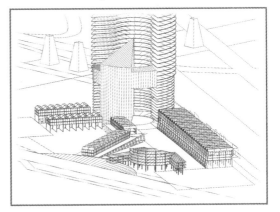

It shouldn't surprise us that in every great awakening, in every national revival, there has been the emergence of new music. From the melodies of German beer songs to contemporary rock 'n' roll, the rediscovery of music as a central form of worship is inseparable from the work of the Holy Spirit in the church of Jesus Christ.

GOD WITHOUT BEAUTY

The apostolic ethos is the world's most fertile ground for

> **To neglect the aesthetics as a part of the ethos of the church is to concede the potential of her constituency to mediocrity.**

the creation of beauty and the elevation of aesthetics. Unfortunately, the church, while reflecting the values of capitalism and pragmatism, has neglected the importance of aesthetics. We have been heavy on reason and weak on romance. I am convinced that this, at least in part, has affected the ethos of the local church. The image we've produced of a biblical congregation has been one in which the teacher taught and the congregants were students in the Bible school of God, but the arts were absent. This has been true not only in the development of unique talents related to literature, sculpture, painting, and dance, but even in the design and structure of our buildings.

The importance of maximizing and utilizing our facilities overwhelmed the value to design for beauty and worship. Why is it that we who worship the God of creativity see so little of it when we come together? If the church is to be an expression of an apostolic ethos, then the fingerprint of God's creative hand should be all around us.

Periodically at Mosaic we create a forum called Velocity. It is an explosion of creativity. It's two hours of dance, drama, poetry, short film, and comedy all wrapped up in one experience. Recently a talent scout from Warner Bros. came to Velocity. After the event he graciously thanked me for creating an environment for emerging talent to develop. In the conversation he expressed his surprise that a church would allow this kind of experience. I responded by reminding him that many of the great talents in the music world came out of the church—from Diana Ross to Whitney Houston to Six-Pence None the Richer. The church is one of the few places where children are actually encouraged to sing. The church is one of the few places where musical talent is nurtured and developed.

It shouldn't have surprised this secular observer that the greatest secular talent grew up in the church. It was exciting to tell him that for us, a local church was the greatest place to be if you want to optimize your talent. We dream of a day when local churches around the world will be known for their wellspring of creativity and the Steven Spielbergs and Quentin Tarantinos will be forced to visit churches to keep up with the newest innovations and the most creative artistry.

> **"Within all of these metaphors, the role of the pastor is inescapably one of spiritual leadership."**

A BRILLIANT USE OF THE AESTHETICS

The influence of the nurture of aesthetics goes beyond the arts. An aesthetic culture is also the environment from which the world's greatest scientists, thinkers, and leaders will emerge. Robert Root-Bernstein, a professor of physiology at Michigan State University and a McArthur Prize fellow, writes in "Hobbled Arts Limit Our Future" concerning the arts: "The arts, despite their reputation of being subjective, emotional, nonintellectual pursuits, make science and invention possible. As a scientist and inventor who has had a lifetime association with art and music, I know whereof I speak...Art done for art's sake is valuable. It is valuable as a source of skills, tools for thinking and inventing, insights, processes and even new phenomena."

Bernstein points out that, in one of their studies, Nobel Prize winners and most members of the National Academy of Sciences "were universally artistic and/or musical, most had several arts-related hobbies as adults and they utilized a wide range of arts-associated mental thinking tools such as three-dimensional mental imagery, kinesthetic feelings and pattern formation." He also notes from another study that "high aptitude in arts and music are much more predictive of career success in any field than the results of grades, IQ, achievement or any other standardized measures."

If we as a church are unmotivated by the importance of aesthetics, then perhaps we should become motivated by the importance of our children. To neglect the aesthetics as a part of the ethos of the church is to concede the potential of her constituency to mediocrity.

A WORLD OF IMAGES

It is important to note that, while past cultures have seen separation between language and art, the emerging culture sees no such separation. Word has blurred into image, and image into movement. The books of our contemporary culture are films. Newspapers and magazines are being replaced by videos and reality television.

In 1964 Marshall McLuhan published *Understanding Media: The Extensions of Man*. It was McLuhan who made famous the edict that "the medium is the message." The integration of language and aesthetics as the primary source of cultural communication in our time is now reshaping who we are and how we see reality. This is more than the message being advocated through a new medium; the medium itself has changed forever the way we communicate the message. The big implication for the church is that we will lose our ability to communicate to culture if we do not regain a commitment to the development of aesthetics.

The role of aesthetics in the work of cultural architecture is expanding, not diminishing. Any leader who engages in this endeavor must go beyond having a value for aesthetics and must understand and use the power of aesthetics for the creating and shaping of ethos.

I am amazed how many pastors of healthy and growing churches have a history in some aspect of the arts. This is a growing and necessary trend. The spiritual leaders of the future will be more artistic than academic. They will embody an integration of what has been commonly known as right brain and left brain thinking. They themselves will be cultural architects, blending engineer and artisan.

When engaging an established congregation in the hard work of transition, the church leader will perhaps at first be best described as a spiritual environmentalist. The leader's primary role will be to nurture and awaken the apostolic ethos that sleeps within the heart of the church. At other times that calling will go beyond this metaphor, and the leader will be best described as a warrior-poet leading God's people to overtake the kingdom of darkness. Such a leader will deliver people from captivity into the freedom of Christ and will expand the kingdom of God, while creating the context from which new stories and songs are written.

Within all of these metaphors, the role of the pastor is inescapably one of spiritual leadership. If leadership is creating and shaping ethos, then spiritual leadership is creating and shaping an apostolic ethos within the local church.

> **In the transmission of human culture, people always attempt to replicate, to pass on to the next generation the skills and values of the parents, but the attempt always fails because cultural transmission is geared to learning, not DNA.**
> —GREGORY BATESON, *MIND AND MATTER*

FUEL FOR THOUGHT

1. What metaphors contain the ethos of our congregation?
2. Is our church more like a crowd than a community? How can we move our group into deeper community?
3. Are we educating or catalyzing? Are we pulling or pushing? Is there movement?
4. Have a "telling": Share some of the great stories of your people.
5. What is your personal story? When have you seen God at work powerfully in your life? How often do you share your stories?
6. Are you a warrior-poet? How can you build on this role?
7. How can we begin to capture the power of beauty to reflect God's creativity?
8. What will be our game plan for nurturing the potential of children and youth?

"Therefore go and make disciples of all nations, baptizing them in the name of the Father and of the Son and of the Holy Spirit, and teaching them to obey everything I have commanded you. And surely I am with you always, to the very end of the age" (Matthew 28:19-20).

THE BAKA PYGMIES HAVE MADE ONE OF THE MOST HOSTILE ENVIronments on this planet their home. They are the people of the rain forest. Without formal education or written language, they pass on to their children skills and knowledge that would equal a Ph.D. in botany. Their children learn not only how to survive but how to thrive in this complex ecosystem. The Baka have created a culture that transmits the secrets of Baka life. And learning the mysteries of the rain forest is nothing less than life and death. We learn from the Baka that some things are best transferred through the multi-textured environment of real life. In the same way, we must pass on the deep teachings of being a disciple of Jesus Christ through the context of a biblical community engaging a broken world. It is in and through this community that God makes manifest his transforming power. Like the Baka, the church must teach her children how to thrive in a dangerous world!

The Cultural Architect

"His intent was that now, through the church, the manifold wisdom of God should be made known to the rulers and authorities in the heavenly realms, according to his eternal purpose which he accomplished in Christ Jesus our Lord" (Ephesians 3:10-11).

模
細
工

THE CULTURAL ARCHITECT

We sat in my office for an informal elders' meeting. I suppose that's an oxymoron. There were five of us, including the former pastor of twenty-five years. The church was doing well. After ten years of plateau and four years of slight decline, the church had started growing again. Our baptisms had doubled in one year, and giving was on the increase. You would think a discussion about my leadership would be a good memory.

Instead, I remember Rick, Enrique, and Robert revealing their disappointment with my leadership. Rick expected more from someone he perceived as having the gift of faith. Enrique had hoped my leadership would be stronger. Robert felt that something was restraining me from fully engaging in my role as lead pastor. I was confronted for being a non-leader! I left devastated. How could this be happening to someone who had taught a doctoral class on leadership?

Seeking comfort, I later told Kim what had happened. We were driving down Beverly Boulevard on a Saturday morning, and all I wanted was for her to lie to me. But she didn't. She did, however, take the opportunity to show her disappointment in me. Apparently, I wasn't the leader that she thought she married. I was so angry that I stopped the car in the middle of the road. I sat there defending myself, all the while knowing the painful truth: I was afraid. I was hesitant. I was apprehensive and uncertain. It wasn't that I didn't know what to do; it was that I understood the consequences. Leadership comes with a price. I thought that I could hide behind a measure of success and never be found out. I was not leading; I was tinkering.

Did I already mention that I followed a twenty-five-year pastorate? The former pastor had done a tremendous job leading a dying church into a new future. He had been the primary shaper of the congregational culture since he was twenty-four years old (by this time he was nearly fifty). In many ways the pastor and the church had grown up together. His personality and the ethos of the church were inseparable.

> **When you alter the methods of a church, you are, in effect, trampling memories.**

There's a reason pastors who follow long-tenured pastors often unintentionally become interims. Bringing about change isn't simply programmatic—sometimes it's personal. When you alter the methods of a church, you are, in effect, trampling memories. Often, you only discover what is sacred once you have moved it.

We tried a transition period in which both of us remained close to the center. But transitioning the congregation was much easier than transitioning us. It could only be described as performing heart surgery on a fully conscious patient. We treated the essence of leadership too lightly. Leadership is not about title; we transitioned that. It is not about position; we transitioned that. It is not about roles; we transitioned that. It is about influence. It is deeply personal. It comes from the soul and connects and shapes the whole of a community. Leadership is a spiritual art form. There is perhaps no better description of a leader than one who creates and shapes culture.

I am so thankful that our elders conducted that leadership intervention. I am grateful that they forced me to engage the real dimension of leadership. I had to face the truth: Churches become like their pastors. If you don't like what you see in your congregation, then you must be the first to change!

REVOLUTIONIZING ORGANIZATIONAL LEADERSHIP

"God is not a God of chaos, but a God of order" has been one of the theological mantras of the modern church. Out of this has come a particular view of leadership: Leaders organize! Yet organizational leadership is different than directional leadership. It is important to acknowledge that there are many different forms of leadership. The term *leadership* can mean different things in different organizations and occupations.

Often, what is described as church leadership is organizational leadership. Value is found in someone who can structure and manage a complex environment, rather than in someone who can create one that needs to be harnessed. The real contribution of the organizational leader is bringing stability and continuity. Mid-size congregations often evaluate spiritual leadership through this template. Success is measured by predictability and order. The danger is going beyond an order of worship to a worship of order!

In many ways the role of a pastor has become that of a spiritual manager. There is a critical distinction between managers who maintain organizations and leaders who create community by catalyzing movement. The former leader creates a corporation of people; the latter, a people with a cause.

Genuine leaders personify the values and vision of the people they lead. They do not simply espouse the vision of the movement; they embody it. What they focus on, whom they empower, and what is rewarded are central to the development of a cultural movement. Sometimes we look to great secular corporations that are led by extraordinary leaders for help. But all too often we ignore the components that make them worthy of emulation. We dissect their skills, disciplines, competencies, and habits in the hope that we can pick up that critical piece in the leadership puzzle. Yet for many of us, especially in vocational ministry, the real essence of leadership is so obvious that it is easily missed. True leadership is spiritual!

SECULAR LEADERSHIP IS SPIRITUAL

Phil Jackson wrote a book called *Sacred Hoops: Spiritual Lessons of a Hardwood Warrior*, describing his experience as coach for Michael Jordan and the Chicago Bulls. Howard Schultz chronicled his Starbucks experience in *Pour Your Heart Into It: How Starbucks Built a Company One Cup at a Time*. Steven Jobs described his creation of Apple as a mission from God, calling his sales force evangelists! Everything that makes leaders unique is spiritual. Many things that make them effective are learned and concrete, but the essence of their true leadership remains intangible. There are others who do the

> **" True leaders are able to influence not only individuals, but also environments. "**

same things they do, yet these unique leaders still rise above the rest. Whether it's in the corporate world, in sports, in politics, or in religion, the ability to create a culture of success is described by mystical language.

We describe it as charisma when referring to the individual and chemistry when speaking of the team. We don't always know what it is, and it clearly comes in many forms and styles; yet we know without question when someone doesn't have it. Soft-spoken or outgoing, it doesn't seem to matter. True leaders are able to influence not only individuals, but also environments. They transform corporate values and their environment on a cultural level.

Successful leaders can rally individuals around shared beliefs and a common vision. As these people work toward the good of the whole, they experience personal fulfillment and intense satisfaction. In fact, if you listened to them passionately describing their experiences within these organizations, you would get the impression that their work itself is a religious experience. Great organizations have an ethos of greatness. It's not just that they do great work, but they literally work out of greatness. Winning teams make average players better and good players excellent. Great coaches create and shape ethos. Great CEO's create and shape ethos. Great presidents create and shape ethos. Each is a spiritual leader.

True leadership affects the soul of the organization and the spirit of the people. The irony is that, while secular leadership has become blatantly spiritual, Christian leadership has become blatantly (and blandly) secular. We need to recapture the invisible aspects of leadership. We must focus our attention on the creating and shaping of ethos and then on the structures that best nurture and harness its potential. In the end leadership is nothing less than spiritual. And spiritual leaders are essentially cultural architects.

THE SCHOOL OF CULTURAL ARCHITECTURE

Architect (n.) A person who creates, founds, or originates: inventor, author, builder, creator, designer, founder, framer, mastermind, maker, originator, planner, prime mover, progenitor, and artificer.

While drifting on a pontoon boat on Big Bear Lake, our leadership team came up with a definition of a cultural architect. Spiritual leadership is both art and science, so the pastor must be both artist and engineer. Frank Lloyd Wright's assertion that form and function are one is nowhere more apparent than in the church. All the material from which God builds his church exists and emerges from the hearts of God's people. The church is a construct of human talents, gifts, intelligence, passions, skills, disciplines, experiences, and commitments energized by the Holy Spirit.

The function of the church is literally to be the Body of Christ in the world, and such is her form. Jesus pours himself into the church as both Spirit and fire, so we must be both wind and light. He comes to us as both living water and as rock eternal; so we must be both liquid and solid. If true leadership is essentially spiritual, then serving as a pastor is the ultimate leadership challenge—leading as a servant of God. The context is invisible, mystical, of the spirit—both the Holy and the human. The product is real, tangible, transforming—both personal and cultural.

THE DESIGN ENGINEER

Engineer (n.) One who skillfully or shrewdly manages an enterprise. 2. To plan, construct, or manage and put through by skillful acts. Engineering. 1. The application of scientific and mathematical principles to practical ends such as the design, manufacture, and operation of efficient and economical structures, processes, and systems. 2. Skillful maneuvering or direction.

> **In many ways, ethos comes from the leader as an artist and then is magnified or optimized through the leader as engineer.**

As engineers, spiritual leaders design structures that shape culture. If part of shaping culture is the generation of momentum—calling people to a common vision and building around common values—then one of the significant skills of a leader is to focus that momentum. A person may be naturally catalytic but lack the skills to maximize what they've catalyzed. This is where the leader as engineer is so critical. The ability to design efficient and economical structures, processes, and systems is critical to maximizing the power of momentum.

This is the most concrete area of leadership. While the artist is in many ways more spiritual, the engineer is more material. The pastor must stand in both those worlds. He must be a genuine spiritual leader and at the same time have the concrete skills of leadership.

When we go to church growth conferences and endeavor to adapt other processes or strategies to our own, we are most often learning the engineering part of leadership. This is critical if you already have momentum but can be extremely confusing if you are hoping that this aspect of leadership will generate momentum. In many ways, ethos comes from the leader as an artist and then is magnified or optimized through the leader as engineer.

At Mosaic the engineering part is a real challenge. We only own three quarters of an acre, have less than a hundred parking spaces, and serve approximately 1,500 people each week. That requires four services in three different locations on Sunday. A part of the challenge in the urban world, where property is a million dollars an acre, is creative engineering. This really stood out to me the other day when we made a minor change of moving our first service from 9:00 to 9:30. Our 9:00 service could never get enough momentum to fill up the building even halfway; but after moving it to 9:30, it suddenly became our largest service. We just didn't imagine a half-hour shift could make such a dramatic difference.

The more complex a situation becomes, the more a nuanced change can have a dramatic impact. One of the most ironic problems we have had to deal with is having our talented dance team perform in all of our services. In our building in east L.A., we have a giant stage area, which simplifies holding a performance. But for our evening service at a nightclub we struggled to organize the space in a way that would allow the dancers to perform. The stage area was just too small, and the problem seemed insurmountable.

We almost gave up and decided to cancel that part of the service at the nightclub. Amazingly, we had somehow forgotten that we had a dance floor all along; we had just filled it with chairs for our worship space! It finally occurred to us to simply move all of the chairs and let the team dance on the dance floor itself. Now whenever we have a dance performance, we begin worship with everyone standing around the edges of the floor. After experiencing the performance, everyone grabs a chair for the teaching time. Sometimes problems stop us simply because we cannot see solutions that are right in front of us. A crucial element of leadership is always having one more solution than you have problems.

> **In some regards the pastor is nothing more or less than the brush through which God paints a masterpiece.**

THE SPIRITUAL ARTISAN

Artist (n.) 1. One, such as a painter or sculptor, who is able by virtue of imagination and talent to create works of aesthetic value, especially in the fine arts. 2. A person whose work shows exceptional creative ability or skill.

The spiritual leader as artist carefully paints a picture of an ideal world—the leader's concept of what the emerging culture should look like. Such leaders use many tools to create this image. They craft images through words. They provoke the imagination through compelling vision. They inspire hearts to believe that, together, a new world can be created.

The pastor's canvas is the soul. Transformed lives make the church a gallery for the searching spiritual connoisseur. The mystery of God working through one person to affect the transformation of another is miracle enough. Yet the mystery of God working through a spiritual artisan to transform a community is greater still. In some regards the pastor is nothing more or less than the brush through which God paints a masterpiece. It is this role of the leader—the spiritual artisan—that is most neglected in studies and treatments of leadership.

The metaphor of a leader as a cultural architect encompasses this dynamic, not on a parallel track in the leadership process but as an integrated component. The cultural architect effects cultural transformation from the wisdom of both disciplines. His work is sacred as he labors to build the house of God, not with brick and cement but through each life that is joined with the community by the transforming power of God's Spirit.

Leading a church must go beyond the utilitarian concerns of numbers and dollars. It is a work of art. The church was intended to reflect the beauty of God's character. Somehow through broken and fragmented people, God creates a divine mosaic. The pastor is both prophet and poet, speaking the living words of God and writing epistles that breathe and feel. The Scriptures tell us that we are God's workmanship, his *poemas*. With every life that is transformed in Christ, a new *poem* is written by God and for God. Our personal stories of faith are nothing more than poetry readings!

DESIGN MATTERS

You feel it every time you enter a building: Shape matters. Buildings with high ceilings create a sense of mystery and awe. The great cathedrals powerfully accomplish this effect. A living room furbished with a fireplace, warm carpet, and rugs on the floor creates a feeling of safety and tranquility. Fast-food restaurants understand design—which is why every single sign is orange! Even colors affect us and create certain responses. For too long the church has underestimated the power of space, shape, and design. And connected to that, the church has underestimated the power of human organization and socialization.

Our building was designed to be all sanctuary and essentially no lobby. We could talk about community all day long, but you didn't feel it when you walked in. There was no place for people to gather, to talk, or to enjoy one another. We were communicating that the most important thing happening in the church came from the podium. After the pastor finished speaking, people had no choice but to exit the building and go home. So we redesigned our space. We brought sofas, love seats, throw rugs, coffee tables, and even a coffee bar inside the sanctuary. We organized the space for community, for conversation. We wanted it to feel more like a person's living room than a dentist's office; and the new setting has dramatically affected the way people feel about Mosaic.

> It's hard to believe that a movement born of visionaries and dreamers would become dominantly known for its traditions and rituals.

In our newest meeting place, which we have named "The Loft," we have chosen to fill our limited space with beanbag chairs and futons. The immediate response we received was how warm and intimate the space felt. Every decision that affects how people interact in large groups has a dramatic impact on the ethos of the community.

I once worked for a man who *said* his door was always open, but it never *was*. Some things communicate more powerfully than words. The leader is a cultural architect, and design matters.

A MOVEMENT OF VISIONARIES AND DREAMERS

In Acts 2:17-18 we read: "In the last days, God says, I will pour out my Spirit on all people. Your sons and daughters will prophesy, your young men will see visions, your old men will dream dreams. Even on my servants, both men and women, I will pour out my Spirit in those days, and they will prophesy."

If you want a certain kind of movement, you enlist a certain kind of person. Looking at the contemporary church, you would almost have to conclude that its founders were administrators and managers or at best theologians and teachers. Yet we find that God chooses visionaries and dreamers. In fact, God promised that when he poured out his Spirit on his people, they would *become* visionaries and dreamers. They would proclaim not only what God was doing, but also what he intended to do in human history.

What would our churches be like if God made manifest the descriptions in this passage? What would be required of spiritual leadership if we understood ourselves to be visionaries and dreamers? This prophesy from Joel was repeated by Peter to young men who were born under the weight of captivity, young men who had never known freedom, young men who knew only Roman oppression. Yet God was going to make them visionaries—suggesting a freedom they had never tasted or known. At the same time God would make dreamers of old men—old men who had lived their lives waiting for the Messiah, old men who believed God would deliver them, old men who would soon breathe their last breaths under the bondage of Rome. This was God's promise—evidence of the outpouring of the Holy Spirit on the people of God. And the new Christians experienced it—sons and daughters, men and women, all who were touched by the Spirit of God.

It's hard to believe that a movement born of visionaries and dreamers would become dominantly known for its traditions and rituals. If you were to look at your own congregation and evaluate honestly what's valued and appreciated, could you say that people are more encouraged to create than to conform? The church should be a place where dreamers are nurtured and visions are realized. The apostolic ethos is a thing of wonder and childlike curiosity, a place where ideas are valued and where a spirit-inspired imagination runs free. God has a lot on his mind, and it is through the church that he makes it happen.

A wonderful thing about being around new believers is that they haven't discovered the limitations the church has embraced. Their ability to believe in God is so pure that it sometimes terrifies older Christians. Do you remember when you believed God could do anything? that God actually heard your prayers with an intention to answer them? Do you remember when you believed that Elijah was an ordinary person just like you and that if you prayed like he did, God would answer your prayers, too?

The first-century church was founded on the adventurous journeys of men like Paul and Barnabus. It was never intended to be a place of safety from the rapidly changing world. The church should be the greatest revolution ever initiated on this planet. She moves from generation to generation through the dreamers and visionaries who believe that nothing is impossible with God. And like prophets, they call God's people to live their lives as if God is truly God.

ETHOLOGICALLY SOUND LEADERSHIP

It's painful but important to realize that our communities reflect our leadership. I'm troubled when pastors tell me what they don't like about their congregations. I could understand this if they had only been there for two weeks or maybe even two years. But I hear this from pastors who have been at their churches more than five years. They're frustrated because people don't "do evangelism" or people are too afraid of risk or a variety of other issues. One of the most difficult things for a leader to do is help a pastor look in the mirror.

If you've been leading your congregation for more than five years, your congregation likely reflects who you are. If you hold the position of leader, and the ethos does not reflect your core values, then you're not the leader—someone else is. If you are genuinely the leader, and you do not like the values of your congregation, the first place you need to bring change into is your own life.

Ethos emerges from the lives of individuals, and whether you realize it or not, you've been shaping the ethos of your congregation from the first moment you gave a message or made a decision. We're going to look at six different areas in which you as a leader have a direct impact in the ethos of your congregation.

CHARACTER

Character (n). 1. The combination of qualities or features that distinguishes one person, group, or thing from another. 2. A distinguishing feature or attribute, as of an individual, a group, or a category. 3. Genetics. A structure, function, or attribute determined by a gene or group of genes. 4. Moral or ethical strength. 5. A description of a person's attributes, traits, or abilities. 6. Public estimation of someone; reputation.

The people you serve will be able to summarize who you are in one core idea or one central characteristic. You need to listen carefully to how they describe you. They may describe you as kind and caring, visionary and courageous, empowering, or something else. Hopefully you will appreciate the description you hear.

When we consider character, we usually think of attributes such as integrity, humility, and trustworthiness. All of these are obviously critical to spiritual leadership. But the kind of character I'm speaking of is more than that. Every leader makes a distinguishing mark, which is the best way to define what we call a character. A character is a distinguishing and defining mark or imprint that communicates something to those who see.

Later in this book, we'll look more extensively at the full implications of character in leadership.

STORIES

All leaders make a distinguishing mark on a culture. One of the ways that happens is through story. People listen to your stories. If your stories are never personal, it will be very difficult for people to embrace a personal faith. People want to know what you're committed to. They want to know how you experience God. They want to know what you know about God, not simply what you've learned. Whatever topic you preach on, the story you choose to tell will reveal your heart.

One thing I've noticed over the years is that even when I teach about tithing, I tell a story about evangelism. I love telling stories about people I meet and the conversations we have about God. It doesn't matter to me what the topic is. These stories are always relevant and fit in with the subject. Your stories of faith, your stories of risk, your stories of failure—all these stories shape the ethos of the congregation. Borrowed stories just don't work as well. Stories communicate what really is important and what kind of experiences others in the community should aspire to have.

> **Stories communicate what really is important and what kind of experiences others in the community should aspire to have.**

EXPERIENCES

When I was in seminary, I was encouraged to hold back on sharing my personal experiences. It was considered more appropriate to tell historical stories, stories of ancient Christian leaders, and generic illustrations that didn't involve my life. It was inappropriate to bring your personal life into the message. The focus was on exegesis and application. I am so thankful I never took this advice. It would have catapulted me into a place of irrelevance within the vast emerging culture.

Leaders shape ethos by sharing their experiences. People want to know about your experiences—even the bad ones. They want to know when you've failed; they want to know when you've been disappointed; they want to know what you've struggled through; they want to learn from your life. Genuine ethos cannot be developed without genuine communication.

REWARD

Another way leaders shape ethos is by what they reward. People long to be blessed. I know I always have. As a child, I would always want to please my mom. I wanted to hear her say not only that I did a good job but that I was a great person. As a parent, I know this to be absolutely true. Kids love the affirmation of their parents and will go to extraordinary extremes to gain it. This is something we never grow out of. We spend our lives looking for blessing.

Bob Buford, the chairman of the board of Leadership Network once asked me what I thought was the most important thing Leadership Network could do for pastors, and I said, "Give them permission." Pastors are looking for blessing from somewhere, but they don't know where to get it. In some sense, all of us need permission givers. It's the adult version of being blessed. It's someone saying to us that what we're doing is important and right. Followers of Jesus Christ look to those in spiritual leadership to give their blessing, and people are incredibly astute to what pastors actually do bless.

Once when I was a young pastor, I found myself creating an environment in which only those who did the wrong things were receiving my affirmation. They were the people I always spent time with. The more you sinned, the more you disobeyed God, the more of my time I would give you. If you did what you were supposed to, you received very little of my time. I was essentially rewarding disobedience and dysfunction rather than affirming obedience and servanthood. I realized that who I gave my time to demonstrated what was important.

I also began to realize that whenever I affirmed someone through a story, it helped shape the culture. If I told stories of the secret servanthood of members in the body, it inspired everyone else to serve. When I celebrated sacrificial giving by individuals, it inspired others to give sacrificially. The power of blessing that the Bible talks about is something very real and very important. A part of spiritual leadership is rewarding those things that Christ would reward, blessing those who are reflecting Christ, and inspiring everyone to follow that example.

BATTLES

Another significant aspect of establishing an ethos is your choice of battles. Both the battles you choose to fight and the battles you ignore are significant in shaping an ethos. Some hills are just not worth dying on. But other hills are key to the future ethos. These strategic battles are critical to leadership.

> **People know what you care about by what you're willing to die for.**

I hate conflict. If I had my choice, I would run from every battle. But I just can't live with being a coward. In my first three years at The Church on Brady, I had endless opportunities to choose strategic battlegrounds. Sometimes I relinquished the fight even though I thought the issue was important because I felt that the price to pay was too high for the potential benefit. But other times, issues were so critical that conflict was unavoidable. This is where wisdom comes in as yet another important attribute of leadership.

A friend of mine from the Washington, D.C. area told me about a pastor who had been confronted by a deacon. The deacon made it clear that this particular church did not have a place for Catholics or gays. It was essential that the pastor make this a defining point for the future of the church. If he didn't, that deacon would later have chosen a different place to engage in battle. The pastor would eventually have ended up getting fired over the style of music or some insignificant change, when the central issue had to do with condition of the heart.

Battles allow you to establish a value system. People know what you care about by what you're willing to die for. If you're not willing to lose your job over a key issue, then your core value is your security. If you're not willing to lose your job, you're not a leader; you're a hireling. Values are not established through verbal repetition. They are established by building your life around them.

The first public battle I had at The Church on Brady was over the establishing of a Saturday night service. We wanted to start a service that would reach a younger crowd. We had virtually no members in their twenties and felt this would help us engage a more postmodern culture. To my surprise, a huge controversy arose over the theological appropriateness of meeting on Saturday. I was told that I was defiling the Sabbath by holding a service on Saturday night. The conflict went as far as having to hold a leadership meeting in my home. It seemed strange having to explain that the Sabbath actually is Saturday and that, if anything, we were honoring the Sabbath. But that, of course, was not the point. We had to establish that the heart of God would want us to create opportunities any day of the week for seekers to discover Jesus Christ.

Another strange battle was over the welcome time in our service. Like many traditional Baptist churches, every week we would have a welcome in the middle of the service where, ideally, members would greet the guests. Upon observation, I realized that the guests were simply obstacles between good friends who were eager to greet each other. It was quite a sight to see the guests sitting awkwardly, excusing themselves, and making room for members enjoying the welcome. So I stopped doing the welcome and created a huge controversy. I was even told that I was destroying the participatory culture of the church. This battle provided a great opportunity to talk about how our guests were experiencing our services and our community. When our leaders realized that they were in fact greeting one another and ignoring those who were new, it created a sensitivity toward the stranger and outsider.

In the first three years at this church, I had conversations I would have never believed had I not been there. One of our leaders came with his wife to meet with another elder and me. Their complaint was that the church had become too evangelistic! I was shocked that anyone would be that honest. They valued the deep biblical teaching that our church provided and felt that the new growth would be detrimental to our strong sense of community. I remember responding that, despite the uncertainty of our church's future, one thing was for certain: If they didn't like how evangelistic we were now, they would not enjoy this place at all next year. They chose to attend somewhere else.

Everything worthwhile has a cost, and the ethos of a community is worth fighting for. Establishing a value system that honors God and reflects his heart is the most important battle in spiritual leadership. All spiritual leaders must be warrior-poets who lead both through courage and suffering.

> **A genuine movement is a leadership culture.**

ADVANCEMENT

One last significant shaper of ethos is the identification and selection of new leadership. I believe that the résumé-style selection of leadership has detrimentally affected the development of an apostolic ethos in the church. The church overwhelmingly hires from the outside. Even mega-churches tend to hire from the outside. Every church seems to have a leadership crisis, whether there are two hundred people or twenty thousand. It seems abysmal that in a church of ten thousand, you wouldn't be overwhelmed with emerging leadership, and yet these churches tend to hire proven leaders from other congregations. We seem to be better at growing congregations than at developing leaders.

The development of indigenous leadership is critical to creating and shaping ethos. It is also essential in generating first-century church momentum. One reason for this is that when you identify leaders from within, everyone realizes that he or she could be the next leader identified. It gives everyone a sense of inspiration and hope that he or she might be selected and invested in. If you're always hiring from the outside, it becomes a mystery how one ever grows to that level of leadership. The obvious conclusion for someone interested in leadership would be that he or she has to leave the church to find a place where that level of leadership could be obtained.

In an organization, leaders must be brought from the outside. In a movement, leaders emerge from within. A genuine movement is a leadership culture. It values the identification, development, and empowering of new leaders. A central component of a movement's success is not the selection of accredited leaders but of proven leadership. Leadership is not about how much education a person has attained but how much they have actually accomplished in a ministry context. In many congregations the only role that members can aspire to is to be a good follower. In the first-century church, there were no other churches to take leaders from. Everybody had to be homegrown.

> **❝The quality of a leader is reflected in the standards they set for themselves.❞** —RAY KROC, FOUNDER OF MCDONALD'S

FUEL FOR THOUGHT

1. Are we managing (organizing) or catalyzing? Explain.
2. Do our structures facilitate healthy processes, or are they stuck in bureaucratic paralysis?
3. Is your leadership more spiritual or secular? Are you leading from biblical or business principles?
4. Are you more like an architect, designer, or artist? How can you grow in all three?
5. In what ways is the ethos of our congregation reflective of our hearts as leaders?
6. What are the ministry non-negotiables of our congregation?
7. Who are the emerging leaders in our community, and what do we need to do to prepare them for spiritual leadership?

CHAPTER SEVEN

SPIRIT DESIGN THEORY

Why is it that you can walk into a room and, without explanation, feel your spirits lift or feel cold and isolated? Design matters, and yet however complicated or extraordinary any structure is, no matter how much the layouts are a work of genius, they all come down to the same three things: circles, triangles, and squares. The worst and best designs are made up of the same three components. We should just stand back in awe of the fact that extraordinary works of art had the same starting point as the most mundane and forgettable structures.

Innovation, beauty, and creativity are all about what is done with lines, curves, and angles. One person could look at circles, triangles, and squares and feel as if the limitations were overwhelming. After all, how much can you do with nothing more than these three? Yet another person sees endless possibilities in the configuration and reconfiguration of lines, curves, and angles. This is also true for the cultural architect.

The pastor also has three textures from which to shape an apostolic ethos. They can be seen as nothing more than circles, triangles, and squares or as the source from which extraordinary creativity, beauty, and innovation can emerge. All a painter has to work with is blue, yellow, and red. Everything else, all the beauty found and formed, is the result of imagination and skill. For the spiritual leader, the three components are faith, hope, and love. When we understand that the primary role of a leader is to create ethos, then it begins to make sense that the primary colors of the leader as artist are spiritual.

In 1 Corinthians 13:13 Paul tells us, "And now these three remain: faith, hope, and love. But the greatest of these is love." So often we hear this statement in the context of poetic readings or in weddings and other ceremonial activities. The beauty of this statement is easily felt, yet most often we overlook its importance.

Only in recent years has the church reawakened to the importance of spiritual gifts. One of the great renewals in the last forty years has been the moving away from programs and methods to an emphasis on spiritual gifts. And every one of us who has sought to discover and use our spiritual gifts has begun to experience a more vibrant and fulfilling life. Certainly a program-based church and a gift-based church are dramatically different, yet Paul says some things are far more important than spiritual gifts, and those are faith, hope, and love.

If spiritual gifts are so critical and essential to a healthy church life and a powerful ministry, then how much more powerful would a church be in which faith, hope, and love prevailed? The question then arises: How do we access and engage the power of faith, hope, and love?

THE FUEL OF A MOVEMENT

In 1 Thessalonians 1:4-10, Paul describes the Thessalonian church in this way: "For we know, brothers loved by God, that he has chosen you, because our gospel came to you not simply with words, but also with power, with the Holy Spirit and with deep conviction. You know how we lived among you for your sake. You became imitators of us and of the Lord; in spite of severe suffering, you welcomed the message with the joy given by the Holy Spirit. And so you became a model to all the believers in Macedonia and Achaia. The Lord's message rang out from you not only in Macedonia and Achaia—your faith in God has become known everywhere. Therefore we do not need to say anything about it, for they themselves report what kind of reception you gave us. They tell how you turned to God from idols to serve the living and true God, and to wait for his Son from heaven, whom he raised from the dead—Jesus, who rescues us from the coming wrath."

The Thessalonian church had become a model to all the believers in the region. In many ways it was the first church-growth model to be commended. The Thessalonians' faith in God had become known everywhere, and their growth and impact on the city was not built on letters of transfer but on radical conversions. Paul describes the impact of the church when he says, "They tell how you turned to God from idols to serve the living and true God."

How many of us long for our own congregations to be described in this way? to be described as a model church for the entire region? a church whose faith in God is known everywhere? a church whose constituency is a result of multitudes turning from idols to the true and living God?

If this church existed today, it would be written up in every Christian periodical and shown on every Christian network, and it would have monthly conferences on church growth and ministry. Don't you wish Paul had expanded on the methodologies of the Thessalonian church? Wouldn't it have been great if 2 Thessalonians were a manual that told us how to reproduce that particular model? Paul doesn't tell us anything about their structure, their methods, their systems, or their programs, but he tells us a great deal about the essence of this church.

In 1 Thessalonians 1:2-3, Paul says, "We always thank God for all of you, mentioning you in our prayers. We continually remember before our God and Father your work produced by faith, your labor prompted by love, and your endurance inspired by hope in your Lord Jesus Christ." Here Paul gives us an inside look into the hearts of the Thessalonian Christians. They were a church that was ignited and fueled by faith, love, and hope. They would be best described as having a work produced by faith, a labor prompted by love, and a perseverance inspired by hope in Jesus Christ.

Could it be that the most powerful ingredients for awakening an apostolic ethos are right before us? Could it be that while we've been searching for innovations and new strategies to effectively engage this radically changing world, the secret to seeing first-century results lies in the first century-church?

At Mosaic we have become convinced that the key to awakening an apostolic ethos lies within the power of these three spiritual essences. We're so sure of this that we have established our congregational mission around them: to live by faith, to be known by love, and to be a voice of hope. How does the pastor, as cultural architect, work with these three components to create and shape an apostolic ethos?

To Live by Faith

A CERTAINTY OF UNCERTAINTY

Larry Clement had confronted me. I could see in his eyes that he desperately wanted to follow my leadership but was unsure if the direction we were heading was right. He looked at me, and with all sincerity requested one thing: "Just tell me that God is in it, and I'll follow you anywhere." We began to unwrap his request. What he wanted me to tell him was that God had spoken verbatim to me, word-for-word, and instructed me in this particular direction. He wanted me to step into that prophetic role and say, "Thus says the Lord."

I looked at Larry, and I told him that some things I knew for certain and some things I certainly did not know. I knew what God was doing in human history; I knew that what we were doing was on the heart of God; I knew without question that there are things God calls us to that we don't need to ask him about again. But did I know that this particular strategy would work for certain? Did I know this particular approach was guaranteed to succeed? No, I didn't.

What Larry wanted from me was something God doesn't often give us. I took Larry to one of the more unusual passages in the Scriptures. In 1 Samuel 14 Israel was at war with the Philistines. Saul and his army of six hundred men were resting under a pomegranate tree. There were only two swords among all the warriors, and only Saul and Jonathan had them. So on the day of the battle, not a soldier with Saul and Jonathan had a single sword or spear in his hands. The situation was desperate. It was not unreasonable for Saul to choose not to engage the Philistines in battle. But in the middle of the night, Jonathan awakened his armor-bearer and said to him, "Come, let us go over to the Philistine outpost on the other side." But he did not tell his father.

They quietly slipped out of the camp. They had to cross a treacherous pass to reach the Philistine outpost. Jonathan looked to his armor-bearer and said, "Come, let's go over to the outpost of those uncircumcised fellows. Perhaps the Lord will act in our behalf. Nothing can hinder the Lord from saving, whether by many or by few" (1 Samuel 14:6b). His armor-bearer responded, "Do all that you have in mind. Go ahead; I am with you heart and soul" (1 Samuel 14:7).

> Could it be that while we've been searching for innovations and new strategies to effectively engage this radically changing world, the secret to seeing first-century results lies in the first-century church?

Most often we read the Bible for comfort, assurance, and certainty, but not for courage—at least not in the truest sense. We're willing to engage in battle if we believe that God has promised ultimate victory. We have somehow convinced ourselves that God has signed a contract with us, promising that we will never fail. Implied in that is that we will never suffer, go through disappointment, or even be inconvenienced in the journey. What Jonathan knew without any doubt was that nothing could stop God from saving, whether by many or by few. But he was honest when he looked at his young armor-bearer and said, "Perhaps the Lord will act in our behalf."

What he was saying is, "I know what God is doing. He is delivering the Philistines to the hands of Israel. It's clear what's on God's heart. He has called us to engage in a battle. I have no doubt that God is powerful enough to give us the victory. So let's act in line with the heart of God to usher in the will of God, and maybe God will help us." Emphasis on "maybe," "perhaps," and "I hope."

After addressing the passage, I looked at Larry and told him I had no doubt that God was calling us to impact the city. It was absolutely clear that Jesus had come so he could save the lost. There's no ambiguity that God is calling on our church to join him in declaring the Gospel to the nations. The decisions that were before us would move us in the direction that God's spirit is moving. So what I knew was that God would be pleased with our action, and I thought maybe he might even help us see the victory.

OBEY AWAY!

What does it really mean to live by faith? The response of faith is nothing more than obedience. Faith begins with God speaking and materializes when we respond. Somehow we've come to believe that faith *removes* ambiguity rather than calls us to *live in* it. As mentioned earlier, we have primarily related to "faith" as a noun rather than a verb. The church tends to live by "the faith" more than it lives by faith. The goal has become to make sure beliefs are doctrinally sound and people have a growing knowledge of the Bible, rather than to live in a dynamic, fluid relationship with God through which we learn to hear the voice of God and move in response to him.

The starting point of living by faith is recognizing that God has revealed so much of his will that we have plenty to live by without ever hearing another word. Some things you simply do not need to pray about. When God has spoken and commanded his people, praying sometimes becomes a way of resisting God's will rather than a way of responding to it.

A church begins to live by faith when its people move the things God has clearly said into the nonoptional category. A church doesn't need to pray about whether it should pray. It doesn't need to pray about whether it should serve. It doesn't need to pray about whether it should evangelize. The list goes on and on. The will of God isn't as obscure as we'd like to make it. Many times what we want from God is not a mandate that requires our faith, but a guarantee that in reality, faith was never needed.

Larry inspired me to go before all of our leaders and come clean, to clearly communicate that the journey I was inviting them to enter had no guarantee of success. I had to tell them that we might even, in the midst of our efforts, find ourselves failing; that there is no promise in the Bible that any one local church will accomplish everything that God has on his heart; and that God's greatest purpose for us might be that we fail falling forward. But could we consider that even our death would be an act of faith if the direction of our bodies pointed the way to God's future?

FAILING TO SUCCEED

Faith has been corrupted by our convenience mentality. We somehow believe that God is more interested in our comfort and our prosperity than his purpose in human history.

I learned the hard way that my own failure is often the context for God's miracle. I was pastoring a small congregation in south Dallas back in 1985. Just a handful of us had begun meeting in a duplex. It took a little while, but after a year or so we moved into a house. We moved from being a half of a house church to a real house church! God blessed our work, and we saw individuals and families come to faith in Jesus Christ. Although we were still small, we felt we were living in New Testament times.

One day we saw an acre of land for sale on Ervay Street. Though our congregation was still less than fifty adults, many of whom were on welfare, we began to talk and pray about purchasing that property. It seemed strange that an acre of land, so close to downtown Dallas, had remained undeveloped while everything around it was built up. I never stopped to reflect on why this property hadn't been developed.

I went to the local Association of Churches and asked the director of missions if they would consider financially undergirding our efforts. Frankly, at first there was little response. South Dallas was not a target community for new growth. It was poor; it was dangerous; it was a transitional community. It was a product of white flight. In my appeal to the director, I even mentioned that it was unlikely we would succeed, and if that were the case, the property would be available for resale. In my mind that eliminated some of the risk on their end.

We ended up buying the land, but not with our money. A gracious church in north Dallas got involved, which allowed the association to partner with us and purchase the property. They put all the money up front. After the purchase, the land remained dormant while we continued to build a stronger base in our congregation. We looked forward to the day we could actually begin to build a facility where we could accommodate a seven-day-a-week ministry to the community. And then we were ready.

We began the process of obtaining the building permits, but a strange thing happened on the way to fulfilling our dream. The city of Dallas had tagged the property "unbuildable." It had been a landfill. It was worthless. We had bought an acre of garbage. Several core samples were taken. From what I understood, they went at least twenty-five feet deep and found nothing but trash. It finally made sense. This was the reason the acre of land had remained undeveloped. You couldn't build on it.

> There is no proper way to stand before the people God has called you to lead and tell them you failed.

Words cannot express the despair that overwhelmed me. I had led our congregation to buy an acre of garbage. I didn't really understand how denominational organizations worked, so I figured I would be kicked out of the Southern Baptist convention. I was ashamed and humiliated and wondered why God would let this happen. My reputation was ruined along with my own sense of self-respect.

Without any doubt, my motivation had been to fulfill God's purpose in this community. My heart was to live out the heart of God. I had been convinced that this property would provide the ministry Jesus longed to do in this needful community.

In moments like these, trying to explain why God would let something like this happen is not an easy thing to do. There is no proper way to stand before the people God has called you to lead and tell them you failed. All I could do was ask our congregation to pray with me to believe that God was with us and that he would use even the worst of human mistakes to perform the greatest of miracles.

FAITH CAN BE A BUNCH OF GARBAGE

So for months and months and months we prayed, and the longer we prayed, the more foolish our request seemed. We began asking God to turn the landfill into a land filled with his people, that he would perform a miracle to make it easier to endure this season. I created personal slogans, "Our trash is God's treasure," "Our garbage to God's glory." There was a church down the highway that was called The Church on the Rock, so I supposed we would be The Church on the Dump. This helped a little, but in the end the situation remained the same.

A pastor, his wife, and some of his youth visited us from out of town to help on a mission project. We were sitting around a little table in the house where Cornerstone met. It didn't take long before the question I dreaded to hear was raised again. What are you going to do with the landfill? We were infamous. Far and wide people knew of our reputation. It wasn't the same as the Thessalonians', but it seemed as extensive.

Also sitting with us was a woman named Delores Rube from Cornerstone. She had served the community all of her adult life. Before I could answer, before I could explain one more time, Delores said something that changed everything for me. She looked at him and said, "It is taken care of. We've prayed and asked God to turn it into soil."

There was a rush inside of me. I had what I can only describe as God goose bumps. It seemed as if God was confirming her words and telling me that he wasn't finished yet. I went back to the association and asked them to take another core sample. Their response was no less than hostile. I understood why, but for whatever reason, they decided to do what I asked. This time, they found soil.

I know what you're thinking—no way! Things like this don't happen in our contemporary society. You have to be in Africa for God to perform miracles through Southern Baptists. I thought about it a lot myself. *How did this happen?* Was it because the core sample was in a different part of the land? Or could it be that God had actually performed a miracle and changed the landfill to good land?

What I do know is that the same realtor who sold the property to me came back and offered me three times the amount he had sold it for once he heard the clearance to build had actually come through. What I do know is that the previous owners could not build on the property, but we could. What I do know is that we were told the property was worthless and unusable. What I cannot tell you is what happened beneath the ground at 2815 South Ervay Street. All I can tell you is what I know—and that is that God took my failure and performed a miracle.

FAITH ON THE INCREASE

Today Cornerstone worships on that acre of land in a sanctuary built by our own hands. Needless to say, we were never the same again. After living by faith, living only by the faith just isn't enough.

The apostolic leader infuses his own life of faith into a culture of faithful living. It is never enough to live on yesterday's faith. We are always required to move into a fresh faith.

> It seems that when God calls us to live by faith, with each miracle he requires more faith.

I am reminded of how God called Moses to stand at the bank of the water and gave him clear instructions to stand firm, raise his staff, stretch out his hand over the sea, and divide the water. You know what happened next: The water divided, and Israel walked through to deliverance and freedom.

For Joshua it was different. When Joshua stood at the bank of the Jordan, God didn't tell him to raise his staff. He instructed Joshua to do something quite different. God told him, "Now then, choose twelve men from the tribes of Israel, one from each tribe. And as soon as the priests who carry the ark of the

Lord—the Lord of all the earth—set foot in the Jordan, its waters flowing downstream will be cut off and stand up in a heap" (Joshua 3:12-13).

In the first situation, God told Israel to stand firm and see the deliverance of the Lord. In the second situation, they had to step into the water first, and only after they set foot in the Jordan did the water stop flowing downstream. It seems that when God calls us to live by faith, with each miracle he requires more faith. I suppose the first time it just took faith to raise the staff and wait for the waters to part. The second time people had to engage the water and set their feet in it.

What took faith yesterday is sight today. When we live by faith, we allow God to take us into new experiences of who he is and how he works. The church cannot live on the faith of the past. The church is called to be the living expression of faith. When a church lives by faith, its people prove that God can be trusted. Faith is the triangle for the cultural architect. Its angles are committed to sharp turns, jagged edges, and extreme redirection.

To Be Known by Love

LOVE NEVER DIES

Stefanie Sakuma was only nine years old, and she was dying. She had a rare and violent disease that the medical professionals barely understood. They were uncertain about the cause and even about how the disease was transmitted. The only thing they knew for certain was that in its advanced stages, death was certain.

Stephanie had severe factor 7 hemophilia, and she had contracted AIDS through a blood transfusion. It was 1983, and the word AIDS was just becoming a part of our vernacular. We were uncertain if AIDS was airborne, which created a tremendous fear of contamination. The Los Angeles congregation that I later came to pastor had decisions to make. They had to decide whether to follow the pattern of many churches across America and ask those who were infected with AIDS to leave the church for the safety of the congregation or to choose to invite the Sakumas to stay at the risk of the congregation's own lives.

Under the leadership of the former pastor and the elders, the congregation decided that they would either live together or die together. Since that time Stefanie Sakuma has died and gone to be with the Lord. She was a tremendous poet with a deep spiritual insight and love for God. Her life inspired a published work that has sold both in the United States and Japan.

When I invited Janice Sakuma, her mother, to be a part of our leadership team, it wasn't simply because of her extraordinary leadership gifts, but also because of the way she and her husband, Steve, personified the kind of love we wanted to express as a congregation. We are called to be known by love.

DEFINED BY LOVE

Love is a romantic word. More songs have been written about love than any other subject or word in the world. And would there even be a movie industry without love? There's an entire genre called romance novels because people so desperately long for love. And yet as much as we write about it, talk about it, and claim to build our lives around it, love is actually a rare commodity. Most of what we call love falls in other categories: from like to lust, passion to possession. We have been so inundated with love imitations that we've become blind to what love is really all about.

In the end love manifests itself in sacrifice. Jesus told us that the way the world will know that we are his disciples is if we love one another (John 13:34). He laid a foundation for an entire movement. Love is so central to the heart of God and the ethos of the New Testament church that without it we have no claim to be the disciples of Jesus Christ.

In John 15:13, Jesus gives us the practical expression of love. He says, "Greater love has no one than this, that he lay down his life for his friends." Of course, Jesus was speaking of his own death, explaining that his sacrifice would be the ultimate expression for the love of all humanity.

> **"Love is so central to the heart of God and the ethos of the New Testament church that without it we have no claim to be the disciples of Jesus Christ."**

The church erupted out of an act of love. It shouldn't surprise us that the church only moves toward God when it is fueled by love. In a world of imitations, real love draws a crowd. It stands out. It is undeniable. It is defining.

I have to admit that for the first ten years of my Christian life, I was far more attracted to faith than I was to love. If my life were a Bible, it would say, "You will be known by your faith—and love is important too." I wanted to be known by faith.

In some ways, that drove me into some pretty extreme situations. It put me in the middle of machine guns, Jamaican drug dealers, and a world of prostitutes, pimps, and johns. My life of faith has carried me to the streets of New Orleans in the middle of the Mardi Gras; it has taken me to street corners to preach the Gospel; and it has even put me face to face with death many times. Yet in the middle of that journey, Jesus changed my core motivation. While he wanted me to live by faith, the only way that I could really know him was to also become known by love.

SERVING LOVE DOESN'T EQUAL NOTHING

It is impossible to come close to God and not have love overwhelm you. And when you realize that the practical expression of love is servanthood, love begins to change everything about your relationships. In fact, this is one of the amazing things about God: He loves to serve.

When Jesus tied a towel around his waist and began washing his disciples' feet, this was not an extraordinary act for God but right in line with who he is. Jesus Christ was a servant. He was doing nothing more than expressing the serving heart of God.

It sounds sacrilegious to say that God is a servant, but that's only because our value systems are so corrupt and distorted. We feel comfortable attributing to God those things we aspire to be. To describe God as all-powerful makes him only what we want more of. To describe God as all-knowing once again reinforces something that we value. To describe God as all-present is not only comforting, but it even affirms our personal value for control. We want God to be all-powerful, all-knowing, and all-controlling. It is not difficult to convince us that these should be attributes of God. But to say that God is a servant seems out of touch with our view of how God works.

If *we* were all-powerful, all-knowing, and all-present, how many of us would choose to let servanthood be the ultimate expression of all that potential? Isn't the whole point of being God to be served? It would be for us, but not for Jesus.

LOVE IS ALL WET

It was a Sunday morning, and it was pouring rain outside. Since it was the early eighties, I was still wearing a suit. It was my Sunday suit, so I didn't want to go outside and get it wet. While everyone else was running to their cars to avoid the rain, I stayed around the podium and pretended that I was doing something important. I knew no one would bother me if I was looking ministerial, except, of course, my wife. She never really seemed to understand that she shouldn't disturb me when I was pretending to do something important.

She came with three or four children who needed a ride home, and she explained to me that she had committed us to take them. This really irritated me, and I tried to explain to her that I wasn't able to leave right now. Shortly afterward, we went to the car through the pouring rain, and I began to drive them to their homes.

> What I said on Sunday wasn't nearly as important as what I did.

My windshield wipers were fighting the rain, failing to clear enough space for me to see the road ahead of me. The water pushed like waves off the side of my tires, and the streets were flooded. As we were driving, all of a sudden Kim cried out,

"Did you see the man? Did you see the man?"

Trying to stay on the road, I responded, "See the man? I can't even see the road. What are you talking about?" She insisted there was a man in the middle of the street who needed help. She said, "We need to go back and help him."

Hypocrisy at full steam, I told her we needed to get these kids home. When she didn't give up, I finally conceded that after we took the kids to their houses, if he was still there, we would help him.

On the way back, I did look for the man, but I saw no one. The rain was still pouring down, and driving was a difficult task. All of a sudden Kim started up again, "Did you see the man? There he is."

I said, "Honey, are you sure there was a man there? I didn't see anyone."

But she insisted so we turned around, and right in front of me was a homeless man with a broken cart and all of his goods floating in a pool of water. Kim was about eight months pregnant, and she looked at me and said, "Honey, we need to help him." I knew she didn't mean her and the baby. "We" meant me.

So I took off my jacket, ran out into the pouring rain, walked into the puddle in the middle of the road, and realized that the man was so disoriented that he kept putting things in his broken cart and it kept tipping over. So I reassembled his cart and began helping him pick up all his stuff that was floating in the water. I realized it was mostly trash, things I wouldn't touch out of my own backyard, but it was everything of value that he had.

After we had recovered everything that was floating away and gathered things into his cart, I experienced a definitive sign that there really is a God. In that moment, it stopped raining and the sun came out. It was as if God were laughing at me and saying, "So you wanted to stay dry, huh?"

I decided that since I had to go through all this trouble, this guy had to receive Christ. So I shared the Gospel with him, but he wasn't at all interested. In fact, he told me he wasn't interested in knowing Jesus Christ, but if we had any garbage at the church, he would be happy to come by and pick it up. That just made the whole experience a little harder to swallow.

I had gotten back in the car and was driving home, when all of a sudden Kim started to cry. I thought to myself, "Oh, what is it now? First I wouldn't do the right thing, and now she's crying because I did it with the wrong attitude."

So I looked at her and I said, "What's wrong, honey?" She responded, "That was the greatest sermon you ever preached." Somehow, deep down inside, I knew that it was true. What I said on Sunday wasn't nearly as important as what I did.

Jesus said we would be known by our love, but that the greatest expression of love is when we lay our lives down for someone else. Until then, it's a call to servanthood.

A WHOLE LOT OF LOVE

Whenever we are known by love, God's reputation is intact. Sometimes the church gets so focused on truth that we forget that the mandate is to speak the truth in love. God's truth is never to be lifted out of or away from the context of love. It's not just important to tell the truth; we have to make sure we are truly motivated by love for the person we are speaking to.

It is the same with faith. Faith is never to be lifted out of the context of love. Paul tells us the only thing that counts is faith expressing itself through love. He goes on to remind us that we were called to be free, but that we are not to use our freedom to indulge the flesh. Instead we are to serve one another in love. That's a pretty strong statement. The only things that count are to serve and love. When love erupts in the hearts of God's people, they become the servants of a lost and broken world.

The apostolic ethos is permeated by love. It grows out of the core of the great commandments to love God with all of our heart, soul, mind, and strength and to love our neighbor as our self. It is a culture born out of a love for the creator God that fleshes itself out in an unreasonable love for all humanity.

When Jesus was asked what was the greatest of all the commandments, he was essentially being asked what is the most important thing to God. His answer could be summarized in one word: relationships. Essentially all the church is, is relationships. Without relationships, the church ceases to exist. Relationship to God and relationship to others are what the church is all about.

One day Kim and Mariah were driving in the car, and Kim turned to our little girl and said, "Mariah, I love you to pieces," and Mariah responded, "Mommy, I love you whole."

This is what happens in an apostolic ethos—God's love makes us whole, unites us, makes us one of heart and mind, heals us, takes the broken fragments of our soul, and makes us new creations.

THROWING IN THE TOWEL

One of our prayers as a leadership team has been that God would truly give us as a congregation a servant's heart and that we could, in a practical way, know that we are being known by love.

> **Love produces servanthood. Servanthood sees sacrifice as a privilege.**

I received a phone call from Asia telling me about a situation related to an event not many months away. Five hundred overseas workers were serving in China and Mongolia for the sole purpose of taking Christ to those nations. They had an annual meeting planned, and support structures to make the event happen had fallen apart. The event was dependent on volunteer teams coming from the United States.

The leaders had asked me to speak throughout that conference, to bring messages to individuals who had spent most of the year without Christian fellowship. I had expected to bring a worship team along with me, but this conversation expanded the request dramatically. When I asked what they needed, the person on the other end said, "Everything: preschool workers, children's workers, junior high and high school workers, worship team, drama team, dance team, any counselor or administrative help." Anything that we could provide was needed.

When we went through the list, it appeared that nearly forty people would be required to fulfill these responsibilities. This would mean that forty of our adult members would need to take two weeks off work and contribute over one thousand dollars each so that they could go change diapers and work nonstop in Thailand.

I wish I could tell you that it was my hard work that resulted in the successful recruitment of forty members to pull off this feat, but it just wasn't that hard. After just a few hours of phone calls and about a week of time, over forty people were committed to taking work off, finding money, and going to serve. We ended up taking forty-two people to serve those five hundred workers.

Love produces servanthood. Servanthood sees sacrifice as a privilege. It is to the servants that the master entrusts the work that must be done. When we are known by love, we are known for the towel wrapped around our waist. Apostolic leaders are servant leaders. They lead not only by serving God, but by serving others.

To Be a Voice of Hope

HOPE IN A DESPERATE WORLD

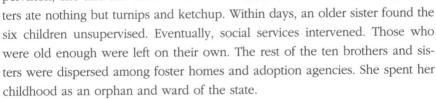

She was eight years old when her parents abandoned her in a house in Asheville, North Carolina. Left without food or supervision, she and her brothers and sisters ate nothing but turnips and ketchup. Within days, an older sister found the six children unsupervised. Eventually, social services intervened. Those who were old enough were left on their own. The rest of the ten brothers and sisters were dispersed among foster homes and adoption agencies. She spent her childhood as an orphan and ward of the state.

As circumstance would have it, the foster home in which she was placed was an open field away from a small church in the mountains of North Carolina. This girl, now nine years old, would walk herself to church every week, despite the fact that her foster family was essentially irreligious.

At the age of fourteen, she told God she would do anything and go anywhere in the world, and she dreamt of perhaps going to Africa as a missionary. While many of her brothers and sisters followed the path of their parents and turned to lives of alcohol, drugs, and promiscuity, she began to walk a different course. Defying the pattern of a family of junior high and high school dropouts, she went on to college, earned awards for her work, and proceeded to postgraduate studies, receiving a master's degree in theology. The story of my wife, Kim, is a reminder that in its essence, the Gospel is a message of hope.

When the Gospel is born in our hearts, it gives us a picture of who we can become in Christ and what God could accomplish through our lives. The gospel has the power to take the orphan and make her the friend of the fatherless; to take the brokenhearted, the outcast, and the lonely and make them instruments of peace, forgiveness, and healing.

We understand that a Christless world is a hopeless world. At the same time we seem to forget that a Christ-filled world is a hope-filled world. Somehow we've lost the mandate given to us by God to stand in a desperate world and offer hope.

IT'S GOOD TO KNOW

The Gospel itself is good news. We know that. We teach it, but we often do not communicate it as good news. When we speak the Gospel of Jesus Christ, we seem to somehow get logjammed around the message of sin, damnation, and hell. No wonder so many people feel that the church has nothing but bad news to tell. We even seem to revel at times in communicating to an unbelieving world that they are godless and condemned.

> Jesus, God himself, the only one who could cast the first stone, would not accept a ministry of condemnation. Why is it that we are all too ready to stand as the condemners of humanity?

The Gospel, as given to us by Jesus, is supposed to be good news. Jesus himself said, "I have not come to condemn the world, but to give the world life." Jesus, God himself, the only one who could cast the first stone, would not accept a ministry of condemnation. Why is it that *we* are all too ready to stand as the condemners of humanity? To understand the full implications of hope, mankind needs to understand the reality of the human condition. But I have a feeling that our message is textured, not by others' inability to understand but by our own passion to reinforce their separation from God.

What would happen if people heard the message of Christ as a message of hope and not a message of judgment? Many times I hear Christians described as hypocritical and self-righteous. How can a message of hope cause us to be perceived in this way? Could it be that people do not hear us acknowledging our own sinfulness but only identifying theirs, and so call us hypocrites? Could it be that somehow those receiving our message feel that we are standing as judges over them rather than servants under them?

The message of Christ and the need for repentance are inseparable, but even in that, the Bible is clear about how we are to relate to people. Paul reminds us that it is the loving kindness of God that brings us to repentance. We are to speak the truth in love. If the truth is extracted from the context of love, it is no longer the message that God is speaking. The Gospel is good news. It is a message of hope. The best indication that we are communicating the Gospel effectively is that broken, sinful, and despairing people receive it as a word of good news.

It's important to remember that the people Jesus continually offended were the religious. Sinners seem to warm up to him quite easily. Many times we mis-apply our prophetic gifts, and instead of preaching to the church the message of repentance and change, we turn it outward to the audience that needs to hear that God offers them forgiveness and healing.

FORGIVENESS MOVES US FORWARD

A forty-year-old Japanese man was visiting because his wife was related to someone at Mosaic. Their spiritual journey involved Buddhism and the Sikh re-ligion of India, but they had never seriously considered the message of Jesus Christ. I asked his brother-in-law at the close of our Sunday morning experience to go talk to him about where he was in his journey regarding Jesus Christ. The brother-in-law came back to share with me that he did not seem to be open. I worked my way to him, and we began talking about his spiritual search. He be-gan by telling me that he had read the entire New Testament that weekend. Sometimes I miss the obvious, but I thought that this probably indicated spiri-tual openness.

He went on to tell me that everything he had read felt true to him and added that the morning message also rang true to him. So I asked what stood between him and God, and he answered with one word: despair. This caught me off guard. I've heard a lot of reasons for not coming to Christ, but I have never had anyone articulate so clearly what lurks deeply in the heart of human beings who are separated from God.

The Gospel, in its essence, is a message of hope to a world full of despair.

I asked, "What do you mean by despair?" He went on to explain that if every-thing he read was true, then the last forty years of his life had been wasted. All of a sudden I understood. Here was a man whose background and religious worldview told him that to fix the problem in his life, he would have to die, be born again, and do better in the next life. When I explained to him that what was more important than the time he had lost was the time that stood before him, he looked at me and said, "Do you mean it's not too late?" When he un-derstood that Jesus Christ could redeem all the years that he felt were wasted and give him new life, he bowed his life to Jesus. The Gospel, in its essence, is a message of hope to a world full of despair.

One of my favorite stories in the life of Jesus is in John 8, where the religious leaders confronted him, wanting to condemn an adulterous woman. I've always been struck by how Jesus, even when others tried to force him into meanness, would not allow it. If there was ever a perfect opportunity to bring down the wrath of God on a sinful woman, it was right then. And yet from that encounter with this woman caught in adultery, thrown naked before him, we have Jesus' famous words, "If any one of you is without sin, let him be the first to throw a stone at her" (John 8:7b). He asked, "Who condemns you?" and she responded, "No one." Jesus revealed the heart of God when he told her that he didn't condemn her. He simply commanded her to go and sin no more. This is an important guide for the church.

We are God's voice of hope. Those who have known nothing but condemnation and shame will find a new beginning in Jesus Christ. This should be one of the markers of a New Testament community. Yet even beyond being a voice of hope for the individual, the church should be a place of inspiration about the future. We are to be a voice of hope because we are a people of hope. A follower of Jesus Christ has no excuse for pessimism.

A FUTURE OF OPTIMISM

The Lord God spoke to Jeremiah and reminded him that he knows the plans he has for us, plans for the future and a hope, plans for our welfare and not destruction. The natural outcome of being connected to God is being optimistic about the future. When this permeates a biblical community, optimism and enthusiasm prevail in the church. The church of Jesus Christ is always looking forward. It always believes in the promise of tomorrow and is never overwhelmed by the difficulty or even the failure of the present.

The cultural architect works with these three primal essences of the church—faith, love, and hope—and unwraps them through his own personal transformation and journey and through the calling out of God's people to live in these realities. When the church begins to live by faith, to be known by love, and to be a voice of hope, she begins to experience the power of an apostolic ethos. The deeper the texture of faith, hope, and love, the more powerfully the momentum can transform culture. People are looking for something worth believing in, somewhere to belong, and something to become. In the context of an apostolic ethos, those intrinsic longings of the human spirit are called out and then find their fulfillment.

Faith, love, and hope are not foundations or pillars; they are wellsprings. They supply the church with the essential ingredients of an apostolic ethos. The deeper the church digs these wells, the more rich and resilient they become.

I cannot emphasize strongly enough that strategy does not create resiliency. It is not through our processes, our methods, or our structures that the church becomes unstoppable or unflappable. When a church prevails, it is not because of the approach toward ministries she has taken, but because of the soul of the church as expressed within the ethos of the community.

Faith, hope, and love build in the church that which is necessary to face not only the challenges ahead, but also the onslaughts and attractions of the evil one that are sure to come. Effective ministry is not the elimination of failure but the ability to thrive in the midst of failure. The mystery is that there are some churches that just can't be stopped. It doesn't matter how many times they fail. There's no problem too great for them to overcome.

HOPE NEVER GIVES UP

Viktor Frankl's groundbreaking work in the area of logotherapy gives us a glimpse of what the Spirit can be like. In his book *Man's Search for Meaning*, he describes the significant insight that he gained through his days in German concentration camps. The torment and violence that the Jewish prisoners experienced were intended not only to kill them, but also to cause them to step into the end of their lives with nothing but despair. Yet Frankl discovered that there were those who had an unusual resiliency and unexplainable ability to stand under the weight that crushed so many others. There seemed to be a unifying theme among these individuals. They all had something yet to do, something left unfinished. This connection to a future responsibility seemed to somehow give them the strength they needed to endure the present hostility. In some ways, the dream allowed them to live through the nightmare.

> **❝I am absolutely convinced that where an apostolic ethos prevails, people move toward optimism; where it is lacking, despair creates pessimism.❞**

Martin Seligman has, in recent times, looked upon this same phenomenon of human spirit from a different perspective in a different environment. His research focused on why some people failed and gave up and why others were able not only to endure failure, but also to use it as a catalyst for success. From one perspective, his research is about pessimism and helplessness. But from another perspective, his findings were linked to something far more powerful. He alludes to this in the title of his book *Learned Optimism*. Seligman submits that there are three crucial dimensions to our ability to engage failure in a positive way. They are all related to how we understand failure and explain it to ourselves.

One style views failure as pervasive, another sees failure as personal, and the third understands failure as permanent. These three arenas describe the context in which Seligman understands our resulting pessimism or optimism.

These explanatory styles are the psychological description of the absence and power of faith, love, and hope. I am absolutely convinced that where an apostolic ethos prevails, people move toward optimism; where it is lacking, despair creates pessimism.

Faith, hope, and love are more than simply poetic words. They are more than spiritual abstracts or religious jargon. Faith, hope, and love are the fuel that ignited the first-century church. They are the very essence of the apostolic ethos. They are the promise that the church of Jesus Christ is unstoppable and that even the gates of hell will not prevail against her.

66Tell me and I'll forget; show me and I may remember; involve me and I'll understand.99 —CHINESE PROVERB

FUEL FOR THOUGHT

1. List practical expressions of the commitment to live by faith, to be known by love, and to be a voice of hope.
2. What areas in which God has clearly called the church to act do we need to address?
3. In what ways are we expressing love to those outside our congregation?
4. In what arenas is there a need to bring a voice of hope to which the church can bring light?
5. What endeavor could we undertake that would be so reflective of the heart of God that even failure would be success?
6. When will we do it?

CHAPTER EIGHT

SOUL ENVIRONMENTS

If the primary role of leadership is the creating and shaping of ethos, then the pastor becomes a spiritual environmentalist. Jesus instructs us to make disciples of all nations. This process involves leading his disciples to publicly declare him through baptism and teaching them to obey all things. We have seen this for too long as a systematic process rather than an environmental one.

This metaphor is both culturally appropriate and biblically grounded. Paul tells Timothy that if someone is to lead the church, the house of God, he must effectively lead his own home. The Greek word for house here is *oikos*. This word refers to the sphere of influence contained within human relationships. But sometimes we forget that *oikos* is also the root word for what has come to be known as ecology. An ecological system that is healthy is essentially a healthy family system.

Paul is saying that if you're a poor environmentalist at home, how can you be an effective environmentalist in the house of God? Paul writes this criterion in the middle of other measures for spiritual leadership, suggesting that they all are connected to this imagery. When you break it down to its primal essence, spiritual leadership is the ability to establish and grow a healthy community.

If you are a parent, you understand that this is no small task. It is an incredible challenge to invest your life in other human beings, especially from birth to adulthood, and to go beyond simply enforcing rules to transferring beliefs and values. Your goal is to shape character and produce a genuinely healthy human being.

An apostolic ethos erupts out of the context of human relationships, not apart from it. The dynamic movement that brings personal transformation and historical change is rooted in the simplicity of right relationships. These relationships begin in a healthy relationship with God that flows naturally into healthy relationships with others.

The birthplace of the apostolic ethos is certainly the great commandment, but the focus of this ethos is found through the commission. The spiritual environmentalist focuses on five environments for spiritual health. At Mosaic we wrap these environments around five elemental images.

Moved-Commission

The first element is wind. The apostolic ethos is fueled by intentionality. God is about something. He is not sitting in heaven, watching human history. God is the wind of history. He moves with power and intent. Those who follow God are children of the wind. Jesus opens his ministry, calling us to follow him. That requires movement. Then he promises he will make us fishers of men. He doesn't promise healing, community, friendship, safety, nurturing, security, or anything of personal benefit to us. He only promises a cause worthy of God.

❝Jesus' mandate to the church covers everyone: "You will be my witnesses." The plural "you," not the singular.❞

The church of Jesus Christ is on mission. Every disciple is a missionary. We are the called-out ones. When God's Spirit comes, we become witnesses. If there is no movement, we must ask, where is the Spirit of the Lord?

The metaphor of wind is inescapable when seeking to understand the environment of an apostolic ethos. From the Spirit hovering over the surface of the earth, to the Spirit coming like a roaring and rushing wind upon the church, to the Spirit closing the book of God, calling us to come; wherever there is Spirit, there is movement.

COMMISSION COMMUNITY

There is great theological debate about what it means to be an apostle and even some debate about who exactly the apostles were. But whether there were eleven apostles or twelve or fourteen or fifteen or perhaps a number that we are unaware of, what we know for certain is that the first-century church was an apostolic community.

To be an apostle literally means to be a sent-out one. From its etymology, this definition encompasses every believer we read about in the New Testament. Jesus' mandate to the church covers everyone: "You will be my witnesses." The plural "you," not the singular. The early church seemed to understand this description to be pervasive. It related to everyone who heard the call of God to follow his Son.

The wind is a reminder that in an apostolic ethos, an environment flows out of the commission; in essence God creates a commission community. He builds a people who fulfill God's purpose together. He unites a community of people who are on mission together. It is no small connection that in the Hebrew of the Old Testament and the Greek of the New Testament, the words *ruach* and *pnuema* both speak of spirit, wind, and breath. "Spirit" encompasses the essence of God himself; "wind" expresses the movement of the awesome God working within human history; and "breath" declares the promise of God's intimate communion and communication with those who hear his voice and follow him.

THE WHISPER OF THE WIND

Intentionality assumes revelation. When Jesus spoke to Nicodemus about the miracle of rebirth, he reminded Nicodemus that the wind blows to and fro throughout the earth. Where it comes and where it goes, no one knows. But later we are reminded that we have the Spirit of God. To an unbelieving world, the wind of God does not exist. Though people see the leaves dance across the lawn and the trees bend in worship, they never see the wind. When we are joined with God, our spirits move from death to life. We become—in our essence—living spirits.

When the Spirit of God moves like the wind, his voice whispers to our spirits, and we hear the call of God. For some of us, this will be like the experience of Samuel, who kept hearing the voice of God but could not recognize him. Samuel needed someone to instruct him. Eli told him what to say when he heard the voice again: "Say, 'Yes, Lord, your servant is listening.' "

The commission environment is more than a military response to evangelism. It is an intense spiritual sensitivity to the prodding and leadership of the

Holy Spirit to move *with* him as he moves forward.

WHERE THE WIND BLOWS

Several years ago my wife, Kim, talked me into going to the *Price Is Right.* I'm not really a big fan of the show, but I'm a great fan of my wife, so I went. We stood in line to get tickets to stand in line to get into the show. This was an all-day affair. If I'd had to stand in line for thirty minutes, I'd have been irritated, but this was close to five hours.

Several hours into the process, we were sitting next to a family from the former Soviet Union. You can only go so long without talking to the people next to you, so we finally struck up a conversation. The person next to me described her journey as an extraordinary opportunity to come from a place like Uzbekistan and be in Los Angeles. As I talked with her about her spiritual background, I led into sharing with her about the saving grace of Jesus Christ.

> The world looks different when you understand yourself to be a child of the wind. You realize that when your sail is up, God's wind blows you to places you never imagined, at just the right moment for someone else.

She asked the question that so many have asked, "How can I believe in a God who only comes to people in America and not to people around the world? What about the person in India or China who has never heard?" I looked at her and asked if she felt that God loved her more than he loved that individual in India that she was concerned about, and she said, "No, that's the whole point."

Then I summarized for her what was so obvious to me in that moment. God had brought me from El Salvador via Miami, to throughout the East Coast, to be sitting in Los Angeles in line at the *Price Is Right* to see a show that I didn't even want to go to. And here she was from the former Soviet Union, having lived in a small town in a nation-state whose name I could not pronounce. If God could bring her from one part of the world and me from another part of the world and move us to the exact same place at the exact same moment so that she could learn that Jesus Christ died for her, didn't she think that God was both creative and powerful enough to bring life to everyone who would cry out to him? There in line at the *Price Is Right,* her heart softened and she turned her life over to Jesus Christ.

The world looks different when you understand yourself to be a child of the wind. You realize that when your sail is up, God's wind blows you to places you never imagined, at just the right moment for someone else. The apostolic ethos is an environment in which all of God's people are guided by the wind. If all are not apostles, at least all are together on the apostolic mission. At Mosaic we say it like this: Mission is why the church exists.

Drenched-Community

The second element is captured in the imagery of water. The apostolic ethos is fueled by intimacy. Jesus prayed that we would be one, even as he and the Father are one. He told his followers that the world would know we are his disciples if we have love for one another.

The early church was united in heart and mind and held everything in common. James goes as far as to say that we are to confess our sins to one another. But we have confused a personal faith with individual faith, sometimes at the expense of community. We see the community of Christ as optional, at best, and more often as an intrusion into our spiritual journey. Yet we are baptized into Christ and joined with his body. Every believer passes through the waters and becomes a part of the river of life. Alone, you are only standing in a puddle. Together, we become an oasis where those searching for genuine love and acceptance can come and drink deeply. Water is a great metaphor for community.

Jesus' calling us to become fishers of men makes us a commission community. At the same time, we discover that it is community that is commissioned. Everywhere Jesus' commission goes, community is created. It is not a cause without community or a community without cause, but the mysterious integration of these two tensions.

THE WATER GRAVE

In the church today, few places exist where people genuinely intersect and share a common experience in a community with cultural, generational, and economic diversity. We must be careful not to miss out on essential, shared, spiritual experiences.

One experience that binds us all together is passing through the water grave of baptism. Others hold varying thoughts and traditions related to baptism, but from where I stand, the metaphor of immersion is both dramatic and significant. Through baptism we are drenched in God, enveloped in God's presence, and brought through death to life. The water grave is a perfect expression of this reality. It is both personal and communal. It declares our individual need for forgiveness and new life, and it binds us to a new community of faith.

This was most dramatically illustrated for me as I listened to the story of Ruth Friesen, as told by her son, Ron. Ruth was baptized by her grandfather in the notorious Krishna River of South India while fellow believers gathered around her in the water, clapping their hands together, and creating a loud chorus of percussion to accent her baptism experience. When Ron described it to me, I thought the clapping was a peculiar addendum to the Christian passage of baptism. But then he explained that the waters were filled with crocodiles. Making loud clapping sounds with their hands was the community's best attempt at keeping the crocodiles away from the new believers! As Ruth herself said, "We were not sure if the crocodiles were just below, at the surface, or right above the water. The crocodiles didn't pull us under before our grandfather did!" In essence, the church risked their lives so that the new believers could publicly declare their faith in Jesus Christ.

Baptism is not simply about being baptized into Christ, but being baptized into the body of Christ. Water is our metaphor for the life-giving essence that is created in the context of genuine biblical community.

LIQUID GRACE

John reminds us that if we say we love God but do not have love for our brother, then we are nothing less than liars. Jesus doesn't call us to *love* God and *tolerate* our neighbor. Many times we think that the miracle is to love God. In actuality, loving God is the most intelligent thing you can do. To love God is not a miracle. God is absolutely lovely. God is breathtaking and awesome in his splendor. When we do not love God, something is wrong with our hearts. Loving God is the most natural thing in the world to do. It's loving *people* that's a miracle.

> **When you come to God, you discover that he is perfect. When you come to Christian community, you discover that God's people are not.**

Have you been outside lately? People are incredibly selfish. We, at our core, are extraordinarily self-centered, self-focused, and self-indulgent. We can be irritable, short-tempered, or easily offended and embittered, and I've yet to describe people who are not Christians. Loving one another is the real miracle. When you come to God, you discover that he is perfect. When you come to Christian community, you discover that God's people are not.

It always makes me nervous when people begin attending Mosaic and, with wide-eyed infatuation, run up and tell me that they absolutely love Mosaic and have finally found the perfect church. My heart begins to sink at the thought of what's going to happen once they get a clear picture of who we are. We are so far from the perfect church that I feel obligated to try to dispel this illusion as quickly as possible.

The Christian community is not a place without interpersonal crisis or challenge. In some sense we are all hypocrites in transition. We're all working it out. Sometimes fighting with God; sometimes working with God. That's why biblical community is such an extraordinary gift. It's not about being perfect or loving people who are always easy to love; it's about loving people through the love of God. It's about being loved even when you blow it, being loved even when you do not deserve it, and being loved by others who know you all too well—even when you find it difficult to love yourself.

When you begin to love people through their imperfections, through the disappointments, you begin to know that it's more than infatuation. Only the love of God creates a bond so deep that not even the greatest betrayal can end the relationship or end all hope. The apostolic ethos is thick with an environment that is more powerful than any single miracle. Those who are searching for the love of God find it through the love of God's people. The church is an oasis of liquid grace where forgiveness flows freely.

LOVE PLACES

A metaphor often used in describing humanity's search for God is that we're all on a journey up the mountain, choosing our own paths, but all paths end in the same place. This metaphor is inadequate. It paints a picture of God being the old wise man who sits on the top of this great mountain in someplace like Tibet, waiting for us to obtain his audience through our personal achievement, when in fact the Scriptures teach us that it is God who has taken the initiative. Being motivated by love, God did not simply come down from a mountain but stepped down from his throne in heaven to walk among us and to create a way to love. Love sent Christ into the world. Love moves God.

A better metaphor for our search for God is that we are all wandering in a desert, dying of thirst and searching for water, when out of the hardened and calloused ground springs up a well of living water which is the presence of God. Jesus said that if we would ask him, he would create in us a spring of water welling up to eternal life, a river from which the water's flow would never end.

The body of Christ is the oasis of God, and God creates love places through the church. At the same time, love places us among those who need God. From a theological perspective, this makes all the more sense. God is relational. God expresses himself through the godhead as three persons: Father, Son, and Spirit. In himself, God experiences perfect community. God is not absent of relationship; God is the essence of relationship. The Father glorifies the Son; the Son glorifies the Father; the Spirit glorifies them both. Within the godhead, there is confounding humility. Even within God's own expression in the Trinity, everything that is necessary for healthy community and genuine intimacy exists. God is relational. It should not surprise us that we cannot properly experience God outside of community. At Mosaic we say it like this: Love is the context of all mission.

Grafted-Connection

The third element of an apostolic ethos is wood. We are all a part of God's ecological system. This ecosystem is spiritual, relational, and personal. Jesus explained that he is the vine and we are the branches. Without the vine, branches are just dead wood. So we are first and foremost dependent on Christ and his Spirit, yet alone we are just twigs. Together we are the vineyards of God.

Still the connection is deeply personalized. Each person fits together with the vine according to his or her unique gifts and talents. There is no assembly-line process here. The organization of the church is built around the unique gifting of each individual and the dynamic relationship to others with which they serve.

Servanthood is the key to connection. Serving others with others is the surest path to having your own needs met. Serving through your own grafting is the surest path to finding fulfillment and to fulfilling your divine purpose. An organic community moves with the life of the Spirit. The Spirit does not dwell in structures, programs, or methods. He dwells in people.

THE BIBLICAL YOU

Wood is our metaphor for connection. When we read the Bible, too often we are reading from a very individualistic Western perspective. We see it through the modern world: "I."

Here's a quick test to see if you have been captured by this filtering system. When you read the Bible, do you read all the "you's" as first person singular? Is what God is saying to you as an individual the first thing you listen for in the Scriptures? Or do you recognize that the Scriptures are not primarily written to "me" but to "us," not to "I" but to "we," not to you specifically but to all of you as God's people? In interpreting the Bible, it's best not to apply it primarily to our own individualized spiritual journey but to our lives in relationship to other human beings, in relationship to the body of Christ; and in relationship to all of humanity. This is important to understand if we are to effectively nurture this third environment.

> Though Jesus warns us that apart from him we can accomplish nothing, he promises us that if we abide in him, we will bear much fruit.

Spiritual maturity cannot exist outside of healthy relationships. In the same way, vibrant, spiritual ministry is the result of a dynamic interdependence on other believers in the service of humanity. With Jesus as the vine, it is critical that we understand the significance of our being joined together as branches. In the context from which Jesus spoke, the role of the branches is significant in accomplishing God's purpose in the world.

We are the vineyard of God, from which the Father produces his new wine. Though Jesus warns us that apart from him we can accomplish nothing, he promises us that if we abide in him, we will bear much fruit. We are living wood joined together in ministry. Our branches are fused together as we take up the task of servanthood, and servanthood becomes for us the practical expression of God's love overflowing in our hearts. We soon discover that God's love places us in ministry to a lost and broken world.

SPIRIT MATTERS

The element of wood deals with how ministries are formed and organized. The modern church has often established programs, structures, and even roles and positions before it is even known who the people are. You have a position, and you've got to find someone to fill it. Recruiting volunteers can become as simple as filling slots.

The connection environment is radically different. It understands that the Spirit of God does not dwell in programs but in people. Strategies are not nearly as important as gifts, and the organizational principle that drives ministry must be the unique gifting of the people that God brings to the body of Christ.

Whenever we receive new members at Mosaic, we remind them that receiving them into our community is our commitment to inviting them to change who we are, that we may become who God desires us to be. Our commitment is not to clone them to who we already are, but that each person who joins our community is a promise from God that he is not finished with us yet. If we respect the gifts, talents, and uniqueness of each individual, then we must be willing to change. If a person's contribution is honored and respected, then he will make a difference.

To empower someone, you must know where that person's power comes from and what his or her power is. God empowers us in different ways. God gives us different passions, different gifts, and different talents. Many times we have demeaned the value of the spiritual power that God has placed in individuals by forcing them to conform into what we perceive the church needs.

A connection environment is a birthplace for dynamic ministry. When people begin to group together, to join together with others who have common passions and gifting, the result is synergistic. Leaders sometimes get frightened when people do not seem to need their help or guidance. But helping people do what God called them to do is like setting fire to a bomb. A leader may begin the process, but people don't need much from the leader after that. And the reward is greater than the risk.

A community with the servant heart of God knows no limit to sacrifice, and when its people are doing what God created them to do, there is no limit to impact. The first-century church had a dynamic organizational system. Long before Transformers became popular children's toys, the individuals of the New Testament church had already embraced the concept, radically adjusting and adapting their forms to fulfill their God-given functions.

In 1988 we pulled together a small group to form a church planting team in an east Dallas community. This was the first and only time I've ever attempted to plant a Spanish-speaking church. As mentioned in an earlier chapter, we named the church *El Pueblo de Dios.* There had been an article in the Dallas paper about a teacher being attacked by a student in that community, and it inspired us to take a team and build a community in the midst of this crisis. We tried to eliminate all of our assumptions of what church needed to look like and formed our structure around the cultural patterns of a dominantly Spanish-speaking, Mexican community.

As a result we would meet together to pray and distribute information to families that were open to the Gospel. We worshipped on Sunday nights, but we would take gifts of *pandulce* to these families on Sunday mornings, knowing they would be home. We determined that the best entry point for reaching Latin men—our primary target—would be to organize a city soccer team, and so we did that.

> **In short, spirit matters. What God's Spirit is doing is what the church needs to be doing.**

We soon discovered that the games were in direct conflict with our worship service, and so for our new congregation, the solution was simple: Move the worship time so everybody can go to the soccer match. Granted, when you're smaller you can make more dynamic decisions at times, but the precedent was set. The church did not exist for its organizers. We were the church, and we were here for the world.

It is important to recognize that the things of the Spirit matter and the work of the Spirit materializes in ministry. In short, spirit matters. What God's Spirit is doing is what the church needs to be doing. And when God's Spirit is working, his work is fleshed out in real ministry through the church of Jesus Christ.

A STICKY SITUATION

When being a church attendee is not a culturally expected responsibility, a person who attends but does not begin to serve will drop out within a year. One can ponder all the research and studies on how to assimilate new members and new believers into the body of Christ, but it comes down to one simple variable. If people begin to serve, they stick. If a person is simply *being* served, it is highly unlikely that person will make it in the long-term.

For some reason, our stickability is related to our servanthood, and it is through serving others *with* others that we genuinely begin to make the connection. It is no small thing to feel that you are needed. And your sense of ownership increases when you see your fingerprint on the work that has been done. To make a contribution is to give of yourself. When you give of yourself, you've become a part of something bigger than simply you. From a leadership perspective, a connection environment unleashes tremendous ingenuity and invention.

Several years ago we needed someone to take responsibility for what we were calling our guest reception area. Frankly, it was just a small desk with a little sign where our guests could meet someone and turn in their communication cards. We asked Catrisha Seward to organize and occupy the station. We gave her a broad stroke of instructions: "Your responsibility is to make the guests feel welcome."

Before we knew it, she was reorganizing not only the reception station or even the lobby, but the entire sanctuary. In a matter of weeks, our sanctuary went from stacked chairs that posed as pews to a room full of sofas, love seats, coffee tables, and throw rugs. The ambiance of our auditorium changed radically, and in many ways the entire culture of our church was permanently transformed.

Catrisha was able to pull together a team to serve our guests because she lived in a healthy environment in which she knew she was allowed to dream, experiment, and create. Her team transformed our entire worship experience: The guest now felt the entire building was the welcome center. When people serve where they are passionate and gifted, you'll be surprised at the potential for genius.

THE SERVANT HEART OF GOD

Two years ago one of our staff people put together a small team to go to Ensenada, Mexico, in an exploratory mission project. The team came back with a report of the tremendous need and the opportunity to serve. I began to share with our elders the possible shift in our ministry philosophy. Up to now, we had only taken those who were in leadership positions outside of the borders of the United States. I proposed that we take to Mexico not only those who were nominal in their faith, but nonbelievers also. The idea was that in the context of an apostolic environment, people would be drawn to the person of Jesus. In a sense they would be invited into the movement in the hope that they would find Jesus in the process.

Over 160 people signed up for the Ensenada service project, and one of those was an art student named Carlos. Carlos studies at the Pasadena Art Center and focuses on the creation of futuristic cars. As he expressed it, he had nothing but negative feelings toward Christianity and Christians, and it was only through the invitation of a friend named Jenn that he decided to come. In the context of our serving community, all his misconceptions began to unravel, and his heart became warm toward God. On the way back that Monday, after three days of serving others, he became a follower of Jesus Christ.

> When we serve others, we more fully reflect the image of God, and our hearts begin to resonate with the heart of God.

There is something mystical about servanthood because God is a servant. When we serve others, we more fully reflect the image of God, and our hearts begin to resonate with the heart of God. We may never be more like God than when we're serving from a purely selfless motivation.

STANDARDIZING UNIQUENESS

If you were to visit Mosaic on a Sunday, you would find four services in three different locations. And if you traveled through each environment, as many of our guests do, you would comment on how each service is so unique. There is no assembly line. Each worship experience is as unique as the people who pull it together: from multimedia to dance to worship to style; from sofas in a sanctuary to stacked chairs in a night club to beanbag chairs in a second-story loft. One can clearly see and feel the uniqueness of the individuals involved in the creation of these experiences.

I remember, early on in my Christian journey, an older ministry leader attempting to espouse the strengths of being Southern Baptist. He made the observation that you could travel anywhere in America, and if you walked into a Southern Baptist church, you would know what to expect. He was saying this as a positive, without realizing that a new culture was emerging to whom this would be a negative.

As I traveled across the country, I found his words to be true. It seemed that in every church the piano was in the same place and the organ across from it. Not only were the pulpits in the same place, but they almost all looked the same. The pews, the architecture, and the carpet were almost always the same, with only slight variations based on size. And then there was the order of worship—always orderly, always predictable, always the same. The same hymnals, the same songs: the elevation of standardization.

An old saying states, "If it ain't broke, don't fix it." I think we need to ask a different question, "If it ain't right, shouldn't we change it?" The work of the Holy Spirit does not create standardization. It unleashes the divine potential in every human being. Structure is good, but it must never become our god. God is always reshaping and remolding. The truth of the Gospel never changes. The Word of God, we are reminded, endures forever. But how that is applied and worked out is disposable. At Mosaic we say it like this: Structure must always submit to spirit.

Consumed-Communion

The fourth element used in describing apostolic ethos is fire. The apostolic ethos is fueled by incarnation. God shows up! He comes as an insider. God is different, not because he is irrelevant but because he is the very best of that

culture. This is where the ministry of the church comes in. We must become relevant and reverent. Worship must become the meeting place between the eternal and the contemporary. We tend to love the altar so much that we refuse to set it on fire. Yet God comes in the flames. Our God is a consuming fire.

> **Our hearts must find passion for those things that enflame the heart of God.**

Fire is an irreversible process. When God inhabits the praises of his people, the process begins. Each generation must build its own altar and then set it on fire. If you worship the wood, you will lose the fire. Perhaps the greatest tragedy of our time is that we have kept our pews and lost our children. Our hearts must find passion for those things that enflame the heart of God. Throw everything into the fire of God, and you will be left with all you need.

Fire is our metaphor for communion. It is a reminder that God in his essence is a holy presence, that God is a consuming fire. Moses first saw this for us as he saw the bush that was consumed by fire and yet not consumed. As he approached, Moses was instructed to take off his sandals, for he was standing on holy ground. He had entered into the presence of God.

FIREPLACES, FIREWORKS, AND FIRE FROM HEAVEN

Sometimes we forget that God is fire. We confuse him with fireplaces and fireworks. We tend to think of him as a fireplace when we make God too much our friend, as if he were a peer. We sometimes conclude that God is our copilot helping us along the way while we remain the pilot. This is the kind of fire that warms you and keeps you comfortable, while at the same time remaining a safe distance away. The fireplace is contained and controlled. But a God-like fire is much different.

Sometimes we see God too much as fireworks: the ecstatic experience of shallow celebration or worship that takes us high but leaves us low. It is the fireworks of praising God on Sunday and forsaking him on Monday. The fireplace and the fireworks each create an illusion of the fire.

God's activity always involves fire. When God spoke, "Let there be light," he introduced fire. Our contemporary minds have a tendency to rescript this primal beginning as if God turned on a light switch or placed cool fluorescent lights into the heavens. When God spoke the existence of light, he created dangerous and illuminating fire. So we should not be surprised that Moses not only met God in a burning bush, but that God led Israel out of Egypt by a pillar of cloud in the daylight and a pillar of fire at night. God sent fire from heaven in response to the prayer of Elijah. And when Shadrach, Meshach and Abednego were thrown into the fire, God was already there, waiting for them.

The fire of God has translated to the New Testament church through John the Baptist in his prophesy that he baptizes in water, but one is coming after him who baptizes in the Spirit with fire. Fire appeared again as the first-century church was ignited when tongues of fire fell upon them. And Paul promises that we will all be tested in the word (crucible) of fire and all that is wood, hay, and stubble will burn away. Only the bronze, silver, and gold will remain.

ENCOUNTER-CULTURE

An apostolic ethos is fueled by an undeniable experience with the living God. When God sends fire from heaven, communion happens and God creates an encounter-culture. In the environment of communion, all individuals are confronted by the reality of God—not simply through the word spoken, but through the presence that presses against them. It is a culture in which even the unbeliever encounters the holy and eternal. It is what Paul describes in 1 Corinthians 14:25b concerning the unbeliever in their midst. "He will fall down and worship God, exclaiming, 'God is really among you!' " At the same time, when the fire of God falls, God moves his people to encounter culture, to become relevant to the now, and to become the genuine expression of Christ incarnate in this particular culture.

Encountering culture takes many forms. Sometimes it's a prophetic voice that speaks to the ills of the culture and calls it to a higher way. At the same time, encountering culture can mean expressing the best of that culture through music and art, creating beauty that reflects the very person of God. Encountering culture means being relevant and transformative. One has to do with being up to date and the other with being up to the challenge.

UNDENIABLE PRESENCE

About five years ago the Los Angeles Times commissioned a story on why churches were growing, bringing in a writer from the D.C. area named Barbara Bradley. They selected five churches in the Los Angeles area that they would research, and one of those was Mosaic. Barbara Bradley called me one afternoon and said she only had one more question in her interview process, and that question was simply this: Is God really there?

I told her she needed to come and see. I thought it would encourage her to experience one of our celebration services. She came to a Saturday night service, and after the experience, I went to her and asked what she had concluded. She said that perhaps God was there. As she walked off that night, I was devastated. I had thought, "This is going to be absolutely wonderful. We're going to be the church in the article where maybe God was there." I could see the L.A. Times having a heyday off this story.

❝The incarnation of Jesus Christ is God's undeniable evidence that relevance to culture is not optional.❞

A few days later she called me back and admitted that she had not been entirely honest with me. When I had asked her what she concluded about the reality of God, she had felt it journalistically inappropriate to answer in a way that honestly expressed her experience, but that in fact she did know God was there.

Here was an intellectual from the Christian Science Monitor who had come with no knowledge of a personal God, with credentials that extend to a fellowship at Yale Law School, and believing that the reason churches grew was savvy marketing and great locations. She was now grappling with the knowledge that somehow she had met God. She later revealed to me that as she sat in the parking lot that evening, gathering her tools to continue her investigative process, she began to shake. And as she watched her hands shake, she somehow knew she was entering the presence of God.

It should come as no surprise that three weeks later, as she was bringing her research to an end, she knelt in my office and committed her life to Jesus Christ. Now five years later, Barbara Bradley is a regular on National Public Radio and a devoted follower of Jesus Christ. It was through her encounter with Jesus Christ that she was able to see the God-story at Columbine High School and broke the story of Cassie Bernall, the teenage Christian martyr who brought hope in the midst of tragedy.

It is not incidental that five times in 1 Corinthians 14, Paul speaks of the unbeliever in the midst of the church. Even in what many would consider the most esoteric congregation in the New Testament, unbelievers were present. It amazes me that we can actually think that genuine worship would not be compelling to an unbeliever. The power of our communion cannot be measured in *our* experience alone. It must also be measured in the experience of those who do not believe in God.

Jesus stepped into this world and into the context of the people to whom he came. Jesus was not acultural. He was a Jew. His skin color, the shape of his face, his eyes, his nose, and his aroma and odor all matched the people of his time. He is our most compelling evidence that we can be relevant without accommodating culture. In fact, the incarnation of Jesus Christ is God's undeniable evidence that relevance to culture is not optional. At Mosaic this is our standard of worship: a communion environment that is an encounter-culture and encounters culture.

Transformed-Character

The final element for describing an apostolic environment is earth. An apostolic ethos is fueled by transformation. The Scriptures tell us that God created mankind in his image and likeness. But as a result of our rebellion and sin, we fell to the ground and shattered like a fragile vase. For too long we have defined the goal of holiness as becoming like God or even being sinless. Our entire pursuit of holiness has been to regain what was lost. In the garden humanity was both good and sinless. Why have we made getting back to zero the highest result of the cross? This goal falls far too short of God's redemptive work. God had big plans for Adam and Eve after he placed them in the garden. The naming of all of the animals gives us a glimpse into the potential that God placed within humanity.

Earth is a natural metaphor for what we often call character. The transformation of our character goes beyond becoming good soil to producing much fruit. Like the earth, we were created to produce life. In an apostolic environment, not only do people change, but they also get better. But what it means to get better needs to encompass the entirety of the Scripture's teaching.

When we focus on character development, we usually emphasize the elimination of sin. What it means to be holy then finds its definition in things that we do not do rather than things we do. This focus can be easily understood and justified. Certainly a significant part of our spiritual journey is the putting off of the old. Early on in this process, the dominant conversation between God and us seems to be around some very concrete lifestyle decisions. Right up front we learn that we should at least begin to live by the standards of the Ten Commandments. If you're a new Christian, it's extraordinarily confirming when you choose to avoid murdering, committing adultery, lying, and stealing. And it makes perfect sense that you stop worshipping false gods and worship only the true and living God.

> **When our hearts are good earth, there's a great harvest.**

The problem is not the insignificance of these areas of change, but that we tend to make them the entire construct for spiritual formation. It's as if all God is trying to do is stop us from sinning. Yet all of us who have walked with Christ know that there's more. We know that beyond being greedy is being generous, beyond lying is being truthful, beyond pride is humility, and beyond slander is encouragement. It is not enough to "put off." We must also "put on." All of us are encouraged when we begin to see the fruit of the Spirit born in the lives of followers of Christ, reconfirming the work of God in the human heart.

RISING AFTER THE FALL

There is still more. Character transformation is more than the elimination of sin. Character transformation is more than beginning to express the fruit of the Spirit. God is about reclaiming the divine potential he has planted within each individual. In its essence the word *character* means a unique shape or mark. Letters are unique configurations that take on meaning. Words are the combinations of characters that communicate more than their symbols alone.

This is also true in the arena of personal character. Each person has been uniquely marked or shaped by God. Our theology of character transformation needs to extend beyond the reestablishment of virtues to the reclamation of the potential in every person. This is no small thing to God. All too often we see the development of human potential to be godless and humanistic. At times we see it as simply an addendum to the need for personal holiness. And yet Jesus describes the human heart as earth.

In the parable of the sower, Jesus tells us that the good soil represents the heart of those who truly accept God's message and produce a huge harvest: thirty, sixty or even one hundred times as much as has been planted. When our hearts are good earth, there's a great harvest. A healthy environment not only nurtures a hatred for sin and a love for virtue, but it also nurtures the potential that lies dormant in the earth of the human heart.

In another parable Jesus spoke of individuals who were entrusted with talents: one with five, one with two, and one with simply one. The master went away for a season and then returned to see what his servants had done with what had been entrusted to them. The one with five had multiplied them to ten; the one with two to five; but the one with one talent explained that he had hid it, believing the master to be wicked and an unfair man. The master described this servant not simply as imprudent, under-motivated, or minimally talented, but as evil and wicked.

A NEW RENAISSANCE

We preach against sin, but have we ever developed the anger of God when it relates to lost human potential? Have we ever looked at human lives and felt our hearts break, not because of the sins committed but because of the potential left unattended?

An apostolic environment sees character development as a commitment to maximizing the life of every individual and seeing each and every human being as a treasure of God. For too long our only conversations related to the image and likeness of God have been about how we have defiled it. We've been negligent in our examination of what it means to be re-created in the image of Christ. We were created not only to declare, but also to reflect God's greatness and beauty. Institutions devalue human potential and minimize the contributions of individuals. An apostolic ethos identifies, nurtures, and develops these capacities as stewardship before God.

> When our hearts are joined to God, our imaginations can be the birthplace of the dreams of God for our lives.

The Gallup organization, from their studies of human talent, have suggested that the unique talent of an individual can be identified by the age of two. Perhaps a difference between a good parent and a great parent is that a good parent forms character, while a great parent unleashes potential through character transformation. If this is true, and I am convinced that it is, then all of us have an opportunity to be prodigies in our own way.

A prodigy is an individual who capitalizes on a unique talent at an extraordinarily young age. When the church nurtures good earth, her children have their greatest opportunity. We've seen glimpses of this. Some of the greatest singers in our contemporary society grew up in church. Church was a place where their gifts were nurtured and encouraged.

At one time, the great art, the great music, the great architecture, and the great literature were born out of the influence and environment of the church. Certainly the emergence of enlightened thinkers and of science itself were born out of the environment of the church. It should not surprise us that if God is the great Creator—and on the seventh day he rested from his work of creating—then those he created in his image and likeness would also be creative beings. It easily follows that the closer we get to God, the more we discover our untapped potential and creativity.

IMAGINE THIS!

Many people do not consider themselves to be creative, often because they can't draw or sing. However, every human being has been given the most essential tool for creativity, and that's the human imagination. There isn't a person alive on this planet without imagination. You may not be very imaginative, or you may limit your travels through your imagination, but you have one.

The imagination is God's gift of creativity to humanity. It is the one way you can see the ideal, go to places you've never been, step into experiences you've never known. In your imagination you have unlimited resources, unlimited capacity, and an unlimited range of influence. In some ways, in our imaginations we are most like God. Unfortunately, the material for our imaginations is primarily filtered through our hearts. When our hearts are separated from God, our imaginations can move to tremendous corruption. But when our hearts are joined to God, our imaginations can be the birthplace of the dreams of God for our lives.

So the Lord invites us: "Call to me, and I will show you things that you could never dream or imagine." I'm convinced that our imagination is the playground of God, a place where God meets us and shows us a future that he can create through us.

What dreams has God placed in your heart? Have you allowed him to take you in your imagination to places that he now desires to take you in history? When God dreams, reality forms. When we dream of God, we are both transformed and become agents of transformation. An apostolic ethos is an eruption of creativity. It becomes the fountainhead of the ideal and the imaginative.

The church can become the place where the great artists of our time paint their first strokes and the great musicians sing their first notes. The church can become the place where the great thinkers and the great scholars and the great writers emerge. The church can become the environment in which the future's poets and film directors, dancers and doctors grow up in community and learn that their talents are gifts from God.

The future leaders of this world will come from somewhere. Shouldn't it be the church? In a world filled with despair, drawn toward darkness, and conceding to existentialism and nihilism, where would the beauty that calls human beings to aspire toward greater things come from if not from the church? At Mosaic we've come to believe this: Creativity is the natural result of spirituality.

> **❝You could not step twice into the same rivers.❞** —HERACLITUS OF EPHESUS

FUEL FOR THOUGHT

1. Why would servanthood be the essential key to an interconnected ethos?
2. If "spiritual maturity cannot exist outside of healthy relationships," how would you describe your community's health and maturity?
3. In the natural world, trees are constantly reorganizing their structure in order to support and create growth. How might this metaphor apply to our community's organizational structures?
4. What ignites the heart of God? How do we burn for the same thing?
5. How could we shatter our illusions of God and enter into a more genuine communion with him?
6. In what ways are we relevant to an unbelieving culture? How might we excel still more in cultural relevance?
7. Let's imagine together and create an ideal church environment. What would it look like? How would it feel? What would be going on?
8. Do we believe that creativity is the natural result of spirituality? How do we demonstrate this connection?

"Consecrate yourselves, for tomorrow the Lord will do amazing things among you" (Joshua 3:5b).

On your mark! Get set! On your mark! Get set! On your mark! Get set!
On your mark! Get set! On your mark! Get set! On your mark! Get set!
On your mark! Get set! On your mark! Get set! On your mark! Get set!
On your mark! Get set! On your mark! Get set! On your mark! Get set!
On your mark! Get set! On your mark! Get set! On your mark! Get set!
On your mark! Get set! On your mark! Get set! On your mark! Get set!
On your mark! Get set! On your mark! Get set! On your mark! Get set!
On your mark! Get set! On your mark! Get set! On your mark! Get set!

GO!

WE LINED UP ON OUR MARKS. THE BRIGHT LIGHTS OF THIS NIGHT track-meet added to the surreal sense of the moment. My heart was pounding within me. I was ready. I was focused. This was my moment. On your mark! Get set! The gun went off. Those on each side of me bolted out like a blur of human lightning. I laid flat on my face, the cold hard pavement my introduction to reality. I forgot to check my blocks. The force of all my effort ripped the spikes right out of the ground. I lost a race and won a lesson I would never forget—secure your starting blocks before you…GO!

"But you will receive power when the Holy Spirit comes on you; and you will be my witnesses in Jerusalem, and in all of Judea, and Samaria, and to the ends of the earth" (Acts 1:8).

Re-Formation

CHAPTER NINE

RE-FORMATION

I've been to a place where pastors have lost their jobs, a place where the abuse and pain have been so severe that pastors have found themselves in professional psychiatric care. In this place, pastors have lost their marriages, sacrificed the health of their children, and even at times nearly lost their faith. In this place the persecution of spiritual leadership is so intense that the survival of the leader, in and of itself, is a miracle. This place is not some foreign land; it is not under the oppression or the rule of another nation. This most dangerous place is where a leader is seeking to transition a congregation from institution to movement.

Transforming a culture is a fragile and volatile undertaking. Countless pastors tell stories of experiencing at a church growth conference the possibilities of what God can do through the church. They come in discouraged and walk out determined. They are filled with vision, enthusiasm, and hope. They've been given tools that would help their churches begin to thrive and reclaim their roles as ambassadors of Christ. It confounds all logic that such spiritual leaders, who would return to their home churches with so much good in their hearts, could reap so much pain as a result.

As these leaders determine to lead the church through this critical cultural transition, the charges that arise span from character assassination to accusations of theological liberalism. While the charges vary, the central theme is the same. Somehow you've changed, and not for the better. All the while, the vision that you've received gives you a new view of who the church can be and a new sense of responsibility of where you need to lead the people God has entrusted to you.

The truth is that you *have* changed. Many times this is what confuses people the most. Churches rarely call pastors who are different from them. Most often pastors are an unusually compatible match to the congregations that are calling them. Churches rarely ask themselves the question, "Who can change us?" The commission given to the pastoral church committee rarely centers around a prophetic ministry but around a pastoral ministry. So the longer we serve a congregation and leave things the same, the more we confirm the status quo we were called to maintain. We do this, not primarily through our words but through our actions.

Whether it is through a personal retreat, a conference, or a seminar, when we are motivated to a new level of leadership, we should not be surprised if we face initial resistance. It's easy to get discouraged when we realize that God's people may not respond enthusiastically to new insight and inspiration from the Holy Spirit. But if as spiritual leaders it took *us* time and experience to come to a new view of God's calling for the church, we should expect that *our people* may struggle with it as well. We must recognize that the principle arena for re-formation leadership is in our ability to transition God's people to move forward in alignment with God's purpose.

BACK TO ZERO

Years ago I was introduced to Joel Arthur Barker's material on *Paradigms: The Business of Discovering the Future.* He explains that one significant aspect of human change is the ability to move from one paradigm to another. When a new paradigm emerges, one's learning in the former paradigm may become irrelevant and in fact detrimental to success in the new paradigm. He explains that the critical rule to both surviving and thriving in this new paradigm is the "back to zero" rule, that when a paradigm shifts, everything goes back to zero. In a sense, it's time to shake the Etch A Sketch, clear the slate, and start afresh.

> **For us to go back to zero means we must reengage the Scriptures, while at the same time detach ourselves from all of our assumptions related to methodology.**

Over the past ten years, I've reflected many times on Barker's observation, wondering what going back to zero looks like for a follower of Jesus Christ. Does this principle apply in the spiritual, and more specifically, the church context? When you listen carefully to the words of Jesus, it is clear that the answer is an emphatic yes! When we begin a process of cultural re-engineering and spiritual re-formation, it is absolutely critical that we begin by expounding the purpose of the church. For us to go back to zero means we must re-engage the Scriptures, while at the same time detach ourselves from all of our assumptions related to methodology.

Jesus accused the religionists of his time of forsaking the Word of God for the traditions of men. What he was saying to them was that they had added so many layers to what God had said that their applications were no longer valid expressions of the words of God. Jesus was calling them to go back to zero.

There are two important points here. One, for a Christian going back to zero never means living in a vacuum. It's not the rejection of truth or moving to a level of innovation without foundation. This has been the concern of many who observe innovation in the local church. Their fear is that the church is losing her roots in a biblical foundation. And we must be careful. The truth is that *not* all innovation is good, and being relevant to culture loses its meaning if you have nothing to relate.

But for those of us who are followers of Jesus Christ, going back to zero means putting aside all of our assumptions and allowing *the Scriptures* to speak to us afresh. In other words, we need to go backward before we go forward. We need to deal with the "why" of our theology and ask ourselves the question, *Why are we doing what we're doing?* We need to ask whether the approach we're using is the best and most appropriate for the present context.

REDEFINING CHURCH

When we evaluate our methodologies or practices, we tend to see them in the context of good and evil. We know to stop doing those things that are wrong and to continue doing those things that are right, but rarely do we evaluate between the good and the best. The difficulty in going back to zero and the process of transitioning a congregation is that the very things that need to be changed are not rooted in evil or even in wrong decisions or actions. They're simply rooted in applications that are now outdated.

It's easy to speak with a prophetic voice when you call the church out because her actions are clearly unbiblical. It is so much more nuanced and difficult to speak prophetically concerning methods that were, in fact, rooted in good, but have over time become disconnected from what they were intended to do.

At some point, though, the preservation of a particular tradition, methodology, or style can move beyond preference and take on an element of sin. This happens when we choose the practice over the principle. When the prophetic leader begins to expound the purpose of God, he begins to expose the heart motivation in God's people.

Many who hear the prophetic call to return and restore the purpose of God for the church are inspired to new levels of obedience and faith. For them, the process of examining every program and expression of the church against the biblical mandate to make disciples of all nations becomes necessary for church health and renewal. Yet for others, this is not true.

For others, the purpose of God for the church and the preservation of the church as they know it move into direct conflict with one another. The expression of religion is far more important to them than the awakening or the embracing of a movement. Any leadership seeking to awaken an apostolic ethos becomes a threat, and their resistance increases as the church moves toward the purpose of God.

The prophetic leader must root the call to change in the fundamental essence of the church and God's calling to her. This is true for both those whose hearts are rekindled by the elevation of God's Word and for those whose hearts are hardened against it. Effective re-engineering happens when you wrap yourself in the Bible. If you cannot defend the *why* from the Scriptures, you are not ready to lead a change process. You need to develop a clear theology of change—a theology that de-

> **The prophetic leader must root the call to change in the fundamental essence of the church and God's calling to her.**

mands transition and transformation. Before you can begin to call God's people to a new way of living and action, you must clearly establish for them the purpose for so painful a process.

KNOWN BY THE SCARS

We need to make sure that we are not so enamored with new methodologies and innovations that our inspiration comes only in the hope of greater effectiveness. A message born out of utilitarian pragmatism does not set the hearts of God's people on fire. People need to know that the purpose of God burns in *your* heart, that people not only matter to God but also genuinely matter to *you*. The people you hope to lead need to see that your life has been reoriented around the very purposes that you advocate.

I remember when things were not going so well at Mosaic. People we love and care for had chosen to leave because of our painful transition process. Three different times I watched the church go from five hundred to about nine hundred and then decline again. The third time seemed the most painful. I wondered if I had the energy to face the challenge again. I identified with the words of the psalmist when he described his own pain as he watched even those closest to him become distant.

I'm a person with a lot of resolve, but I remember one day coming to the end of myself and telling my wife, Kim, that I just didn't think I could do it again. One phone call made all the difference in the world. One of the elders called me at home and informed me that the other elders had met without me. You can imagine how that information up front was not all that encouraging, but what he then said filled my heart with strength. He said, "Erwin, we've talked as elders, and I'm calling on their behalf. We want you to know if there are only three families here with you, that we're with you because where you're leading us is right."

Reflecting on this scenario after the call, I could almost see the three elders and their families, and Kim and I and our children, meeting together on Sunday morning for worship. Yet I was reminded from the encouragement of spiritual men that what's important is not that everything *goes* right, but that what you're *doing* is right. If you are to lead God's people in the way of God, then you must prepare yourself for spiritual warfare ahead. If your motivation is the approval of men or being measured as successful in this world, then this journey may not be for you. But if you can live and die on the knowledge that you have given your life for the purpose of God, then you can move to the next step in the process of spiritual re-formation.

SEEING THE OBVIOUS

After you expound the purpose, you then expose the problems. There is no true leadership without facing problems. In many ways before you ever get to the issue of how to solve problems, you have to deal with the issues related to avoiding problems. Prophetic leadership understands that problems are road guides on the journey to spiritual health and life.

Three kinds of congregational problems must be addressed. The first is problems that are obvious to everyone. Strangely enough just because a problem is obvious to everyone doesn't mean it has been addressed. In an unhealthy community, such problems are what we've come to know as "family secrets." Everyone knows what's going on, knows there's a problem, and knows what the problem is, but no one has the courage to talk about it out loud. In many cases no one will even acknowledge that it exists. If someone alludes to the problem, such an immediate denial will likely follow that the conversation will be shut down.

> But sometimes speaking the truth in love is so difficult and painful that the help that could result from it is never engaged or experienced.

I've found that simply having the courage to say the problem out loud and in public is perceived as a tremendous act of leadership. But sometimes speaking the truth in love is so difficult and painful that the help that could result from it is never engaged or experienced.

Declining congregations of fifty sit in auditoriums which seat five hundred, and no one has yet stood up and said what was obvious: "Our church is dying." The average age of the congregation is in the late fifties to early eighties, and no one stands up and states the obvious, "We have lost our children." A Caucasian congregation sits in the middle of an African-American community, and again no one states the obvious: "We do not reflect the people who live around us." If such problems have ever been publicly stated, they live on the back burner. Other issues take priority. The magnitude of the problem or its significance seems to be lost.

The role of leadership in declaring problems that are obvious to everyone is clearly not to bring new insight, but to establish the credibility to lead. We sometimes avoid speaking about congregational issues to avoid conflict or maintain harmony, yet what is lost is the credibility gained from a demonstration of our perceptivity. If a part of leadership is painting a compelling picture of the future and inspiring people to a new vision for life and community, how will anyone have confidence in your ability to lead or create that new world if you can't even engage the present reality effectively?

When you ignore problems, you relinquish a place of truth. When you ignore problems, you communicate a lack of confidence that God can overcome obstacles that have debilitated or even paralyzed God's people. Identifying the clear problems is not expressing pessimism or negativity. It is not judgmentalism or condemnation. It is standing to face whatever Goliaths stand before God's people and speaking with confidence about a future gained after Goliath's defeat. Identifying the clear problems is the beginning point of spiritual warfare in leadership. It gives the spiritual leader an opportunity to call God's people to prayer and usher in the promises of God, promises of a future and a hope.

JUNGLE WARFARE

The second kind of problems is camouflaged problems, problems that are not so clear but need to be uncovered. If stating the obvious can seem like a courageous act of leadership, then unwrapping problems that have remained unseen is even more dangerous. Clear problems are often related to the present condition of the church in its relationship to the mission of Christ. Camouflaged problems, on the other hand, are often hidden within the human heart. Camouflaged problems usually involve core values and human motivation.

Camouflaged problems may appear when blame is being assigned. It's amazing how the local church will blame the outside world for the struggles within. While acknowledging that greater is he that is in us than he that is in the world, we attribute the decline

> **If the root issues or core problems are not identified, a church can spend too much time and energy addressing the wrong issues.**

of the church to the darkness outside or the apathy of those without Christ. We are too quick to blame the decline of the church on the disinterest of the unchurched.

A part of spiritual leadership is as simple as reconnecting cause and effect. We must help God's people see the spiritual connection between our priorities, values, and heart motives and the effectiveness of the church to engage culture and bring people to Christ. If the root issues or core problems are not identified, a church can spend too much time and energy addressing the wrong issues.

A church in southern California made dramatic changes in response to a significant decline. They took "Baptist" off their name. They changed from First Baptist Church to a community church. They went from hymns to contemporary music and changed the approach of their teaching from dominantly doctrinal to a greater emphasis on felt needs. But through all these changes, they were never able to turn the corner.

The community around this church had become dominantly ethnic minority and underprivileged. The tens of thousands of people who lived within walking distance did not even speak English as their first language. This church continued to decline and has virtually ceased to exist.

The church made changes in style but never dealt with the real issues of control that kept it from growing. The changes they made reflected a suburban baby boomer congregation. The only problem was that those changes had absolutely no relevance to the real problem. Any new congregation to be birthed in this facility would have to successfully reach the emerging community that in no way reflected the old congregation.

BECOMING A PROBLEM

The third area of problems to be exposed—though seemingly paradoxical—is the ability to create problems. Great leaders create great problems. If you're not willing to create problems, you're not willing to lead. Leaders create problems by changing expectations. Many churches that have been stagnant for years do not consider themselves to have any real problems. Only when a leader begins to call them out of the status quo does it begin to be perceived as a problem.

> ❝I guarantee that the only problems you will solve are ones that you engage, and the only problems that you engage are ones that you perceive.❞

When a church has reached a level of financial stability and numerical growth, it usually works from an assumption of health and vitality. You would think that in this context vision would be enthusiastically embraced, but that's not always the case. If vision is anything at all, it is an invitation to excel beyond the present condition. In a sense, when a leader begins to cast vision, he begins to create problems. No matter how healthy or vibrant a church is, once a people begin to aspire to greater heights than presently experienced, problems are created. Before a leader casts a vision, there may not have been a problem in that arena at all. Only when the standards have been raised does a crisis ensue.

Leaders create problems not only by changing the expectations, but also by creating a greater sense of urgency. Sometimes the crisis is not only about what the church is shooting for, but also how quickly or how slowly the church is willing to move. If people perceive that they have all the time in the world, even if they have lofty and noble goals, they may not feel any sense of crisis or problem.

When leaders increase the level of urgency, they begin to accelerate the need for immediate response. This urgency is obviously a tremendous source of crisis. What once may have been seen as an area of great calm may now become the center point for problem solving.

When the focus of our congregation was primarily the local community around our facility, the distance and accessibility of our worship center from the rest of Los Angeles was in no way considered a problem. But when we began to embrace responsibility for the whole of Los Angeles, our vision began to create logistical and sociological problems. I guarantee that the only problems you will solve are ones that you engage, and the only problems that you engage are ones that you perceive.

THE PROBLEM WITH VISION

When a church has too few problems, that may be because it has too little vision. When you begin to address the issues of reaching tens or hundreds of thousands or even of wanting to touch millions with the Gospel of Jesus Christ on a budget of one thousand dollars, you begin to grapple with new problems at a new level. Our structures are usually adequate for the vision that they contain; but when vision increases, the structures become inadequate. Our processes for decision-making may be more than adequate in the context of minimal change or urgency; but when urgency increases, our processes turn into cumbersome bureaucracies incapable of engaging the challenges before us.

When we began to embrace the burden of reaching the city of Los Angeles, we asked God to reveal our mission to us. In the process, we were forced to address every level of problem solving. The clear problems were obvious: We owned three quarters of an acre and had less than a hundred parking spaces.

The camouflaged problems were many, but one stood out. We had yet to work through our dependence on and our emotional attachment to our present facility. It appeared as if our main problem was our inability to buy properties around the building—we felt that we should create parking for the number of people we intended to reach. But the real issues revolved around our heart values and pliability before God. Were we willing to leave the security of our present facility and take on the financial responsibility, not to mention the added manual labor, of meeting in rented facilities?

The created problem we faced grew out of the way we responded to the clear and camouflaged problems. Every Sunday, I drive approximately sixty miles to lead four worship services in three different locations. This is a solution to a problem that didn't exist five years ago.

PROPHETIC WHISPERS

After we have expounded the purpose of the people of God in human history and exposed the problems that must be addressed, we must turn to a third step that is critical to effectively change leadership. This step is the identification and equipping of point men and women. In this step, we must remember that the critical issue in momentum is not the establishment of structures or the implementation of methodologies but the transformation of a corporate culture. The selection of a transition team can determine one's success or failure in implementing change. The individuals you are looking for are men and women who personify spiritual pliability and responsiveness, reflecting an apostolic ethos.

> **❝Too many times, pastors begin a radical transition process without solidifying the key spiritual leaders necessary for healthy transition.❞**

Required for this role are the abilities to understand the issues, embrace the direction, and transition others emotionally. One of the most significant evidences of the work of the Holy Spirit in the change process is the emergence of these spiritual leaders. Too many times, pastors begin a radical transition process without solidifying the key spiritual leaders necessary for healthy transition. The whole of God's people will be led into a wilderness experience— through the work of these indigenous leaders.

In our present context, most pastors are, at best, welcome guests. They are what sociologists might call "the acceptable outsider." As much as a pastor may love his congregation and have a deep sense of calling and commitment to its people, the nature of his position makes him a voice coming from the wilderness. It is essential, in leading a congregation with an already established ethos into a new future, to call out from within that community those who would hear the prophetic voice and respond by embracing the calling of God.

Without question, our transition process has flourished as a result of our elders and lay leaders. Had the success of our transition depended on my abilities alone, we would have, without question, failed in this endeavor. The voice of the spiritual leader, when echoing the heart of God, resonates in the hearts of those who are already seeking after God.

The key to cultural transition is not to bring something alien into a new culture, but to call out from within that culture those things that are most true and right. Deep within the heart of the local church is the heart of God. The local church cannot live without the heart of God pounding vibrantly within her. When a church loses the heart of God, she ceases to truly be the church. When the leader endeavors to awaken an apostolic ethos, he should not be surprised when men and women rise up to this higher calling of God.

DO NOT PASS GO!

The fourth step in the process of effective transition is energizing the possibilities. If the first three steps have been effectively engaged then the question that ruminates throughout the community should now be *how* and not *why*.

Many leaders make the mistake of beginning with *what* rather than *why*, so the *what* is quickly rejected. Sometimes the reason we as leaders do this is because we've thought about the *why* so much that we think it's obvious to everyone. And so we begin the conversation with what needs to happen rather than with what has led

> ❝It is when we move from the strategic to the tactical that the people of God can be most powerfully unleashed.❞

us to this place. Once the *why* is clearly understood and embraced, the *what* can be received well. The *what* is the strategic aspect of leadership. The *what* is a response to the *why*.

Peter's first message spoke from the heart of God to the core of the heart of man and the response of the hearers was "What then must we do?" We need to lead God's people to that place where the *why* is weighty in their hearts—hearts that would cry out with the question, "What then should we do?" Getting to the *what* is part of effective leadership, yet the *what* is still a broad stroke that needs to be detailed. It is when we move from the strategic to the tactical that the people of God can be most powerfully unleashed. Once the dominating question becomes *how*, creative juices begin to flow.

If the question in your congregation is still *why*, then you need to go back to step one. If the question is still *why*, it means that the purpose of God for the church has not yet been embraced. *Why* deals with purpose and essence. *How* deals with implementation. If you listen carefully early on, almost all the questions are about *why*. Why do we have to change? Why can't we keep the organ? Why did you change your translation of the Bible? Why do we have to go to two services?

When the conflict is still centered around the purpose of the church, most committees and meetings will center around the *why*. Every time there is an attempt to move to the *how*, there is either a filibuster—which delays the decision and in the end kills it—or an insistence that committees and subcommittees be established to decide whether it should be done or not. Often the language will be that of process. We're not against the idea, we just think we need to be cautious. Curiously, the question is not about how long the process is; the real debate is about when the process will begin. In a healthy apostolic ethos, the *why* is both quick and clarifying. It is obvious to those who have embraced the church as a movement if something actually flows out of its purpose.

THE CREATIVE ENTERPRISE

The apostolic church seems capable of moving on instantaneous notice simply because the *why* is no longer in conflict. The focus and energy move quickly to the *how*. This is where the creative process really begins. Our purpose creates intentionality, and intentionality brings focus. A strange freedom comes when you have clearly defined a reason for existing. Once you're settled on what the church is about, you'll be able to innovate and create without fear.

As tightly as a leader must grasp the purpose of the church, he must equally relinquish his grip on the creative process of how the church accomplishes the mission of Christ. Too many times, we confuse a call to leadership as a monopoly on the creative process. Just as some churches are unwilling to follow genuine spiritual leadership, some pastors find it difficult to entrust and empower God's people. Along with the creative implementation of ministry often comes an attitude that the *how* always has to come from us. But we should see ourselves as stewards of a community of dreamers, and perhaps our most important role is to be able to identify a great idea when we hear it.

For creativity to flourish, it has to be nurtured and affirmed so that people get a clear sense of whether their ideas are genuinely valued. You can energize an environment in which the best ideas emerge by allowing questions, affirming ideas that are not your own, and asking questions rather than giving answers. Perhaps most important of all is inviting people into the process before you get too close.

EMPOWERING SPIRITUAL ENTREPRENEURS

❝When you acknowledge failure for what it is, you gain the confidence of others as you speak on God's behalf.❞

After you've journeyed together through the dream process, you move to the phase of encouraging pilot projects. Many times, there's a fear of new ideas or approaches that's based on a sense that change or failure will be pervasive. If you can affirm everything that *isn't* changing, while highlighting something that strategically *is* changing, you'll more easily gain adherence and support.

Pilot projects can become cultural catalysts for change. A church that has been institutionalized often has a difficult time believing that the church can be a movement. Through pilot projects, an apostolic environment can be introduced and affirmed one layer at a time. Projects that are formed around a view that the church exists to impact culture can be the source for newfound faith. Many of us have to see it to believe it. That's why pilot projects allow those who believe first and see later to take initiative and create the groundwork for those who struggle to believe.

Through these kinds of spiritually entrepreneurial endeavors, you will begin to lead the church into an apostolic ethos. Even failure can build credibility in this process. When a particular project fails and you acknowledge its failure but don't lose hope, it does two things. It teaches your people that you are more committed to the purpose than you are to the particular project. And secondly, it demonstrates to them that you have integrity when faced with failures and successes. When you acknowledge failure for what it is, you gain the confidence of others as you speak on God's behalf.

In many situations, failure is the very thing that restrains God's people from doing great things for God. They've been taught that failure is equivalent to sin, and so they'd rather not try at all than risk failing. When you face failure with humility and hope, you teach others how to risk. When you affirm those who risk great things for God and count them as successful even if their particular endeavor has failed, you have affirmed something far deeper than any particular project or strategy could ever encompass. It is not so much the experiment that is of greatest value, but the affirmation of spiritual entrepreneurialism among God's people.

ENGAGE

The final step in creating an effective change culture is to integrate the change process into all you do. The affirmation of entrepreneurialism and innovation must move to the center of the apostolic community. The church must be understood as a catalyst for change and every process related to the church must be interpreted through this filter. Early in the process, it's important to make sure you don't change everything and to remind those who are being introduced to the process of change of all the things that will not change. Now it's important to call people to *change* and not just to *changes*. And since change cannot be experienced without loss or the hope of potential gain, it is again essential for the leader to lead the way in change.

Spiritual leadership in the change process is not so much about being the primary advocate of change but being the primary example of change. When the people of God see in their spiritual leaders a willingness to sacrifice for the sake of others and to be the first to change for the sake of the Gospel, they're more likely to make the changes that they need to make. The ultimate outcome of the change process is not the implementation of any one single change, no matter how significant. It is to move the people of God through a journey that leads them from transition to transformation.

"To ask the hard question is simple." —W.H. AUDEN

FUEL FOR THOUGHT

1. What have we successfully transitioned in our community? How did we do it? What did it cost us? What have we gained by making the change?
2. Are we holding on to any "sacred cows" that God may want us to sacrifice?
3. Why are we doing what we're doing? Why are we doing it the way we're doing it? Do we need to do something completely different or in a fresh new way?
4. What is our theology of change? What Scriptures provide the foundation for our theology?
5. What may be the personal cost to you in leading a transition?
6. Do you see any "clear problems" in your community? Have you ever failed in transition due to a camouflaged problem?
7. What problems are worth creating in order to change the status quo? Are our standards of expectation high enough? Do we express a sense of urgency?
8. What is a pilot project that we could launch as a spiritually entrepreneurial endeavor?

"There was once a small city with only a few people in it. And a powerful king came against it, surrounded it and built huge siegeworks against it. Now there lived in that city a man poor but wise, and he saved the city by his wisdom. But nobody remembered that poor man. So I said, 'Wisdom is better than strength.' But the poor man's wisdom is despised, and his words are no longer heeded" (Ecclesiastes 9:14-16).

WHAT CAN ONE HUMAN BEING REALLY DO? AFTER ALL WE'RE ONLY human! So we look to superheroes to inspire us. They are unfettered by human frailty and limitation. If only we could be like them. Then we could really change things. Then we would make the world a different place. If only we could be more than human. Then we, too, could set the city free!

Or

Perhaps we have underestimated our capacity. Maybe being created in the image and likeness of the Creator God still means something. Could one poor man with the wisdom of God really rise up to set an entire city free? And what would motivate those he delivered to despise him? Is there a conspiracy of mediocrity? Are we unwitting enemies of nobility and heroism? In Australia it's called "cutting the tall poppy." We choose to live where apathy is normal and average is the goal. Occasionally, some refuse to cooperate. They rise out of the rubble of decadence and conformity, and by the power of God, they show us a new way. They shock us into reality. They force us to accept responsibility. They inspire and require us to consider a new way to be human.

"His divine power has given us everything we need for life and godliness through our knowledge of him who called us by his own glory and goodness" (2 Peter 1:3).

A Radical Minimum Standard

CHAPTER TEN

A RADICAL MINIMUM STANDARD

On August 20, 1978, I walked to the altar at the first Baptist Church in Orlando, Florida and gave my life to Jesus Christ as my Lord. I remember standing there, looking up at Jim Henry, the pastor of the congregation, as he held his Bible and asked the question, "Do you confess Jesus as Lord, and will you obey his Word?"

I have to admit that, at that moment, I had virtually no idea what was inside the Bible other than what I had learned from Brother Jim's preaching. It could have been a copy of *War and Peace*. It could have been a leather-bound version of *Winnie-the-Pooh*, but I figured if it was connected to Jesus and affirmed by this people I had come to trust, it was good enough for me. I was genuinely a blank slate to the whole process of what it meant to be a Christian. Soon I discovered that I had a terrible misconception of what I had done on that Sunday night.

After I left Orlando and returned to college, I ran head-on into a layered view of Christianity. I began learning that it was necessary to not only receive Jesus as your Savior, but also to accept him as your Lord. I learned this not only through osmosis, but also through listening carefully to Christian vernacular from people who claimed to be Christians, yet somehow lived extraordinarily worldly lives. It was explained to me that these people had Jesus as Savior but not as Lord.

Another misconception I had was that every Christian was called to proclaim the Gospel. I remember coming back home from college around Thanksgiving and sitting in a room with a bunch of guys. I pondered aloud about how amazing it would be when all of us ended up all over the world, telling people about Jesus.

Everyone else in the room proceeded to tell me that they did not feel called to "preach the Gospel." They explained to me that that required a "unique" calling.

So now I had discovered that there were at least three callings: a calling to be saved, a calling to Lordship, and a calling to ministry. Again, this concept was confirmed by simple observation. There were all kinds of Christians who were not involved in ministry. In fact, in most places only the pastor seemed to do ministry. Sometimes his wife would, but not always. Ministry was what pastors did in relationship to their congregations. If you were called to the ministry, then your life focus was to care for and nurture the Christians in your congregation.

Later I discovered there was even a higher level of calling. At a missions conference the speaker began inviting people to give their lives to missions. I was somewhat confused since I was still a new Christian. I asked the person next to me what the invitation was specifically asking for. She said, "If you feel that God is calling you to missions, to take the Gospel of Jesus Christ to the world, then you're supposed to go forward." I went forward again.

This was my third calling. I went forward for the purpose of salvation, I went forward to respond to a call to full-time ministry, and now I was going forward in response to a call to be a missionary. But this time I discovered that there were two levels of missionary calling. One was to be a home missionary and one was to be a foreign missionary.

So now I had discovered five levels of callings from God—a calling to be saved, a calling for Jesus to be Lord, a calling to ministry, a calling to home missions, and a calling to foreign missions. These five levels of calling don't even take into consideration my conversation with someone from the Church of God of Prophesy in which I was told about my need to be sanctified. They don't take into account my engagements in the charismatic community, where it was explained to me that I needed to receive a second baptism.

HOW MANY TIMES DOES HE HAVE TO CALL?

Why are there so many levels of Christian calling in our contemporary Christian community? Where are they found in the biblical text? I have a strange suspicion that the nuances of these "callings" have less to do with theology and more to do with the condition of the church.

Paul seemed to think there was only *one* calling. He writes to Timothy, "So do not be ashamed to testify about our Lord, or ashamed of me his prisoner. But join with me in suffering for the gospel, by the power of God, who has saved us and called us to a holy life—not because of anything we have done but because of his own purpose and grace" (2 Timothy 1:8-9a).

The Scriptures seem to simplify the process of calling. The one call is to lay your life at the feet of Jesus and to do whatever he asks. It is a calling that says "to live is Christ and to die is gain" (Philippians 1:21). It is a calling that declares, "I have been crucified with Christ and I no longer live, but Christ lives in me. The life I live in the body, I live by faith in the Son of God, who loved me and gave himself for me" (Galatians 2:20). It is the calling that challenges us to make ourselves a living sacrifice, holy and pleasing to God, that we may know and do his will.

An honest evaluation of the dramatic number of callings that the church has created would reveal that we have found extraordinary ways of describing the overwhelming amount of Christless living in the church. If we got the first calling right, would any of these other callings be necessary?

> **The one call is to lay your life at the feet of Jesus and to do whatever he asks.**

Jesus said, "Follow me and I will make you fishers of men." He did not say, "Believe in me so that you can go to heaven." In fact, he laid down extraordinary criteria. He said, "Deny yourself, take up your cross and follow me." He expands by saying, "Unless you hate your father and mother, your brothers and sisters, your wife and children, yes even your own life, you cannot be my disciple." He is emphatic in the condition that unless we deny ourselves, we cannot be his disciples. He describes the response to his calling as the end of ourselves. If we try to save our lives, we will lose them. But if we lose our lives for his sake, we will find life.

LET'S CALL IT WHAT IT IS

What we now consider to be the highest level of calling in the Christian community was, for Jesus, the basic entry point. It was to the whole church that Jesus said, "Therefore go and make disciples of all nations, baptizing them in the name of the Father and of the Son and of the Holy Spirit, and teaching them to obey everything" (Matthew 28:19-20a). It was to the whole church that Jesus said, "But you will receive power when the Holy Spirit comes on you; and you will be my witnesses in Jerusalem, and in all Judea and Samaria, and to the ends of the earth" (Acts 1:8).

In the process of creating a theology that accommodates apathy, disinterest, compromise, and even rebellion, we have lost the essence of the movement for which Jesus died. We made a mistake of making heroes out of those who were simply living a normal Christian life. There may be no more significant ingredient to the apostolic ethos than establishing a radical minimum standard. The gatekeepers for our culture are not the heroes or supermen, but the common person. The individuals who represent the ideal inspire masses to pursue the values and virtues of their people; but it is the common person within each society who establishes the boundaries that are required to remain a part of the clan. It is not the extraordinary standard but the minimum standard that is the critical boundary in shaping a culture. To unleash an apostolic ethos, it is essential to establish a radical minimum. It is essential to call people to a radical minimum standard.

It's easy to confuse the minimum with the extraordinary. We do it all the time. In fact, organizations continuously face that crisis. Whenever someone fails to live up to an understood expectation, we are forced to make some kind of reevaluation. Either our standard should change or our actions have to change. When we live below a standard, it is simply human nature to redefine the standard as unreasonable and establish standards that our patterns are already accomplishing. We keep lowering the bar until we clear it.

BOTTOM DWELLERS

Look, for example, at the Ten Commandments. For years I have heard people describe God as unreasonable and unfair, all because of the Ten Commandments. It's easy to view God as a legalist, thinking that he has unfair expectations and that, by giving us the Ten Commandments, he is expecting us to live at his level rather than ours. The Ten Commandments, even for those who revere them, are often seen as a divine standard, something that we should live up to, a cultural ideal. This would seem to be reinforced by the Scriptures, which make clear that the Ten Commandments condemn us. When we measure our lives against the Ten Commandments, we see clearly that we are sinful and unworthy of communion with God. It might appear as if the Ten Commandments describe that place between man's best attempt and God's divine expectation. Nothing could be further from the truth.

The Ten Commandments are not heaven's standards. They are not the standards by which the angels live. They are not God's attempt to pull us up beyond the human into the spiritual. The Ten Commandments are the lowest possible standard of humane living. Stop and consider what they demand of us. Maybe it would help if we just rephrased them in everyday language. Here goes: "Hey, could you stop killing each other? Oh, yeah, by the way, could you not steal each other's stuff? And it would be really helpful if you wouldn't lie to each other, either. And here's a thought, could you not take other people's husbands and wives and just, sort of, like, keep your own?"

Upon reflection, these are unreasonable, right? How could anyone be expected to live up to these? Only God could do that, right?

> **The Ten Commandments are the lowest possible standard of humane living.**

Why don't we get it? Anything below these standards is choosing to live like an animal, a barbarian. The Ten Commandments don't call us to the extraordinary spiritual life; they call us to stop dehumanizing one another. The law is the minimum of what it means to be human. The reason the law condemns us is not because of our inability to live up to an extraordinary measure. We couldn't even pass the test with a D. When God gave Moses the Ten Commandments, he was establishing a nation for himself. God was giving them the tools to form an ethos that, through honoring him, would result in the nurturing and elevation of the human spirit.

THE GRACE TO BE MORE

Can you imagine a nation in which simple things like honoring your parents actually happened? A nation in which people were honest and upright in their business endeavors? Can you imagine a nation in which you could leave your possessions outside and no one would take them? in which you could leave your wife with a friend and he would not take her? Can you imagine a society in which no one is slandered, gossiped about, or falsely accused? And that's without even looking at the first four commandments.

God gave us a map for a healthy society, and the map was not a picture of the ideal but a definition of the minimum. The same was true for the church. God was establishing a new people, a new nation. In the same way, he established a basis from which this new culture would draw its ethos. In a word, it could be summarized as grace. Grace deals with the generosity of God, his gracious work in the hearts of those who would turn to him. Yet many times grace is misunderstood or even cheapened at times. Grace has been seen as the liberty to live beneath the law rather than the capacity to soar beyond the law.

We have a new members' seminar that meets in our home. It's the last seminar before people are received into our community. While every person is required to take a five-week seminar that focuses on his or her personal life in Christ, this one-day seminar is about the life of the church and, specifically, the ethos of Mosaic.

I was sitting on the hearth of the fireplace with an individual who was considering becoming a part of Mosaic. He turned to me and asked me if Mosaic was a law church or a grace church. It was pretty obvious to me that he was setting a trap, so I thought I would go ahead and jump in. I said, "Well, of course we're a grace church." "I thought so," he replied. "I was concerned that you were one of those law churches that told people they had to tithe."

"Oh, no," I said. "We're a grace church. The law says, 'Do not murder.' Grace says you don't even have to have hatred in your heart; you can love your enemy. The law says, 'Do not commit adultery,' but grace says you don't even have to have lust in your heart for another woman. The

law says, 'Give 10 percent,' but grace always takes us beyond the law. You can give 20, 30, or 40 percent. We would never stop you from living by grace." He looked at me and said, "Oh"—a profoundly theological response.

RISING ABOVE THE FALL

Isn't it interesting how we think of grace as something less than the law? When Paul spoke of generosity and giving, he could have never imagined that a Christian would give less than a religionist. Paul was a Pharisee. Ten percent was the law. It would have been inconceivable to him that any Christian who gave less than a tithe would ever be considered generous.

Jesus said, "I have not come to abolish the law, but to fulfill it." Jesus lived a truly human life, not just an extraordinarily divine one. He was fully human and fully God. But it's the fully human part that ought to take your breath away. Too many times we attribute the life and acts of Jesus to the God part when we should be attributing them to the human part.

Jesus lived the life we were created to live. When humans sinned against God, they fell from grace. They began to live beneath the law. They couldn't even live up to what it meant to be human, much less begin to live up to their birthright of a supernatural life.

"Jesus lived the life we were created to live."

Before we are able to clearly see the radical minimum of the first-century church, we must first change the lenses from which we view our reality. We've been looking at the book of Acts as extraordinary acts of God performed through extraordinary people. We have rescripted the text to be a picture of heroes of the faith rather than the simple lives of the faithful. The list of names given to us in Acts, such as Peter, John, James, Andrew, Philip, Thomas, Paul, and Barnabus, have become the historical highlights of our heroes of the faith. We read their story and, without any conscious intent, place them in the category of the extraordinary and unusual as we speak of their era as apostolic times.

ALL THE WAY BACK

The history of the contemporary church seems to stop just past the first-century church and fails to find its roots at Pentecost. You see this in subtle ways, even among what are being identified as postmodern expressions of faith.

I remember sitting in a seminar dealing with postmodern Christianity. For the first time I understood that, though we shared a common language, we had dramatically different frameworks. Many of the young leaders were advocating a return to the pre-modern era and the medieval church in contrast to the modern expression of the church. Around the country, new expressions of the faith have attempted to discard modern frameworks in favor of a zealous commitment to the church of one thousand years ago. They seem less interested in going back two thousand years. The key to regaining an ancient faith is not the reclamation of the icons and rituals of pre-modern medieval Western Christianity. We must go back further than this. It is essential that we return to the origins of the church and reestablish the elemental faith of the first disciples.

The disciples of Jesus were not extraordinary individuals. In fact, their actions confounded everything that was known about them. They were best described as ignorant and unlearned men. Their spiritual pedigree was far from pure. This was a band of fisherman, tax collectors, and social outcasts. Yet it was with men like these that God began his revolution of faith, love, and hope.

At significant times and places in the book of Acts, the only way to describe what was happening was through the word *all*. Let me encourage you to go back into your own Bibles and highlight every place you see this word emerge. Acts tells us that *all* three thousand were baptized after Peter's introductory message. It tells us that *all* the believers met together constantly and shared everything they had. It tells us that *all* the believers were of one heart and one mind, and they felt that what they owned was not their own. They shared everything they had. This was a movement of the *all*, not of the elite.

QUALIFIED TO SERVE

The power of the New Testament church was shown in what happened to the common person, not simply to the extraordinary hero. Even one infamous moment in Acts 6 has been reinterpreted, effectively diminishing the value of what it means to be a follower of Christ. The Scriptures are pretty clear. They tell us that the problem was a combination of logistical and cultural disagreements. The group consisted of Hebraic and Hellenistic Christians, or those who spoke Hebrew and those who spoke Greek. Their practical problem was determining how they could distribute food to the widows who were joining the movement.

> Are we actually seeing mere glimpses of what the normal Christian life looked like in the book of Acts, rather than a highlight reel of spiritual superstars?

The apostles were being overwhelmed by the administrative responsibility of this task. Many argued that they should spend their time on preaching and teaching the Word of God, rather than administering a food program. After much discussion, they came to a conclusion: "Now look around among yourselves, brothers, and select seven men who are well respected and are full of the Holy Spirit and of wisdom. We will put them in charge of this business. Then we can spend our time in prayer and preaching and teaching the word."

The passage tells us that everyone thought it was a good idea, and they promptly listed seven men to fulfill this duty. Two of them, of course, were Stephen and Philip. These men were described as full of faith and the Holy

Spirit. Some traditions base their theology concerning deacons around this experience from the book of Acts. They look to this passage as the criteria for "spiritual leadership." The story is essentially reconstructed to fit into our paradigm of how Christianity works.

This is not a picture of pastoral leadership but what we've come to know as lay leadership. The apostles were looking for seven men with hearts to serve who could simply be trusted to be honest and fair. But we soon discover that Stephen preached a message so powerful that he became the first Christian martyr. Philip got so dynamically engaged in the work of evangelism that he brought the first Ethiopian to Christ. This encounter established the longest standing Christian nation in the world.

Contrary to our perspective, Philip was never commissioned in any unique way to go into a "vocational ministry." In fact, as described in Acts 8:4, "the believers who had fled Jerusalem went everywhere preaching the good news about Jesus. Philip, for example, went to the city of Samaria and told the people there about the Messiah."

It was through the persecution and dispersion of ordinary believers that these people whom we would consider to be ordinary Christians had extraordinary experiences with God. Could it be that the minimum standard of faithful fellowship of Jesus Christ can be described as being full of the Spirit and wisdom? Are we actually seeing mere glimpses of what the normal Christian life looked like in the book of Acts, rather than a highlight reel of spiritual superstars?

HIGH JUMP OR LIMBO?

I'm convinced that what we see unfold in the book of Acts is the radical minimum standard of an apostolic movement. This is the only way to make sense of the tremendous gap between the mandate that Jesus gave his first disciples and their reality. Why would he commission a handful of ordinary people to transform the entire planet? To instruct a group of eleven men—who had already experienced attrition through the loss of Judas—to be his witnesses, not only in Jerusalem, not only in Judea, and not only in Samaria but to the very ends of the earth, would be a malicious act if he did give them the power to carry out the command.

A mission as expansive as this has no room for spectators. In fact, it requires the sacrificial investment of every adherent to the cause. But now, statistics say that approximately 1 percent of all Christians have ever led someone to faith in Jesus Christ. What would have happened in the first-century church if our reality had been the reality of this fledgling movement?

Advocating a radical minimum standard is not a call to legalism. It is not an attempt to put an unbearable yoke on the lives of believers who are joined with

God through faith and by grace. It is a cry for liberation. It is a declaration that the freedom for which Jesus died is yet to be experienced in the hearts of many who confess him as Lord. Like Israel, which knew nothing but captivity and slavery, we too need to be taught what it means to be truly free.

This may be the very tragedy that holds the church in bondage: We have been telling people that Jesus came to save them from the punishment of hell, that the ultimate goal of the Christian faith was to be able to go to heaven, and that the fundamental promise of grace was an assurance of our salvation. We've been telling them these things for so long that we have neglected to bring the children of God into the greatest experiences of their freedom. Through our omission, we have destined them to a bondage of mediocrity.

MISUNDERSTOOD IT CORRECTLY

Sometimes misperceptions can actually be perceptions. Through the people who loved me into the kingdom of God, I developed tremendous misperceptions about the whole of Christianity. I thought every follower of Jesus Christ sacrificially gave of himself to those who were lost without Christ. Every Christian I met was like that. They all served in that way. I could come to no other conclusion. I thought every follower of Christ joyfully shared the Gospel through the natural outflow of relationships. It was an honest misperception.

> **I had a misperception that the life of every believer revolved around the person of Jesus Christ and activity of the Holy Spirit.**

It appeared to me that every Christian I knew was constantly and continuously telling me about Jesus. I had a misperception that every Christian had a calling from God to change the world and saw their vocation as both the context of their ministry and the resource from which they ministered to others. I had a misperception that the life of every believer revolved around the person of Jesus Christ and activity of the Holy Spirit. Yet to my defense, how could I come to any other conclusion? My experience gave me overwhelming evidence that this was reality.

To my regret, over the years I have found these perceptions to be misperceptions. Most of us would confess that the overwhelming experience in the life of the church is that these people modeled the exception to the rule and not the commonplace. But again sometimes misperceptions can be perceptions. What I didn't know changed my life. And what I misperceived helped me see what God could do both in and through me.

ACCIDENTAL WITNESS

A guy named Gary handed me the little cards and told me to start memorizing Scripture. I thought every Christian did this, so I didn't argue. In that first week, I learned what I now know as the Romans Road. On that first Friday night, on

August 25th, I was invited to go with the high school/college group to a juvenile detention center, a prison for people under eighteen. I had no desire to go to the prison until they told me that there was a football game afterward. It was a combination experience—prison and entertainment. This was my first Christian date.

I'll never forget the strangeness of that experience. All the Christians sat on one side of the room, and all the convicts sat on the other. A Christian rock band was there, entertaining the inmates with the hope that the rest of us would have an opportunity to share the Gospel with them. There was no small sense of terror when the inmates walked in: hard faces, crew cuts, butches—and these were the women! When it came time to sit with them and share the faith, no one wanted to go.

Having more in common, in many ways, with the inmates' hearts than I had with the hearts of the Christians, I sat down at a table and I looked at three inmates. I said, "I've only been a Christian a few days. I wish I could tell you what Jesus means to me." And to my surprise one of them said, "We're listening."

Soon after, he lost his place at the table, and I went over to him and asked him if he really wanted to know about Jesus, and he said yes. I took my brand-new leather bound Thomas Chain Reference King James Bible and began desperately looking for the book of Romans. I had been memorizing the Bible from those cards. I had no idea where the book of Romans was.

He looked at me and explained that he could not read or write. Not wasting one more second, I pretended to find the book of Romans and recited the verses the best I could remember. I know I misled him, yet as I shared those verses, they pierced his heart and he bowed his life to Jesus Christ that day.

SOME THINGS COME NATURALLY

Up to that point, I had only heard one prayer of salvation in my life, and that was mine. I had only seen one person ever lead someone to faith in Jesus Christ, and that was the man who led me to Christ. Though my limited knowledge could only be described as ignorance, I did what I thought was natural to any Christian. I helped another person find God.

I left the prison that night wishing I could stay. I realized that there were perhaps hundreds of inmates whose hearts may have been open to Christ. The misperception was now a perception. There was nothing unique or different about me. I was just another follower of Christ swept up in this revolution of faith, love, and hope. I had entered the kingdom believing that every believer lived by a  radical minimal standard and lived for the expansion of the kingdom of God. The standard was no extraordinary thing, just ordinary Christianity. To hear the voice of God, to be led by God's Spirit, to be God's witness among the nations, and to see God's power translate into the transformation of the human heart—this was our one calling.

Looking back I realize that this misperception was pervasive to my understanding of the Christian life. I learned to immerse my life in the Scriptures and to believe that God speaks through them. I learned that God speaks in a personal, intimate voice through his Holy Spirit, and that I could not live the Christian life without a sensitivity to his voice. I learned that prayer is the fuel of spiritual life and that God hears our prayers and answers them. I learned that the stories capturing the lives of individuals like Elijah were not to inspire us to admire Elijah but to become like Elijah in his connection to God. And all this that I learned, I learned through what I saw, what I experienced, and what I came to know through the community of believers in which I came to faith.

> **I had entered the kingdom believing that every believer lived by a radical minimal standard and lived for the expansion of the kingdom of God.**

LIFE IS NOT A STAGE

I didn't experience the stage theory of discipleship, a view that the spiritual journey is a series of building blocks or spiritual Legos. You build into a person one aspect of the Christian faith at a time, and if a person follows Christ long enough, then all the elements of spiritual maturity will be finally engaged.

The stage theory approach to discipleship is often doctrinally heavy and spiritually light. The first stage of Christian discipleship is to have all the right beliefs in place. And so we begin to indoctrinate our disciples, making sure they have a proper theology. This would include a broad range from Christology to eschatology, depending on the denominational tradition of the church.

Only after a proper theological foundation has been established do we begin to expect the fruit of ministry to emerge. For most people the extent of this expression relates to faithful attendance at church. If a Christian has a sound theological perspective and is a regular attendee in church life, he or she is perceived as qualified for the highest levels of leadership in most churches. Around these two foundational commitments of sound doctrine and regular attendance, we build another level of commitment: church participation and service.

Tragically, the basics of spiritual formation are seen as expressions of extraordinary Christian maturity. Some people move to an extraordinary level of faith and actually become evangelistic. Some begin to express an unusual connection through prayer. Others seem compelled to extraordinary sacrifice and begin to tithe, and still others receive a unique missionary distinction characterized by their willingness to uproot and go anywhere for the sake of the Gospel. The stage paradigm for Christian discipleship works on an assumption that the core is proper beliefs and the journey is adding on the different components of spiritual life.

This is essentially an organizational construction of discipleship. Unfortunately, the New Testament biblical image of discipleship is not the constructing of an organization but the creation of an organism. Jesus did not tell Nicodemus that he needed to be rebuilt; he told him that he must be reborn. The best biblical metaphor for the discipleship process is that new Christians are new babies, not new buildings. To make disciples is not to add a second floor and a third floor and a fourth floor, but to nurture what is already there and allow it to grow naturally. A lot of us treat discipleship as if we were brought into the world with missing parts. Newborn babies are disproportionate to their adult shape, with large heads, very small bodies, and tiny fingers and toes. But they have every part they're ever going to have.

DECODING THE DNA

Contemporary discipleship would suggest that babies are born with only their heads, and maybe six months later they will develop their necks and bodies. Two years later they'll finally have arms and legs. And by the age of five, those cute little fingers and toes begin to pop out. But we all know it doesn't work like this. In fact, everything that a healthy adult needs to function effectively in this world already exists in his DNA.

> Jesus did not tell Nicodemus that he needed to be rebuilt; he told him that he must be reborn.

Before a person takes his first breath, his uniqueness as an individual already exists. A healthy adult has two arms, two legs, ten fingers, ten toes, two eyes, two ears, one nose—not because they gradually emerged but because they were all there at the beginning and were nurtured to adulthood. It is the same in the spiritual journey. What we will become is all in the DNA. It's there from the very beginning. Everything that would be the spiritual equivalent of arms and legs, heart, essential organs, and brain, is there; it just needs to be nurtured, developed, and optimized.

The capacity to live out a radical minimum standard is within every genuine follower of Jesus Christ. If you hadn't walked in twenty years, your legs would be atrophied from their lack of use. If you spent your whole life being fed by someone else, your manual dexterity would remain underdeveloped; your ability to use your hands, both for work and for art, would be painfully limited. But the capacity and the potential would still be there. Just because a person cannot read doesn't mean she lacks the capacity to learn. One's present condition is not an indication of potential, but of development. The radical minimal standard that our "heroes" from Acts aspire toward is not intended to be a yoke of burden on our backs, but to inspire us to see who we could be if we allowed God to unleash his potential in us.

I am convinced that the local church can be a place where every believer experiences the fullness of the life for which Jesus died and where every believer can find healing and transformation. It can be a place where every believer can pray in such a way that history changes and where every believer can die to himself and become a source of unbelievable sacrifice and generosity. The church can become a place where, for every believer, relationships become the core value of life, helping the lonely find acceptance and those without Christ experience unconditional love.

RESILIENT TRANSFORMATION

The marvel of leading a New Testament community is that the genuine measure of leadership is not simply in the calling out of the extraordinarily gifted and talented. Instead, it is in the creation of an environment where each individual discovers and develops her unique gifts and talents. The measure of an apostolic community is not in the legends created by heroic acts but in the quality and texture of what that community considers ordinary living. Perhaps the images the gospels give us are glimpses into the future of God's people.

> **The measure of an apostolic community is not in the legends created by heroic acts but in the quality and texture of what that community considers ordinary living.**

The Samaritan woman who met Jesus at the well and asked him one question brought the entire city of Sychar to the person of Jesus by testifying, "Come, see a man who told me everything I ever did. Could this be the Christ?" (John 4:29). The Gerasene demoniac was so dangerous that even chains were unable to keep him from wandering naked and homeless in a cemetery. Yet he was not only delivered from his demons by the person of Jesus, but commissioned by Jesus to return to his people. He begged to go along with Jesus, but Jesus refused him this privilege and instead sent him back to be a witness among the people with whom he was infamous.

Modern discipleship would tell us that this event was improper and, in fact, immoral. Modern discipleship would say that a baby Christian should never be left to fend for himself in a harsh world, that he must first be protected, and that only if he obtained a certain level of maturity should he be sent out. Yet Jesus instructed the former demoniac to go back to his family and city to tell them of all the wonderful things God had done for him. So he did. When Jesus returned, the masses awaited him, all the result of the life of one man who was still ignorant and unlearned.

ON THE JOB TRAINING

We sometimes speak of the disciples being trained for three years and then being entrusted with the movement of the church. We seem to forget that early on in the public ministry of Jesus, he commissioned his disciples to represent him and to minister in his name.

Luke tells us that one day Jesus called together his twelve apostles and gave them power and authority to cast out demons and to heal all diseases. Then he sent them out to tell everyone about the coming of the kingdom of God. He instructed them to take nothing—not a walking stick, not a traveler's bag, not food, not money, not even an extra coat. He told them how to proceed, warned them of the likelihood of rejection, and sent them out to the villages to preach the good news and heal the sick.

If the three years of Jesus' public ministry were meant to prepare his disciples, then his method of preparation was to send them into the world. The disciples never enjoyed insulation from realities of ministry and the pressures of the world around them. They were trained in the context of real life and were expected—from the very first moment—to begin the process of becoming fishers of men.

At times it seemed Jesus' expectations were unreasonable. When five thousand people came to hear Jesus speak and became weak from hunger, Jesus looked on the famished people, turned to Philip, and instructed him to feed the multitude. Already knowing how he would meet the needs of the people, Jesus was determined to push his disciples to a different level of faith, which would result in a different level of living. Jesus' rebuke and assessment that his disciples had too little faith rings true in our own lives and congregations. He draws a bottom line for all believers when he says, "He who believes in me, the works that I do, he shall do even greater works than these because I go to my father in heaven."

Jesus began by establishing a radical minimum standard that would permeate his church long after his ascen-

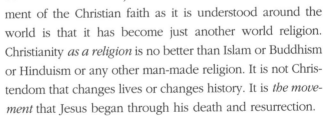

Jesus began by establishing a radical minimum standard that would permeate his church long after his ascension to heaven.

sion to heaven. We must evaluate our own preconceptions and assumptions about what it means to be a Christian. An objective assessment of the Christian faith as it is understood around the world is that it has become just another world religion. Christianity *as a religion* is no better than Islam or Buddhism or Hinduism or any other man-made religion. It is not Christendom that changes lives or changes history. It is *the movement* that Jesus began through his death and resurrection.

At Mosaic, we have been forced to reevaluate what it means to be a member of a church. I have never felt comfortable with the word "membership." Whenever I think of membership in an organization, I can't help but think of when I was a member at Bally Total Fitness health club. I joined with an incredible enthusiasm for regaining my youthful physique. I was going to lose weight, gain muscle, and move from an A-frame back to a V-shape. I was even willing to pay an exorbitant amount of money to a place that might possibly help me achieve these unrealistic aspirations for my life.

The first month went really well. I was in there three or four times a week, enjoyed breaking a good sweat, played a little racquetball, and felt good about my progress. The next month didn't go quite as well. I made it to the health club only once or twice a week, but was working under the strong delusion that I was still making tremendous progress. By the third month, I was there once a week to justify paying the bill for the multiple-year contract I had signed. Soon I was driving by the Bally sign on the I-10, trying to ignore it; there was a twinge of guilt and maybe even a bit of conviction.

Six months later I was an average member of this elite health club. In other words, I never went. I had heard that hundreds if not thousands of people were members in these health clubs that had space for only a fraction of their membership. They were able to continuously sign up new members because of the dramatic drop in attendance by those who signed on enthusiastically but quickly lost their passion to burn the fat.

For a lot of people, church membership is not that different from a membership at Bally. They're a part of something that they do not take part in. Another problem with the word *membership* is that many times it is associated with being exclusive. Many people struggle with churches having membership rolls because it feels exclusive and alienating to those outside.

I certainly understand the biblical imagery of membership. Paul describes the church as the body of Christ and all of us are members of that body, members in the same sense that arms and legs are members of the human body. To be dismembered is to be cut away from the body that brings life. I can imagine how inconceivable it would be for Paul to think of a Christian as someone who was not a member of the body. But time corrupts language and the word *member* in our present context is quite different from the time in which Paul used it.

DISMEMBERED BODIES

Within the church we see multiple levels or kinds of membership. One of the most peculiar is "inactive" membership. It is sometimes described as nonresident membership. I once studied a church that grew from 10,000 to 26,000 in a period of sixteen years. But each year the nonresident membership grew by a thousand. And so nearly a decade and a half later, while the membership had grown to 26,000, the attendance had remained exactly the same.

In the early '80s, I traveled to California and had an opportunity to share in churches across the state. I was always caught by surprise when I would see that the membership of a congregation was over a thousand, but only one hundred or two hundred real-life human beings were present. In many churches the only time you see those individuals who are classified as inactive or nonresident is when the church is in turmoil. It seems that when there is an opportunity to vote against the direction of spiritual leadership, inactive members become instantly active and nonresident members immediately renew their residency. Many churches have done away with the concept of membership entirely, at least partially in response to the corruption and the dilution of the meaning of membership.

We chose a different direction at Mosaic. We decided that everything that we could do for a person we would do regardless of membership. If you want to learn the Scriptures at Mosaic, you don't need to be a member. If you want to receive counseling, you don't need to be a member. If your desire is to be loved, accepted, cared for, or encouraged, you certainly do not need to be a member. Everything we can do, it is our intention to do for everyone, regardless of membership. There is really only one reason to become a member at Mosaic.

THE BENEFITS OF MEMBERSHIP

Several years ago three leaders from a Presbyterian denomination came to visit our congregation. They asked me what I thought was a very curious question: "What are the benefits of membership at Mosaic?" I had never been asked that question. It kind of took me by surprise. I suddenly felt like we were American Express.

This question drove me to a staff meeting at which I asked our pastoral team what exactly were the benefits of being a member at Mosaic. One responded, "Well, members are entrusted with responsibility." As we began breaking down our process, we realized that membership was the entryway to public service. We started laughing at the irony of this discovery. The only benefit in membership was the privilege to serve.

> **The motivation behind becoming a member is not what can be received but what can be given.**

Today we delineate clearly what it means to be a member at Mosaic. Becoming a member of Mosaic is a declaration that you are moving from being a consumer to being an investor; that you are joining not simply the community of Christ, but the cause of Christ. The motivation behind becoming a member is not what can be received but what can be given. And yet on a deeper level, membership is an invitation to genuine intimacy. When people become members, they are saying that they submit their lives to the spiritual authority of this community and welcome genuine accountability in their spiritual journeys. What once was our standard for leadership is now our standard for simple membership. We have established a radical minimum standard.

People who come to faith through Mosaic never have a problem with this standard of living. The greatest tension and difficulty comes from those who are accustomed to being members of churches without any expectations on their lives.

We have broken the membership standard into four basic areas of commitment for every person considering membership. The first is that they live a holy life, acknowledging that every person is imperfect and that there is a high likelihood we will all blow it at some time or another. This commitment entails that we be honest about where we are and that when we sin we come clean and trust the body of Christ to restore us to fellowship.

The second commitment is to be an active participant in ministry. This is a commitment to move beyond a spectator mentality to a participatory one. Involvement is understood—on a minimum level—to be a faithful worshipper in corporate celebration, to be actively involved in a small group committed to life transformation, and to find a particular place of service in which to use gifts and talents.

> It's amazing how much people can accomplish if you'll simply have confidence in them and call them out to give God the very best of their lives.

The third commitment area is in tithing. We ask every person who feels called to be a part of Mosaic to be a generous giver, and by generosity we mean to give 10 percent of our income and beyond.

And finally, the fourth commitment of all members is to live an evangelistic lifestyle. People commit to using their many gifts and unique personalities in building meaningful relationships with those who do not know Christ and, through a genuine expression of love, help others come to faith.

So up front, we ask all members to invest their passions, their service, their resources, and their relationships for the sake of the kingdom.

After I tell other church leaders about these four commitments, I am often asked if we monitor people to insure their adherence. And the answer is no. We have tremendous confidence in both the integrity of our people and the work of the Holy Spirit in their lives. We simply ask for a sincere, God-motivated commitment to allow God to work in and through them. It's amazing how much people can accomplish if you'll simply have confidence in them and call them out to give God the very best of their lives.

THE BEAUTY OF HOLINESS

Mike had dropped out of UCLA. Beatrix, his live-in girlfriend, was a student at Otis School of the Arts. They'd been living together for over a year, and during that time, had a series of experiences that led to Mosaic becoming a part of their lives. Through a young couple in our congregation—who are now serving in

Indonesia to reach Muslims for Christ—Beatrix was invited to our Saturday night service, and she began to investigate the claims of Christ.

Earlier in Beatrix's life, the claims of the Bible had seemed unworthy of her honest consideration, but now she was on a sincere search for God. A car acci-

dent that had left her and Mike nearly dead made her question what was going on in her life and caused her to search for answers. Before long she submitted her life to Jesus Christ and began dealing with the realities of her relationship to Mike. As Mike tells it, he knew that Beatrix loved him, so he wondered who this man was that was coming between them. He began to attend Mosaic, and shortly after Beatrix came to faith in Jesus Christ, Mike did the same.

Some people at Mosaic were concerned that Beatrix and Mike were going to be baptized while they were living together. I think many times we have too little confidence in the power of the Spirit to convict and transform. Before I could even talk with them about the meaning of Christian baptism, which includes public identification with Christ and upholding his honor and the integrity of his name, they came to me and explained that they were still living together but had stopped being physically intimate.

At first they felt this was sufficient—they knew in their hearts their relationship was purely platonic. But through further conversations, they decided that their unbelieving friends would never believe that they were living together without "living together." So they came to the conclusion that one of them needed to move out and that they would live a life of celibacy until they were married. They could never have imagined how complicated the journey that followed that commitment would be.

> **On a practical level, this is what it means to hold commitment number one—to invest your passions for God.**

Mike's family had no room for God in their lives, and Mike had been groomed to be a successful atheist. News of his faith did not bring joy to his parents but tremendous concern. Mike's desire to be a convincing witness of Jesus Christ and gain the blessing of his parents before marrying Beatrix led them to an engagement of over four years! Mike's parents' approval of the wedding was conditional; he had to go back to school and get his college degree before they would give it. But with limited financial help, he was on his own.

So while Beatrix was finishing her degree at Otis with hopes of being a fashion designer, Mike began all over again. He wanted to serve as a living validation to his parents that Jesus Christ was alive, but also to reestablish a relationship of respect toward Beatrix.

For four-plus years, Mike and Beatrix were steadfast. Not only did they remain abstinent, but they also chose to neither kiss nor even hold hands throughout that period. At the same time, Mike began to reestablish his parents' trust through his discipline and economic achievements. A young man who had once sent false reports of his academic achievements at UCLA to cover up his failing grades, Mike was now pursuing a pre-med degree from Cal State L.A. Who could have imagined that his commitment to live a life that honored God would result in his graduating magna cum laude from that university? At the same time, Beatrix, before the age of twenty-five, became a successful fashion designer for a major national retailer.

Today Mike and Beatrix, at the age of twenty-six, hold the highest level of lay leadership at Mosaic other than eldership. Mike and Beatrix's commitment to a radical minimum standard of personal integrity and holiness has allowed them the tremendous personal satisfaction of career success—Mike has just been invited to interview with Johns Hopkins and Harvard Medical School and has already been accepted at USC Medical School in Los Angeles. But more importantly, they've gained the respect of those who know them day in and day out and have observed their journey with God. On a practical level, this is what it means to hold commitment number one—to invest your passions for God.

MASTER SERVANTS

Kim was watching *Nightline*'s coverage of a crisis in Rwanda. Two rival groups, the Hutus and the Tutsis, were at war, and the human devastation was almost unimaginable. Reporters spoke of the desperate need of countless infants and children for food, water, and shelter. An invitation that expressed the horrific condition of the children and how outsiders could help captured her: They were asking for people just to come and hold the children. Surrogate parents, even in the short term, were desperately needed.

> When a person begins to invest their service out of a love for God and for people, it has a magnetic effect on those around them.

At a women's event in our church, the call went out to take emergency vacations from work and go to Africa to serve in this crisis. Many in our congregation responded instantaneously. We contacted the United Nations but were told that only medical personnel were being allowed to enter this volatile region.

Four nurses in our congregation decided to find a way to help anyway. With the financial support of spontaneous offerings from our congregation, these four women were able to travel to Zaire and work through this crisis time. It was the beginning of a medical ministry that we could in no way foresee. One of those nurses, Susan Yamamoto, was recruited for a two-person team led by another registered nurse, Matt Shriver, to help the underprivileged in Ensenada, Mexico. They began a medical ministry in a congregation with few medical personnel available. It was amazing to see what two individuals with a passion for God could accomplish with so little in so short a time.

Susan Yamamoto would never describe herself as a leader or person of great influence. In fact, she once explained to me that she could never find her place of meaningful service and never felt she could make a significant impact for the kingdom. Within a span of eighteen months, her fledgling medical ministry took a team of 115 medical personnel to serve in the impoverished *colonias* of Ensenada, Mexico. Not only were they able to recruit individuals from within the congregation who had tremendous interest in alleviating human suffering, but they generated such excitement and enthusiasm around the cause that other doctors started coming to our congregation through their ministry. Even unbelieving doctors gave sacrificially of their time and energy to serve the poor alongside the Christian doctors.

When a person begins to invest their service out of a love for God and for people, it has a magnetic effect on those around them. Today our medical ministry is one of the most significant avenues through which Mosaic ministers, both outside of U.S. borders and in the Los Angeles community.

A GENEROUS REVOLUTION

Early in my ministry at Mosaic, I was faced with harsh financial realities. Aside from being about a million dollars in debt, we had nearly a $100,000 deficit—and a little over $1,000 in the bank. Our annual budget was projected to be in the area of $280,000. But with an enormous mortgage payment in relation to our income, staff salaries were extraordinarily low and many ministry budgets were a couple hundred dollars a year.

Church leaders everywhere seemed to be saying that growing younger meant less giving. The general assessment of Gen X and post-baby boomer congregations was that the younger the church went, the lower the giving went. The older the congregants, the more sacrificially they gave.

Around the country, as people have learned that our congregational average age has decreased by nearly thirty years, I am inevitably asked how that has affected our financial condition. It's always exciting to tell how going younger has actually affected the financial condition of the church in a positive direction. Our last year's financial experience defies all the patterns out there, and certainly defies all logic.

The average attendee age moved into the low twenties. Even those in their early thirties were starting to feel old and complained about the sudden youth movement! But at the same time we were able to swallow up a deficit of over $50,000, go beyond our projected budget of $780,000, and finish the year at nearly $900,000. In the meantime, we mobilized over a quarter of a million dollars beyond the normal budget in resources for overseas ventures and raised nearly $700,000 over three years for a potential property we might find someday, somewhere in Los Angeles. Our experience shows that a church that grows younger does not have to grow poorer, and that those under forty can demonstrate tremendous generosity and sacrificial giving.

When people ask us what the difference is, we simply respond that Christians give. I think many times what happens is that we teach stinginess by default. We are so afraid to talk about money and touch on issues of giving that we've taught people they can be deeply spiritual and not be generous. In many ways we have communicated that how we deal with money is irrelevant to our spiritual lives.

Each week when we stand before our guests at Mosaic, we give the classic disclaimer, "If you're a guest, please feel no obligation to give today." But every six weeks, when we introduce new members, we explain that that disclaimer no longer applies to them. The reason we can invite our guests not to give is because we as a people openly and unashamedly make the insane and unreasonable decision to give of our own hard-earned money for the cause of Christ through the local church. We believe that the use of money is a deeply spiritual issue and that how you give is an honest reflection of your heart toward God.

> **If people are selfish with money, you'll never get their real contributions.**

Paul described the Corinthian church as generous in their poverty, not generous once they were wealthy. Jesus spoke without reservation about the importance of our relationship to our material possessions. It can't get any clearer than when Jesus tells us we cannot love God and money both, but that we have to decide where to put our treasure.

MORE THAN MONEY

Calling believers to a minimum standard of tithing and into exploring the joy of generosity is not a call to legalism but an invitation to freedom. You can only imagine the encouragement we felt when believers sent out from our congregation to serve in places like China and Turkey and India were found to be contributing thousands upon thousands of dollars to the purpose of Christ at Mosaic. Mosaic is intent on accomplishing God's calling, not only throughout the world but specifically in Los Angeles.

I can honestly say that the Mosaic community is crazy about giving. Their generosity seems unlimited, but not unexpected, and this goes far beyond money. The sacrifice of time and energy, of unique skills and talents, is the overflow of a spirit of generosity. If people are selfish with money, you'll never get their real contributions.

For me, a powerful personal illustration of this is in the process of writing this book. For the last ten years, I've struggled with both a conviction to share with the broader Christian community the things that God has shared with us and with the obstacles that seem to make that impossible. The biggest obstacle, of course, being me. A part of my own approach and style of preparation and communication each week is that I essentially prepare everything in my head. I type at the blinding speed of about one word a minute. You can imagine how difficult and overwhelming the writing process would be for a person with this kind of disability.

For two years I have known someone by the name of Holly Rapp, a regular attendee of Urban Mosaic, our service that is held at a nightclub. Early in our conversations, I learned that she worked as the executive assistant to Sidney Sheldon. For those of you who don't remember, Sidney Sheldon was the creator of *The Patty Duke Show*, *I Dream of Jeannie*, and *Hart to Hart*. He has written over two hundred television scripts, twenty-five major motion pictures, six Broadway plays, and seventeen novels that have sold over 300 million copies.

In the back of my mind, I kept thinking to myself, "If I just had Holly Rapp, I might be able to pull this off." But Holly Rapp worked for Sidney Sheldon, and as you may have already noted, you have not found any of my books at Barnes & Noble or Borders. What were the chances that someone who worked at this level in the literary world would come to work helping me write my first book, with an outside chance that someone might actually buy it and read it? Yet even now as you read these words, they are proof that generosity goes beyond what a person gives financially.

> **When we are afraid that the minimum is an unreasonable maximum, we limit the Spirit of Christ from working in the hearts of those who genuinely desire to be used of him.**

As a volunteer, Holly began transcribing many of my lectures (and insisting that these things should be in a book). Our conversations eventually moved to my asking her when she was going to leave Sidney to work for me. Of course I forgot to mention that I could not pay her the extraordinary salary that she made working for him. In actuality, I had no money at all to offer her. Why would somebody sit at a court-reporting machine, typing up to 240 words per minute with no guaranteed compensation, serving someone else and expecting no personal gain whatsoever? Because generosity is a genuine expression of the heart of God; it is part of God's radical minimum standard. And that's what Holly did.

When we are afraid that the minimum is an unreasonable maximum, we limit the Spirit of Christ from working in the hearts of those who genuinely desire to be used by him. I am convinced that in every believer, there's a generous heart waiting to be born, and generosity can never be expressed without sacrifice. Every letter written in this book, every word that is formed, every sentence that communicates any level of truth, every chapter, every paragraph, every page, and every bit of help this book might be to you have come only through the sacrificial generosity of someone you will likely never meet.

RELATING THE MESSAGE

Our radical minimum standard applies to investing our relationships—being an active vessel of Christ's love. We've only begun to tap the surface of the unlimited spiritual potential that exists within this community of faith, hope, and love. I can't wait to see what the future holds as its potential is unleashed.

It seemed that every week at Mosaic, I kept meeting a first time guest who was brought by Marge. These people were being introduced not only to Christ, but even to evangelical Christianity for the first time, through this extraordinarily kind and gracious person. You might describe her as a wide-eyed evangelist, always looking for someone who was open to the Gospel. She was a great inviter. It didn't hurt that she was winsome and magnetic, both in her character and her personality.

What's amazing about Marge is that not only was she a new Christian who had erupted on the scene as an evangelist, but she was one of the few senior adults that our congregation had brought to faith in Christ. Marge is a reminder to me that having a heart for those who are lost is not limited to the young in age or the tender in spirit.

> ❝When evangelism is not reserved for the elite, kingdom relationships become everyone's responsibility. This is the radical minimum standard.❞

My little girl, Mariah, loves writing music. When she was seven years old, she wrote her first song. I was struck by her lyrics: "God, I want to see you; God, I want to know you; I hope I can help more people to know you." At seven, she was expressing a heart passion to God that her life might make a difference in the lives of those who don't know Christ.

In a thirteen-month period ending last year, from a congregation of eight hundred people, over four hundred left the borders of the United States to serve in a missionary endeavor. For the last three years, an average of one adult a month has been commissioned out of our congregation to serve as a career overseas worker in a closed-access nation. One-tenth of our congregation now lives overseas, predominantly in nations where the sharing of the Gospel is illegal.

In a recent Gallup study of our congregational church life, approximately 85 percent of our attendees were found to be actively involved in the lives of unbelievers for the purpose of bringing them to faith. And if I were to tell you that this was the result of a specific evangelism program that we have implemented,

I would imagine that curriculum for that program would soon be jumping off the bookstore shelves. But evangelism is not a program within Mosaic's organizational strategy. In fact, our training is not systematic in this area and may even be inadequate.

What has happened is that individual believers understand that giving their lives to those without Christ is a part of God's radical minimum standard for Christian living. The idea that you could become a mature Christian and not have a heart that is broken for those who are lost is inconceivable. No measure of Christian maturity exists in our context without an evangelistic lifestyle.

People have different levels of gifting; some have a unique anointing through which multitudes come to faith with what seems to be minimal effort. Some are so uniquely gifted that every time they get onto a plane, they get off a church because during the flight everyone has come to faith in Christ.

Others establish one friendship at a time. Their strength is not the crowd or the masses. They are in no way social butterflies or honeybees that can move from one flower to another without any effort. Nevertheless, their relationships are committed to Christ, and—one person at a time—they build relationships deep into the lives of those who don't know Christ. Sometimes it takes years to see the fruit of their labor, but there is fruit in their labor. They are as faithful to an unbelieving world as those whose gifts are more obvious. Our commitment is not to become like someone else whose giftings flourish and inspire us all, but to be faithful in loving a lost and broken humanity and in opening up our lives to those who are willing to establish a meaningful relationship with a follower of God.

This final commitment is an investment of relationship. It is the fulfillment of the great commandment to love God with all of our heart, soul, mind, and strength, and to love our neighbor as ourselves. It is a belief that God looks on how we treat others, care for others, and serve others as the genuine measure of what is in our hearts toward him.

At Mosaic you will rarely hear the word evangelism, but you'll always hear the word relationships. When evangelism is not reserved for the elite, kingdom relationships become everyone's responsibility. Paul tells Philemon, "I pray that you may be active in sharing your faith, so that you will have a full understanding of every good thing we have in Christ" (Philemon 6). When we only call an elite force to the work of evangelism, we rob the rest of God's people from Christ's fullness in their lives. Only when people are active in sharing their faith can they fully grasp and experience every good thing we have in Christ. And then when they are living in that fullness, they are once again compelled to be active in sharing their faith.

A NEW HUMANITY

Caleb Bryant has already passed his first birthday and has yet to learn to eat and drink on his own. Because of a birth defect, he was unable to eat the way most babies do during their first days and weeks. To this day, he must be fed through a tube that connects to his stomach. His parents, Eric and Debbie, have discovered a surprising phenomenon of human development: All healthy infants are born with an instinct to suckle and swallow, but if they don't begin eating within the first three months, the reflex fades. If that happens, they have to learn to eat and drink the same way they have to learn to walk and talk. The instinct is gone, and they must learn by instruction.

When we come to faith in Jesus Christ, we are born again. Our hearts are made new by the Spirit of God. We are re-created to live in a new way. We instinctively drink deeply of God and seek his kingdom. In Ezekiel, God tells us that our new hearts will long to obey the voice of God.

If we wait too long, the spiritual craving begins to fade. Discipleship moves from instinct to obligation. But when we capture the fuel placed within a heart that is newly God's, the fire spreads. Those with faded reflexes are renewed. When we catch the wind of a fresh follower of Christ, our sails go up and our speed increases. When we allow the Holy Spirit to soften our hearts and impassion us anew, it rekindles our first love. And when we cling to our first love, it results in a radical minimum standard.

This is how your church can become an unstoppable force.

66 Do not seek to follow in the footsteps of the men of old; seek what they sought. 99 —BASHO

FUEL FOR THOUGHT

1. How well do you and others in your community grasp your singular calling to lay your lives at the feet of Jesus and to obey whatever he says?
2. How does our community express that we believe the Great Commission applies to everyone?
3. How do we call one another to a radical minimum standard? How does our community's bottom line stack up to this radical minimum standard?
4. How does our community express a dependence of the "all" rather than on an elite few?
5. Do we apply a "stage theory" of discipleship within our community? Explain.
6. How can we facilitate an "as you go" holistic approach to discipleship?
7. How might our outlook on membership and its benefits need to change?
8. How is our community doing with investing passions, service, resources, and relationships?